The End of Times

The End of Times

Connie Joslin

Horizon Publishers
Springville, Utah

© 2008 Connie Joslin

All rights reserved.

No part of this book may be reproduced in any form whatsoever, whether by graphic, visual, electronic, film, microfilm, tape recording, or any other means, without prior written permission of the publisher, except in the case of brief passages embodied in critical reviews and articles.

This is not an official publication of The Church of Jesus Christ of Latter-day Saints. The opinions and views expressed herein belong solely to the author and do not necessarily represent the opinions or views of Cedar Fort, Inc. Permission for the use of sources, graphics, and photos is also solely the responsibility of the author.

ISBN 978-0-88290-836-6

Published by Horizon Publishers, an imprint of Cedar Fort, Inc.
2373 W. 700 S., Springville, 84663
Distributed by Cedar Fort, Inc., www.cedarfort.com

LIBRARY OF CONGRESS CATALOGING-IN-PUBLICATION DATA

Joslin, Connie R. (Connie Ruth)
 The End of Times / Connie R. Joslin.
   p. cm.
 ISBN 978-0-88290-836-6
 1. Eschatology. 2. End of the world. 3. Church of Jesus Christ of Latter-day Saints--Doctrines. I. Title.
 BX8643.E83J67 2008
 236'.9--dc22
                                2008000617

Cover design by Nicole Williams
Cover design © 2008 by Lyle Mortimer
Edited and typeset by Melissa J. Caldwell

Printed in the United States of America

10 9 8 7 6 5 4 3 2 1

Printed on acid-free paper

Table of Contents

1. The Eleventh Hour 1
2. The Sixth Seal 11
3. Signs of the Times 21
4. The Voice of Warning 31
5. God's Sermons 39
6. America's Future 51
7. The Middle East Conflict 59
8. Islamic Jihad 65
9. The New Jerusalem 71
10. Mustering for Armageddon 79
11. An Evil Alliance 87
12. Gog and Magog 99
13. The Second Beast 109
14. The Destruction of Babylon 115
15. The Invasion of Israel 123
16. The Abomination of Desolation 129
17. Unusual Phenomena 137
18. Gathering For Safety 147
19. Return of the Lost Tribes 155
20. A Solemn Assembly 167
21. Gathering to One Place 173
22. Where the Eagles Are Gathered 181
23. Adam-Ondi-Ahman 187
24. The Second Coming of Jesus 197
25. The Millennium and Beyond 207
    About the Author 222

One

THE ELEVENTH HOUR

With each setting of the sun, the earth's inhabitants are another day closer to the Second Coming of Jesus Christ. We do not know how much time we have left before we arrive at that momentous day, but we know that the time we have left is short. In fact, it has been said that we are living in the final hour of the "Saturday night of time," just before the "midnight" hour when Jesus will appear and the earth's millennial Sabbath will begin. A latter-day apostle, Orson Pratt, said in 1873, "We, the latter-day Saints, are living in the eleventh hour, that is in the eleventh period of time"[1] before Jesus comes. And in a revelation to the Prophet Joseph Smith in 1830, the Lord declared, "For behold, the field [the world] is white already to harvest; and it is the eleventh hour" (D&C 33:3). Jesus had told his early apostles that "the harvest is the end of the world" (Matthew 13:39), that is the end of the world in its present corrupt condition.

For more evidence that we are living in the eleventh hour, we can turn to the writings of the apostle John. In an apocalyptic vision, he saw the extent of the earth's temporal history in a book "sealed with seven seals." He recorded, "And I saw in the right hand of him that sat on the throne a book written within and on the backside, sealed with seven seals" (Revelation 5:1).

The Prophet Joseph Smith inquired of the Lord about the meaning of the book with seven seals and was given the following revelation: "We are to understand that it contains the revealed will, mysteries, and the works of God . . . concerning this earth during the seven thousand years of its continuance, or its temporal existence . . . the first seal contains the things of the first thousand years, and the second also of the second thousand years, and so on until the seventh" (D&C 77:6–7). In other words, the earth's temporal history is divided into seven periods of one thousand years each.

The seventh seal will be the millennial period during which Jesus will reign upon the earth. The apostle John stated that "when [Jesus] had opened the seventh seal . . . the mystery of God should be finished . . . And the seventh angel sounded; and there were great voices in heaven, saying, The kingdoms of this world are become the kingdoms of our Lord, and of his Christ; and he shall reign for ever " (Revelation 8:1, 10:7; 11:15).

Although we know that Jesus will come in the beginning of the seventh seal, we do not know how much of that seal's time will lapse before the Lord actually appears. According to latter-day revelation, he will not come the very moment that seal begins. There is a short space of time after the seventh seal opens in which the Lord will finish his work before he appears. A revelation to the Prophet Joseph Smith states, "We are to understand that . . . in the beginning of the seventh thousand years will the Lord God sanctify the earth, and complete the salvation of man . . . and the sounding of the trumpets of the seven angels [mentioned in the eighth chapter of Revelation] are the preparing and finishing of his work, in the beginning of the seventh thousand years—the preparing of the way before the time of his coming" (D&C 77:12).

Not only will the Lord finish his work during that short space of time, but the war of Armageddon will also occur then. It was revealed to Joseph Smith that the things written in Revelation 9 (regarding Armageddon) "are to be accomplished after the opening of the seventh seal, before the coming of Christ" (D&C 77:13).

Jesus will come during that final world conflict. The prophet Zechariah declared, "His feet shall stand in that day upon the mount of Olives, which is before Jerusalem on the east, and . . . [the Jews] shall flee to the valley of the mountains . . . and the Lord my God shall come" (Zechariah 14:4–6).

The early part of the seventh seal is thus a critical time in the history of the earth, and people living in that era will need to be aware of, and prepared for, the life-changing events that will occur. However, since no one will announce when the seal opens, how will anyone know when it begins?

There is evidence that it may have already begun. We cannot know with certainty that it has, but it is a possibility when viewed in light of current world events. The world scene has shifted dramatically since the horrific 9/11 disaster. It is becoming more apparent that we may be living in the era in which the war of Armageddon will be waged. Current terrorist strikes against Jews and Americans throughout the world—especially the Jews in Israel—are an indication that the stage is being set for the final world war. The tiny nation of Israel will be the target during Armageddon, and that country is already surrounded by hostile nations. The situation in the Middle East is extremely volatile; even a small incident could ignite an all-out war. In the summer of 2006, the whole world watched as a violent confrontation between Israel and Hezbollah terrorists in Lebanon almost spun out of control.

Latter-day apostles provide further evidence that we might be living in the beginning of the seventh seal, the Armageddon era. In 1918, Elder Orson F. Whitney said, "According to received chronology—admittedly imperfect, yet approximately correct—four thousand years, or four of the seven great days given to this planet as the period of its 'temporal existence,' had passed before Christ was crucified; while nearly two thousand years have gone by since. Consequently, Earth's long week is now drawing to a close, and we stand at the present moment in the Saturday Evening of Time, at or near the end of the sixth day of human history."[2] Keep in mind that Elder Whitney's statement was made before the year 2000, the approximate beginning of the seventh seal.

In 1978, Elder Bruce R. McConkie stated, "We are now living during the final years of the sixth seal, that thousand-year period which began in AD 1000 and will continue through the Saturday night of time and until just before the Sabbatical era when Christ shall reign personally on earth."[3]

Elder Wilford Woodruff also said (in 1874) that "we are at the end of the sixth thousand years, and are bordering upon the coming of the Son of Man."[4]

It could be argued that we cannot know when the seventh thousand-year period will begin because our calendar system is not completely accurate. But according to a reputable encyclopedia, the Gregorian calendar which we use today "is so accurate that the difference between the calendar and solar years [upon which the calendar is based] is now only about 26 seconds."[5]

The apostle Orson Pratt observed,

> We know that God set up and established this [church] 1800 years from the date of his crucifixion, preparatory to his coming in the clouds. . . . Perhaps this is sufficient on the history and chronology of the world. . . . It is also acknowledged by the greater portion of the learned men of the day, who have carefully examined the subject, that Jesus was crucified on the 6th day of April; and according to the true Christian era, it was precisely eighteen hundred years from the day of his crucifixion until the day that this Church was organized.[6]

It could also be argued that we cannot be living in the seventh seal because there are too many prophecies yet to be fulfilled. But evidence suggests that most of those prophecies will be fulfilled during the war of Armageddon. (They will be discussed in later chapters of this book).

If we are living in the beginning of the seventh seal, we are not only living in the Armageddon era, but we are living in the era in which the Lord will sanctify the earth, as a previously quoted scripture indicated (see D&C 77:12). Sanctify means to purify or make holy. To become sanctified, the earth must be cleansed of wickedness. The cleansing is necessary in order for the earth to be prepared for the millennial reign of Jesus Christ, for he cannot dwell amidst evil. Therefore, people who fail to repent of their wickedness before the Lord comes will be destroyed. Elder Bruce R. McConkie stated, "Before this earth becomes a fit habitat for the Holy One, it must be cleansed and purified. The wicked must be destroyed."[7]

President George Albert Smith once exclaimed, "The world is in for a housecleaning unless the sons and daughters of our Heavenly Father repent of their sins and turn to him. And that means the latter-day Saints . . . along with all the rest."[8]

Unfortunately, it appears that most people are failing to repent. In fact, in 1974 Joseph Fielding Smith was prompted to say, "Now I believe that the world today is as wicked, just as corrupt as it was in the days of Noah."[9] In Noah's day, "the earth . . . was corrupt before God, and the earth was filled with violence . . . for all flesh had corrupted his way upon the earth" (Genesis 6:11–12).

Because the earth must be cleansed, the Lord warned the saints in 1839 that:

> Not many years hence [the wicked] shall be swept from under heaven, saith God. (D&C 121:15)

> The Son of man shall send forth his angels, and they shall gather out of his kingdom all things that offend, and they which do iniquity. . . .
>
> So shall it be at the end of the world: the angels shall come forth, and sever the wicked from the just. (Matthew 13:41, 49)
>
> Behold . . . the angels are crying unto the Lord day and night, who are ready and waiting to be sent to reap down the fields. (D&C 86:5)
>
> [For] the field is white already to harvest. (D&C 33:3)

Many latter-day events, including recent startling and unprecedented disasters, are evidence that the Lord is proceeding to harvest and sanctify the earth in preparation for his return. His latter-day judgments (destruction of evil) which began in the sixth seal (see chapter 5 of this book) are now accelerating and will continue until all corruption is swept from the earth.

In 1823 the Prophet Joseph Smith was "informed . . . of [the] great judgments which were coming upon the earth, with great desolations by famine, sword, and pestilence; and that these grievous judgments would come on the earth in this generation" (Joseph Smith–History 1:45). The Lord declared,

> For behold . . . the time is soon at hand that I shall come in a cloud with power and great glory. . . .
>
> But before that day shall come . . . great destructions await the wicked. (D&C 34:7, 9)
>
> And it shall come to pass, because of the wickedness of the world, that I will take vengeance upon the wicked, for they will not repent; for the cup of mine indignation is full. (D&C 29:17)
>
> Thus will I sweep away the bad out of my vineyard. (Jacob 5:66)
>
> The righteous shall never be removed: but the wicked shall not inhabit the earth. (Proverbs 10:30)

The Old Testament prophet Enoch "saw the day of the coming of the Son of Man, in the last days, to dwell on the earth in righteousness for the space of a thousand years; But before that day he saw great tribulations among the wicked . . . and men's hearts failing them, looking forth with fear for the judgments of the Almighty God which should come upon the wicked" (Moses 7:65–66). Aware of those coming judgments, the apostle

Paul remarked, "This know . . . that in the last days perilous times shall come" (2 Timothy 3:1).

Armageddon will be the final latter-day judgment before the Lord appears. During that war, "the wicked shall slay the wicked" (D&C 63:33), and "the third part of men [shall be] killed" (Revelation 9:18). For "behold, the judgments of God will overtake the wicked; and it is by the wicked that the wicked are punished" (Mormon 4:5).

Whether sinners die as a result of the latter-day judgments or some other way, their eternal condemnation will be the same. For coupled with the coming of the Lord will be his great Day of Judgment, a time when the lives of the wicked will be weighed in the balance and their sins will tilt the scales of justice against them forever. The moment Jesus appears, there will be "time no longer" for the living to repent and change their eternal destiny; their fate will be irrevocably sealed. The apostle John recorded,

> And the [seventh] angel which I saw . . . lifted up his hand to heaven, and sware . . . that there should be time no longer [and] in the days of the voice of the seventh angel, when he shall begin to sound, the mystery of God should be finished. (Revelation 10:5–7)
>
> And [God's] wrath is come, and [he] . . . shouldest give reward unto . . . them that fear his name, small and great; and shouldest destroy them which destroy the earth. (Revelation 11:18)

Although it has been prophesied that the righteous will, in general, be spared from the destructive judgments, they should not become complacent about the future—especially the Day of Judgment. Jesus' parable of the ten virgins indicates that half of the virgins will be unprepared for the Second Coming of Jesus Christ, the Bridegroom. The parable reads,

> And five of them were wise, and five were foolish. They that were foolish took their lamps [to meet the Bridegroom, but] took no oil with them: . . .
>
> And while [the foolish] went to buy, the bridegroom came; and they that were ready went with him to the marriage: and the door was shut. Afterward came also the other virgins, saying, Lord, Lord, open to us. But he answered and said, Verily I say unto you, I know you not. Watch therefore, for ye know neither the day nor the hour wherein the Son of man cometh. (Matthew 25:2–3, 10–13)

President Spencer W. Kimball suggested that the ten virgins represent members of the Church. He said, "I believe the Ten Virgins represent the people of the Church of Jesus Christ and not the rank and file of the world. All of the virgins, wise and foolish, had accepted the invitation to the wedding supper; they had knowledge of the program."[10]

Church members who are not preparing and watching for the coming of the Lord will be caught offguard, for his appearance will be as unexpected as a thief coming in the night. Jesus taught, "But know this, that if the goodman of the house had known in what watch the thief would come, he would have watched, and would not have suffered his house to be broken up. Therefore be ye also ready: for in such an hour as ye think not the Son of man cometh" (Matthew 24:43–44).

On the other hand, people who are watching and preparing are like those to whom the apostle Paul said, "But ye, brethren, are not in darkness, that that day should overtake you as a thief. Ye are all the children of light . . . Therefore let us not sleep, as do others; but let us watch and be sober" (1 Thessalonians 5:4–6).

The Lord also remarked, "Ye look and behold the figtrees, and ye shall see them with your eyes, and ye say when they begin to shoot forth, and their leaves are yet tender, that summer is now nigh at hand; even so it shall be in that day when they shall see all these things, then shall they know that the hour is nigh. And it shall come to pass that he that feareth me shall be looking forth for the great day of the Lord to come, even for the signs of the coming of the Son of Man" (D&C 45:37–39).

The signs that the Lord referred to are being seen all around us, "in heaven above and in the earth beneath" (D&C 29:14). (The signs will be discussed more in chapter 3). However, most of the earth's inhabitants are not recognizing them as indications that the Lord will soon appear. Some people believe that "Christ delayeth his coming" (D&C 45:26). Thinking they have plenty of time left, many are procrastinating the day of their repentance and preparation like the five foolish virgins. But the Lord will not delay his coming; he will come at the appointed hour, which may be sooner than we think, "for thus saith the Lord, I will cut my work short in righteousness" (D&C 52:11), and "for the elect's sake those days shall be shortened" (Matthew 24:22).

President Joseph Fielding Smith warned in 1936, "Do not think that he delayeth his coming. Many of the signs of his coming have been given, so we may, if we will, know that the day is even now at our doors . . . The day of the coming of the Lord is near. . . . And yet many, even among the Latter-day Saints, go about their affairs as though this coming of the

Lord Jesus Christ . . . had been indefinitely postponed for many generations."[11] Elder Wilford Woodruff also remarked, "The Lord will not delay his coming . . . and the signs both in heaven and earth indicate that it is near."[12]

Jesus himself prophesied, "As I live, even so will I come in the last days, in the days of wickedness and vengeance. . . . And the day shall come that the earth shall rest, but before that day . . . great tribulations shall be among the children of men, but my people will I preserve" (Moses 7:60–61).

Time is required to become sufficiently righteous to avoid being swept away with the those who will be classed among the wicked when God's judgments come. The calamities and disasters which we have already observed are reminders to repent before it is too late. However, although calamities will continue to increase, the warnings will generally go unheeded until Armageddon erupts and the last of the wicked are destroyed.

President Joseph Fielding Smith has admonished members of the Church to prepare before it is too late. He said, "The day of the coming of the Lord is near . . . It behooves us as Latter-day Saints to set our houses in order."[13]

When the Prophet Joseph Smith considered the rapid approach of the coming of the Lord, he remarked, "When I contemplate the rapidity with which the great and glorious day of the coming of the Son of Man advances . . . [and] that soon the heavens are to be shaken, and the earth tremble and reel to and fro; and that the heavens are to be unfolded as a scroll when it is rolled up; and that every mountain and island are to flee away, I cry out in my heart, What manner of person ought we to be in all holy conversation and godliness!"[14]

Because the Second Coming is rapidly approaching, the Lord has counseled the Latter-day Saints to prepare "today." He said, "Behold, now it is called today until the coming of the Son of Man, and verily it is a day of sacrifice. . . . For after today cometh the burning . . . for verily I say, tomorrow all the proud and they that do wickedly shall be as stubble. . . . Wherefore, if ye believe me, ye will labor while it is called today" (D&C 64:23–25). The Lord also said, "Hearken, O ye people . . . and hear my voice while it is called today, and harden not your hearts" (D&C 45:6).

Although the vista of time may seem endless, the final era in which we live is getting shorter, and one day soon, whether we are ready or not, the Lord will come as prophesied, for the earth's clock will inevitably tick through the last few minutes of the Saturday night of time until it reaches the appointed midnight hour.

Notes
1. Orson Pratt, *Journal of Discourses,* vol. 10 (London: Latter-day Saints' Book Depot, 1854–86), 328.
2. Orson F. Whitney, *Saturday Night Thoughts* (Salt Lake City: *Deseret News,* 1921), 12.
3. Bruce R. McConkie, *Doctrinal New Testament Commentary,* vol. 3 (Salt Lake City: Bookcraft, 1973), 485–86.
4. *Journal of Discourses,* 17:247.
5. *World Book Encyclopedia,* vol. 3 (Chicago: World Book, Inc., 1991), 31.
6. *Journal of Discourses,* 15:263, 45.
7. Bruce R. McConkie, *The Millennial Messiah: The Second Coming of the Son of Man* (Salt Lake City: Deseret Book, 1982), 378.
8. Jerreld L. Newquist, *Prophets, Principles, and National Survival,* 2nd ed. (Salt Lake City: Publishers Press, 1964), 427.
9. Joseph Fielding Smith, *The Signs of the Times* (Salt Lake City: Deseret Book, 1974), 6.
10. Spencer W. Kimball, *Faith Precedes the Miracle* (Salt Lake City: Deseret Book, 1972), 253–54.
11. Joseph Fielding Smith, *Doctrines of Salvation,* vol. 3 (Salt Lake City: Bookcraft, 1956), 2, 55.
12. *Journal of Discourses,* 16:35.
13. Smith, *Doctrines of Salvation,* 3:2–3.
14. Joseph Fielding Smith, *Teachings of the Prophet Joseph Smith* (Salt Lake City: Deseret Book, 1976), 29.

Two

THE SIXTH SEAL

If we are now living in the seventh seal, then every event associated with the sixth seal should have already occurred. Even if we are still living near the end of the sixth seal, most of that seal's events have passed. We learn from the apostle John what some of those events were. One was a great earthquake. He related, "I beheld . . . the sixth seal, and lo, there was a great earthquake" (Revelation 6:12).

The question arises, if the earthquake has already happened, why have we not heard about it? There are at least three possible reasons. First of all, when the sixth seal opened in approximately AD 1000, the world was in the middle of the Dark Ages, long before we were born and long before the invention of seismographs or other earthquake-recording devices. In addition, there were no telephones, television, or telegraphs with which to report it.

Second, the earthquake may have occurred simultaneously with another major event that overshadowed the earthquake. For example, the atomic bombs of World War II caused the earth to quake to an extent, but people were more concerned with the destructive power of the bombs than they were with the quaking of the earth. Deke Parsons, one of the war's nuclear scientists, stated that the bomb dropped over Hiroshima had the potential to crack the earth's crust.[1] But people may have focused on the bomb rather than on the earthquake.

Third, the earthquake might not have been literal. The Revelation of John contains much symbolism, so the sixth seal earthquake could have been symbolic of all earthquakes that the Lord said would occur in the last days. It is a statistical fact that earthquakes have been increasing in number and intensity since the opening of the sixth seal. During the 1900s alone, there were at least thirty-six major earthquakes measuring 7.9 and higher on the Richter scale.[2]

That raises another question: Why are earthquakes increasing? The answer could be that, to become a fit millennial planet, the earth must return to the paradisiacal condition it was in before the fall of Adam. The tenth article of faith states, "We believe . . . that the earth will be renewed and receive its paradisiacal glory." The Prophet Joseph Smith also indicated that the earth will "resume its paradisean glory, and become as the garden of the Lord."[3]

The initial stages of the transforming process may have begun during the sixth seal. Evidence of that is found in John's Revelation. He wrote, "And I beheld when [the] . . . sixth seal [opened] . . . every mountain and island were moved out of their places" (Revelation 6:12, 14). That movement is still occurring. Mountains and islands are constantly shifting with the earth's crust, which is no longer a solid land mass.

Before the earth "fell" to its present telestial condition, its crust was apparently one seamless and unbroken land mass. The continental drift thoery suggests that all the continents at one time formed an enormous land mass called Pangaea.[4] Sometime later in the earth's history, the land mass was divided into continents. This event may have occurred during the time of "Peleg; for in his days was the earth divided" (Genesis 10:25). At that time, the earth's crust may have split into the shifting tectonic plates which scientists now believe are responsible for earthquakes.

The surface of the earth was further broken up at the time of Jesus' crucifixion. Samuel the Lamanite prophesied, "Yea . . . the rocks which are upon the face of this earth . . . which ye know at this time are solid, or the more part of it is one solid mass, shall be broken up; yea, they shall be rent in twain, and shall ever after be found in seams and in cracks, and in broken fragments upon the face of the whole earth" (Helaman 14:21–22).

The Lord said that at his coming, or just prior to it, the land will return back to its former condition. "And the land of Jerusalem and the land of Zion shall be turned back into their own place, and the earth shall be like as it was in the days before it was divided" (D&C 133:24).

Although the earth's transforming process may have already begun, the biggest changes will occur at the Second Coming of Jesus. At that time, there will be "a great earthquake, such as was not since men were upon the earth, so mighty an earthquake, and so great" (Revelation 16:18). "Every valley shall be exalted, and every mountain and hill shall be made low: and the crooked shall be made straight, and the rough places plain" (Isaiah 40:4).

Thus it was prophesied that there would be "a great earthquake" during both the sixth and the seventh seals, but the latter one will be the most cataclysmic. When the seventh seal earthquake shakes the earth, "The earth [will be] utterly broken down . . . the earth [will be] moved exceedingly" (Isaiah 24:19). "The earth shall tremble and reel to and fro as a drunken man" (D&C 88:87).

Besides a great earthquake during the sixth seal, John recorded that "the sun became black as sackcloth of hair, and the moon became as blood" (Revelation 6:12). This phenomenon will also occur twice, once during the sixth seal and again during the seventh, near the end of the war of Armageddon. Jesus described the latter in the book of Matthew: "Immediately after the tribulation of those days shall the sun be darkened, and the moon shall not give her light, and the stars shall fall from heaven, and the powers of the heavens shall be shaken: And then shall appear the sign of the Son of man in heaven" (Matthew 24:29–30).

John's Revelation clearly indicates that something similar would also occur during the sixth seal. But if that seal has passed, has the sun ever been darkened and has the moon ever looked like blood? According to several sources, it has. When the volcanic island of Krakatoa in Indonesia erupted in August, 1883 (during the sixth seal), its blast was equal to 1000 atomic bombs and the sound was heard about 3000 miles away, over one-twelfth of the earth. It shot twelve cubic miles of volcanic ash into the air, causing the sun and moon to become darkened, and the skies to become "blood red." As far away as England, the skies appeared red, and at times the sun, itself, "was the color of blood."[4] The painter Edvard Munch witnessed this incredible event. He observed, "All at once the sky become bloodred. . . . It was as if a flaming sword of blood slashed open the vault of heaven [and] the atmosphere turned to blood."[5] Munch was so affected by this event that he painted it. (His painting, which he entitled *The Scream,* became famous.)

World Book Encyclopedia also states that the 1815 eruption of Mount Tambora in Indonesia "released 6 million times more energy than that of an atomic bomb."[6] The resulting amount of ash and dust in the air from that eruption also caused extreme atmospheric changes such as a darkened sun and blood-red sky and moon. Whenever large amounts of dust, smoke, and gas enter the atmosphere, the sun becomes obscured and the moon can appear red.

This type of phenomena is also descriptive of what happens after an atomic or nuclear bomb explodes. Two such bombs were dropped over Japan during the sixth seal (in 1945), and hundreds more have been tested. Even during the 1991 Gulf War, the skies over the Middle East became darkened and the moon appeared red from the extreme amount of smoke and gas from burning oil wells in Kuwait. "Observers in the surrounding areas noted that the chemicals released in the atmosphere by the fires created an illusion that caused the moon to appear to be blood red."[7]

Another sixth seal event was recorded by John the Revelator: "And the stars of heaven fell unto the earth, even as a fig tree casteth her untimely figs, when she is shaken of a mighty wind" (Revelation 6:13). Many "falling stars" are seen in the heavens every day. It is quite possible that they began falling more frequently during the sixth seal. Or they began to be observed more easily because of the invention of the telescope in 1608.

Falling or shooting stars are usually meteors.

> Scientists estimate that as many as 200 million visible meteors occur in the earth's atmosphere every day. These and invisible meteorites are estimated to add more than 1000 short tons (910 metric tons) daily to the earth's weight . . . The earth meets a number of meteoroids [meteor showers] every year. At such times, the sky seems filled with a shower of flying sparks. . . .
>
> The most brilliant meteoric shower took place on November 13, 1833 [during the sixth seal]. . . .
>
> Another brilliant Leonid meteor shower occurred in 1966. . . . In 1908, the famous Tunguska meteorite crashed into the earth in Siberia. People as far as 466 miles (750 kilometers) away saw it in full daylight, and felt its blast at a distance of 50 miles (80 kilometers). The meteorite had a weight estimated at a few hundred tons. It scorched a 20-mile (32 kilometer) area and flattened forests. In 1947, a meteorite exploded into fragments . . . in eastern Siberia. It left more than 200 craters in the earth. . . .
>
> In the 1950's, scientists discovered a 400-mile . . . wide depression on the eastern shore of Hudson Bay in Canada, which may be the earth's largest meteorite crater. Canada also has four other craters found in the 1950's.[8]

It has been estimated that the earth gains tens of thousands of tons each year as foreign bodies hit the earth. During the Leonid meteor shower in 1966, over 100,000 meteors fell through the sky every hour.[9] These meteoric showers and falling stars were seen between AD 1000 and 2000, the approximate time of the sixth seal. If John's Revelation has been translated correctly, and if the sixth seal has passed, then the "stars of heaven fell unto the earth" during that time just as John prophesied.

John recorded another unusual occurrence of the sixth seal. He said that "the heaven departed as a scroll when it is rolled together" (Revelation 6:14). Joseph Smith indicated that the word *departed* should have been translated "opened" (JST, Revelation 6:14). Both of the mushroom-shaped clouds of World War II's atomic bomb blasts made the heavens appear to open as each cloud pushed up into the atmosphere. They even looked like scrolls opening as they extended upward.

In addition to bombs opening the atmosphere during the sixth seal, the heavens also opened in another way. When God restored his kingdom to the earth in these last days, the heavens opened between God and mankind. After a long time of spiritual famine during the Dark Ages, the Lord began once more to pour out revelation to his prophets who have been called to direct the latter-day work of his restored church and kingdom (D&C 107:19).

Joseph Smith, the first prophet chosen to direct the work, recorded that when the heavens opened to him in the spring of 1820, he "saw a pillar of light . . . which descended gradually . . . [and] two Personages, whose brightness and glory defy all description" appeared before him and gave him instructions (JS—H 1:17). The heavens opened to him many times thereafter as he received further revelatory instruction and keys with which to carry out the work of the Restoration. On one occasion, in April of 1836, the Lord opened the heavens and appeared to both Joseph Smith and Oliver Cowdery (D&C 110:2–3). On another occasion, Moses appeared to them. Joseph recorded, "After this vision closed, the heavens were again opened unto us; and Moses appeared before us, and committed unto us the keys of the Gathering of Israel" (D&C 110:11). Thus the revelatory opening of the heavens during the sixth seal was one of the greatest events of these last days.

The sealing of 144,000 is another event of the sixth seal. John recorded, "And I saw another angel ascending from the east, having the seal of the living God: and he cried with a loud voice to the four angels, to whom it was given to hurt the earth and the sea, saying, Hurt not the earth, neither the sea, nor the trees, till we have sealed the servants of our God in their foreheads. And I heard the number of them which were sealed: and there were an hundred and forty and four thousand of all the tribes of the children of Israel," 12,000 from each tribe (Revelation 7:2–4). (The earth, sea, and trees will be hurt the most during Armageddon; the 144,000 must be sealed before then, according to the scripture quoted above).

The tribes of Israel are descendants of the twelve sons of the Old Testament prophet Jacob, whose name was changed to Israel. Over the centuries, most of Jacob's descendants, who number in the millions by now, have passed on to the other side of the veil. The 144,000 were to be chosen from Jacob's enormously huge posterity, whether on this side of the veil or the other. And they were to be sealed during the sixth seal, according to John.

The Lord also revealed to the Prophet Joseph Smith that the sealings were "to be accomplished in the sixth thousand years, or the opening of the sixth seal" (D&C 77:10). Thus the Prophet said in 1844, "The selection of persons to form that number had already commenced."[10]

Many people have assumed that the 144,000 cannot be sealed yet because their location is unknown. However, although we do not know where all the living descendants of Jacob (Israel) are today, we do know where his deceased descendants are. They are in the spirit world awaiting their resurrection. Because the 144,000 were to be sealed during the sixth seal which may have already passed, then those that were sealed must have been among Jacob's deceased posterity, and they were in the world of spirits when their sealing work was done. People need not be alive to be sealed. Sealing work is done for the dead as well as the living.

Sealing work commenced during the sixth seal when the sealing powers were restored to the Prophet Joseph Smith. The Lord said to him, "And of as many as the Father shall bear record, to you shall be given power to seal them up unto eternal life" (D&C 68:12).

Referring to the 144,000, the Prophet Joseph taught that "the servants of God are sealed in their foreheads . . . thereby making their calling and election sure."[11] That is, their exaltation in the highest heaven is assured.

Scriptures tell us that those men, 12,000 from each of the tribes of Israel, "are they which follow the Lamb whithersoever he goeth. These were redeemed from among men. . . . And in their mouth was found no guile, for they are without fault before the throne of God" (Revelation 14:4–5). They "are high priests, ordained unto the holy order of God, to administer the everlasting gospel . . . to bring as many as will come to the church of the Firstborn" (D&C 77:11).

When the Lord comes, he will bring the 144,000 with him. A revelation received by the Prophet Joseph Smith says, "For the hour of his coming is nigh—When the Lamb shall stand upon Mount Zion, and with him a hundred and forty-four thousand, having his Father's name written on their foreheads" (D&C 133:18). That group of faithful priesthood leaders will likely include apostles and prophets (most of whom were in the spirit world before the sixth seal opened). The Lord said,

> Mine apostles, the Twelve which were with me in my ministry at Jerusalem, shall stand at my right hand at the day of my coming in a pillar of fire. (D&C 29:12)

> Yea, and Enoch also, and they who were with him; the prophets who were before him; and Noah also, and they who were before him; and Moses also, and they who were before him; and from Moses to Elijah, and from Elijah to John, who were with Christ in his resurrection, and the holy apostles, with Abraham, Isaac, and Jacob, shall be in the presence of the Lamb . . . when he shall stand upon Mount Zion, and upon the holy city, the New Jerusalem. (D&C 133:54–56)

It appears that the 144,000 may have been ordained and sealed to direct the affairs of the millennial church. In particular, they will probably supervise the missionary and temple work that will be done during that time in order to bring "as many as will come to the church of the Firstborn" (D&C 77:11), the millennial church. Members of that church "shall come forth in the resurrection of the just' as heirs of exaltation in the celestial kingdom. "They are they who are the church of the Firstborn" (D&C 76:54).

It was also revealed to Joseph Smith that the 144,000 will administer the gospel (see D&C 77:11), meaning they will have charge of, direct, and manage the work of the gospel. They could only do that during the Millennium, for now the current prophet of God administers and directs the work of the gospel. Joseph Smith recorded, "We are to understand that those who are sealed are high priests, ordained unto the holy order of God, to administer the everlasting gospel; for they are they who are ordained out of every nation, kindred, tongue, and people, by the angels to whom is given power over the nations of the earth, to bring as many as will come to the church of the Firstborn," the millennial church (D&C 77:11).

The temple work which the 144,000 will likely oversee will probably be their most important work. Elder Bruce R. McConkie tells us, "Temple work will be the great work of the millennium."[12] President Joseph Fielding Smith also stated, "The great work of the millennium shall be performed in the temples which shall cover all parts of the land and into which the children shall go to complete the work for their fathers, which they could not do when in this mortal life for themselves."[13]

President Wilford Woodruff declared, "When the Savior comes, a thousand years will be devoted to this work of redemption; and temples will appear all over this land of Joseph—North and South America—and also in Europe and elsewhere; and all the descendants of Shem, Ham, and Japeth, who received not the Gospel in the flesh, must be officiated for in the Temple of God, before the Savior can present the kingdom to the Father, saying, 'It is finished.' "[14]

What an undertaking for the 144,000! But they will not be alone in that great work. They will be part of a great multitude of "saviours [which] shall come up on mount Zion" (Obadiah 1:21) to "bring out the prisoners from the prison" (Isaiah 42:7). That multitude of people, which John the Revelator saw in vision, will serve God day and night in his temple. John said of them, "These are they which came out of great tribulation, and have washed their robes, and made them white in the blood of the Lamb. Therefore are they before the throne of God, and serve him day and night in his temple" (Revelation 7:14–15).

There is no way of knowing with certainty that the sealing of the 144,000 and all the other events of the sixth seal have already transpired, but it must be acknowledged that most of that seals events have certainly passed by now. Furthermore, the restoration of the church in 1830, and everything associated with it, makes the sixth seal one of the most important times in the history of the world. Much was accomplished to prepare for the Lord's return. It was a time when the sealing powers were restored to the earth through the Prophet Joseph Smith, and sealings can now be performed not only for the dead, but for anyone who is worthy to enter the temple of the Lord. Now the righteous can be "sealed up to eternal life" with their families, to come forth in the first resurrection as members of the millennial Church of the Firstborn.

John the Revelator exclaimed,

> Blessed and holy is he that hath part in the first resurrection: on such the second death hath no power, but they shall be priests of God and of Christ, and shall reign with him a thousand years. (Revelation 20:6)

> And they shall see his face; and his name shall be in their foreheads. (Revelation 22:4)

> And I saw thrones, and they sat upon them, and judgment was given unto them. (Revelation 20:4)

Whether we are living in the sixth or the seventh seal is not as important as what we do with our time while in mortality. We are living in a time when the blessings and ordinances of the restored gospel are available to us. The wise virgins of Jesus' parable are those who are living the gospel and are participating in the saving ordinances before the Lord comes to dwell with those who have been obedient.

Notes

1. Deke Parson, "Second World War: Hiroshima," http://www.spartacus.schoolnet.co.uk/2WWhiroshima.htm.
2. *World Book Encyclopedia,* vol. 6 (Chicago: World Book, Inc., 1991), 33.
3. Smith, *Teachings of the Prophet Joseph Smith,* 248–49.
4. *World Book Encyclopedia,* vol. 4 (Chicago: World Book, Inc., 1991), 1022.
5. Marilynn S. Olson, et al., "Marilynn S. Olson, Donal W. Olson, and Russell L. Doescher on the Blood-red Sky of Munch's *The Scream," Environmental History,* Vol. 12, No. 1, Jan. 2007, http://www.historycooperative.org/journals/eh/12.1/olson.html.
6. *World Book Encyclopedia,* vol. 20 (Chicago: World Book, Inc., 1991), 457.
7. Perry Stone, Jr., *Unleashing the Beast* (Cleveland, TN: Voice of Evangelism, 2003), 198.
8. *World Book Encyclopedia,* vol. 13 (Chicago: World Book, Inc., 1991), 431–432.
9. Robert Roy Britt, "The 2001 Storm: How it Stacks Up Against History," http://www.space.com/scienceastronomy/astronomy/leonids_2001.html.
10. Gerald N. Lund, *The Coming of the Lord* (Salt Lake City: Bookcraft, 1971), 174.
11. Smith, *Teachings of the Prophet Joseph Smith,* 321.

12. Bruce R. McConkie, *Mormon Doctrine* (Salt Lake City: Bookcraft, 1966), 501.
13. Joseph Fielding Smith, *Doctrines of Salvation,* vol. 2 (Salt Lake City: Bookcraft, 1955), 252.
14. *Journal of Discourses,* 19:230.

Three

SIGNS OF THE TIMES

When Jesus came to the earth in the meridian of time, his disciples asked him about signs which would indicate the time of his second coming. "And as he sat upon the mount of Olives, the disciples came unto him privately, saying, Tell us . . . what shall be the sign of thy coming, and of the end of the world?" (Matthew 24:3). Jesus replied with a description of several signs that will precede his return. He said, "I will shew wonders in heaven above, and signs in the earth beneath; blood, and fire, and vapour of smoke" (Acts 2:19). "And there shall be signs in the sun, and in the moon, and in the stars" (Luke 21:25).

Beginning in the sixth seal, new things began to be observed in the heavens, and in the sun, moon, and stars, which heretofore had remained unseen by the human eye. The invention of powerful telescopes made possible a greater view into the starry vistas, bringing to sight such things as the Milky Way, quasars, black holes, asteroid belts, new planets, and even new galaxies, among other things.

In addition, extraordinary man-made objects also began to be seen in the heavens. President Joseph Fielding Smith referred to those signs when he said, "In speaking of the heavens, reference is made to that part which surrounds the earth and which belongs to it. It is in the atmosphere where many of the signs are to be given. Do we not see airships of various kinds traveling through the heavens daily? Have we not had signs in the earth and through the earth with the radio, railroad trains, automobiles, submarines, and satellites, and in many other ways?"[1]

Another sign that Jesus prophesied would foreshadow the end of the world was "false Christs and false prophets." He said that those false spiritual guides "shall shew great signs and wonders; insomuch that, if it were possible, they shall deceive the very elect" (Matthew 24:24). Christ also said, "If any man shall say unto you, Lo, here is Christ, or there; believe it not.... Wherefore, if they shall say unto you, Behold, he is in the desert; go not forth: behold, he is in the secret chambers; believe it not" (Matthew 24:23, 26).

Elder Bruce R. McConkie commented on the false Christs of which Jesus prophesied:

> Since then untold millions have worshipped before the thrones of false Christs. Some deluded fanatics have bowed before persons professing to be saviors or to have the power to confer salvation. Other hosts of misguided souls have trekked to desert monasteries, to mountain hermitages, to Jesuit retreats, and to the meeting places of secret cults—all acting under the specious assumption that in the place of their choice they would find Christ. Still others have made money, power, worldly learning, political preferment, or the gratification of sensual lusts their God. And virtually all the millions of apostate Christendom have abased themselves before the mythical throne of a mythical Christ whom they vainly suppose to be a spirit essence who is incorporeal, uncreated, immaterial, and three-in-one with the Father and Holy Spirit.[2]

The world is also full of false prophets. They are people who claim to be speaking for God, but they are preaching false doctrine. The Lord said of them, "I have not sent them, saith the Lord, yet they prophesy a lie in my name" (Jeremiah 27:15).

Another sign that Jesus said would point toward his Second Coming was the preaching of his gospel throughout the world. He said, "And this gospel of the kingdom shall be preached in all the world for a witness unto all nations; and then shall the end come" (Matthew 24:14). Only one church today is coming close to achieving that—The Church of Jesus Christ of Latter-day Saints.

Jesus' early apostles were the first to be given the commission to preach the gospel throughout the earth (see Mark 16:15), but they were eventually killed or were otherwise prevented from accomplishing that goal. The Great Apostasy followed, plunging the world into the Dark Ages. False prophets stepped forward to fill the leadership void, but without inspiration and revelation from God, the gospel of Jesus Christ became corrupted and the Church "fled into the wilderness" (Revelation 12:6).

Finally in 1830, following centuries of spiritual darkness, the true Church was restored in its fulness in a place where it could flourish. That place was America, a land of religious freedom. Its God-inspired Constitution preserves for America's citizens the right to worship how, where, and what they may.

The Lord said the restoration of the priesthood to Joseph Smith in America in 1829 was "the beginning of the rising up and the coming forth of my church out of the wilderness—clear as the moon, and fair as the sun, and terrible as an army with banners" (D&C 5:14). The Church's "banners" are now seen by millions of people as Church wards and stakes are organized throughout the earth. The Church has been established in 160 nations, and its membership has grown from a mere six people in 1830 to over 12 million, as of December 2004.[3] A *Newsweek* article reported in October of 2005, "Two centuries after the birth of founding Prophet Joseph Smith, Mormonism is America's fastest-growing Christian denomination."[4]

Because the Church is growing rapidly, it has been able to expand its missionary force to over 51,000 full-time missionaries,[5] serving in 341 missions worldwide, as of September 2005.[6] God has also inspired the development of technology, which is assisting his great missionary force in spreading the gospel. It is no coincidence that technology has developed at a phenomenal rate since the Prophet Joseph Smith was given the commission to carry the gospel throughout the world. President Gordon B. Hinckley stated that technology becomes more available as the Church grows.[7]

Since the Church has been established now for nearly two centuries, it appears that the pre-millennial goal of spreading the gospel has almost been achieved. We do not yet have missionaries in every country, but through technology, gospel messages are being received by satellite in nearly every part of the earth except the tip of South America and western Africa.

Printed in the August 2005 *Ensign* is the following information:

> The ability to broadcast more often in an increasing number of languages began after the [Church] Conference Center was built in 2000. . . .
>
> Until recently, church satellite broadcasts were limited to North and South America, the Pacific, Europe, and South Africa. In 2002,

to Asia, [and] signals now also reach into India. The Church's broadcast system uses five satellites to relay satellite signals to most of the globe. A few remote areas such as the tip of South America and western Africa cannot receive a signal from one of the five satellites. Areas not served by satellite can receive audio by Internet or telephone lines. . . .

On average, the Church broadcasts two events per weekend . . . "We have made a very long jouney in reaching out to the nations of the world," President Hinckley said. "There is much more to be done, but what has been accomplished is truly phenomenal."[8]

In addition to technology, a few individual Latter-day Saints, as well as the Tabernacle Choir and BYU performing groups, have been able to enter countries where proselyting is not allowed, but those dedicated Church members have, unofficially, been able to spread the light of the gospel among those with whom they visit. Thus, with the help of God and his righteous Saints, the gospel voice cannot be silenced. The Prophet Joseph Smith said, "No unhallowed hand can stop the work from progressing; persecutions may rage, mobs may combine, armies may assemble, calumny may defame, but the truth of God will go forth boldly, nobly, and independent, till it has penetrated every continent, visited every clime, swept every country, and sounded in every ear, till the purposes of God shall be accomplished, and the Great Jehovah shall say the work is done."[9]

The Lord indicated that during the beginning stage of the seventh seal, he would finish his work and complete the salvation of man (see D&C 77:12). That does not mean, however, that every single person will be taught the gospel before Jesus comes, for there is evidence that many "heathens" (non-Christians) will not be taught until the Millennium. A revelation to the Prophet Joseph Smith states, "And then the Lord shall set his feet upon [the] mount [of Olives]. . . . And then shall the heathen nations be redeemed, and they that knew no law shall have part in the first resurrection" (D&C 45:48, 54); for "then cometh the day when the arm of the Lord shall be revealed in power in convincing the nations, the heathen nations . . . of the gospel of their salvation" (D&C 90:10). It seems, therefore, that if there will be those who "knew no law," there will be those who were never taught the "law" of the gospel.

According to Joseph Fielding Smith,

> There will be a need for the preaching of the gospel, after the millennium is brought in, until all men are either converted or pass away.[10]

The gospel will be taught far more intensely and with greater power during the millennium until all the inhabitants of the earth shall embrace it.[11]

In that day there shall be no "divided Christianity." All who will not repent and receive the gospel shall soon be removed, and they who shall remain shall learn to worship the true and living God in spirit and in truth. The Church of Jesus Christ shall have sway over all the earth, for Christ shall be the King and Deliverer.[12]

People who have the opportunity to hear the gospel before Jesus comes will be in jeopardy if they do not accept and obey it. The prophet Joseph Smith said that "in consequence of rejecting the Gospel of Jesus Christ . . . the judgments of God [rest] upon people, cities, and nations."[13] The apostle Paul taught that at the Second Coming "the Lord Jesus shall be revealed from heaven with his mighty angels, In flaming fire taking vengeance on them . . . that obey not the gospel of our Lord Jesus Christ" (2 Thessalonians 1:7–10).

According to President Heber C. Kimball, without a testimony of the gospel we will never have enough spiritual strength to withstand the trials that are coming. He stated, "To meet the difficulties that are coming, it will be necessary for you to have a knowledge of the truth of this work for yourselves. The difficulties will be of such a character that the man or woman who does not possess this personal knowledge or witness will fall. If you have not got the testimony, live right and call upon the Lord and cease not till you obtain it. If you do not, you will not stand. . . . The time will come when no man or woman will be able to endure on borrowed light."[14]

As the Saints strive to live righteously, their testimonies are strengthened, and the Church, the Kingdom of God on earth, grows in power and dominion. However, as it grows, the power of Satan also grows, and wickedness increases. President Spencer W. Kimball remarked that "the progress of the church will be paralleled by a growing wickedness among mankind . . . in proportion to the spread of the Gospel among the nations of the earth so would the power of Satan arise."[15]

Extreme wickedness is another sign which Jesus said would point to the end of the world. He stated:

> Iniquity shall abound [and] the love of many shall wax cold. (Matthew 24:12)
>
> And the day speedily cometh . . . when peace shall be taken from

the earth, and the devil shall have power over his own dominion. (D&C 1:35)

> As the days of Noe [Noah] were, so shall also the coming of the Son of man be. (Matthew 24:37)

The moral decay of today's society is very evident. President James E. Faust said in June 2006, "Values have shifted. Basic decency and respect for good things are eroding. A moral blackness is settling in."[16] As early as 1831, the Lord was prompted to say, "All flesh is corrupted before me, and the powers of darkness prevail upon the earth, among the children of men . . . and all eternity is pained. . . . [Therefore] the angels are waiting the great command to reap down the earth" (D&C 38:11–12).

As wickedness increases, violence and wars are also increasing. The inordinate amount of warfare in these last days is another sign of the times. Jesus said, "And ye shall hear of wars and rumors of wars. . . . For nation shall rise against nation, and kingdom against kingdom" (Matthew 24:6–7). And there will be "wars and rumors of wars among all the nations and kindreds of the earth" (1 Nephi 14:15). And "they shall behold blood, and fire, and vapors of smoke" (D&C 45:41). "And thus, with the sword and by bloodshed the inhabitants of the earth shall mourn" (D&C 87:6).

God will allow wars to occur in order for the earth to be cleansed of the wicked people who live upon it. He said,

> I have sworn in my wrath, and decreed wars upon the face of the earth, and the wicked shall slay the wicked, and fear shall come upon every man. (D&C 63:33)

> The judgments of God will overtake the wicked; and it is by the wicked that the wicked are punished for it is the wicked that stir up the hearts of the children of men unto bloodshed. (Mormon 4:5)

> Men will harden their hearts against me. [Therefore] they will take up the sword, one against another, and they will kill one another. (D&C 45:33)

There will eventually be so much bloodshed that Elder Bruce R. McConkie remarked, "Carnal men will consider war as a way of life and a norm of society, not as a scourge sent of God to cleanse the earth preparatory to the return of his Son."[17]

Without Jesus' intervention, earth's inhabitants would self-destruct because they have chosen to do things their way instead of God's. When the laws of God are not obeyed, order breaks down and the "law of the jungle" takes over. That law is "every man for himself," which results in chaos and violence. Consequently, in recent decades, war has ravaged the earth as never before. It has been reported that during the twentieth century, over 200 million people died as a result of warfare.[18]

In 1934 President Joseph Fielding Smith read a study of war conducted by two Harvard sociologists who concluded that wars are increasing. It said, "Two scientists charting the European record find that the indexed number of wars rose from 2.678 in the twelfth to 13,735.98 in the twentieth century."[19] President Smith went on to say, "If prophecy is to be fulfilled, there awaits the world a conflict more dreadful than any the world has yet seen."[20] He was, of course, referring to the war of Armageddon. War does not, therefore, tend to decline as nations become more civilized.

Because of modern technology, wars are also becoming more destructive. Hundreds of nuclear weapons have been developed and are being stored in various parts of the world. In 2005, Martin Sheen hosted a television documentary called *Stockpile: The Nuclear Menace*. The alarming statistics that he presented are summarized here: Two atomic bombs were dropped over Japan on August 5, 1945. In August 1949, Russia tested an atomic bomb. Later, the more powerful hydrogen or thermo nuclear bomb was tested (in October 1952). That bomb was four times more powerful than all allied bombs of World War II put together. Bombs were tested again and again until both "super powers" (United States and USSR) moved the testing to underground in 1963. Mr. Sheen said that the arms race in the 1960s resulted in the development of 32,000 nuclear weapons by the United States and 45,000 nuclear weapons by the Soviets. In 1961, the largest nuclear weapon ever built was tested by the Soviets—a 100 megaton bomb. It was tested at half capacity because of radioactive fallout. Many of the unused bombs are still being stored.[21]

There is no doubt that nuclear scientists today are developing plans for even more powerful and destructive bombs. And there is little question that such weapons will be used during the war of Armageddon. It has been prophesied that the warfare waged at that time will result in the death of a "third part of men" (see Revelation 9:15). The scriptures read, "For then shall be great tribulation, such as was not since the beginning of the world to this time, no, nor ever shall be. And except those days should be shortened, there should no flesh be saved: but for the elect's sake those days shall be shortened" (Matthew 24:21–22).

That may be the time when "every man that will not take his sword against his neighbor must needs flee unto Zion for safety. And there shall be gathered unto it out of every nation under heaven; and it shall be the only people that shall not be at war one against another" (D&C 45:68–69).

That final gathering of the righteous is another sign which Jesus mentioned. He said, "Behold, wheresoever the carcass is, there will the eagles be gathered together; so likewise shall mine elect be gathered from the four quarters of the earth" (JS—Matthew 1:27). That gathering will be distinct from the gathering which is already taking place. (It will be discussed at length in a later chapter.)

The rest of the signs which Jesus mentioned were primarily "judgments" (natural disasters or other calamities). They too will be discussed later.

It is clear that most of the signs have already been seen. They began to be observed as early as the mid-1800s, according to the Prophet Joseph Smith. He declared, "I will prophesy that the signs of the coming of the Son of Man are already commenced. One pestilence will desolate after another. We shall soon have war and bloodshed. The moon will be turned into blood. I testify of these things, and that the coming of the Son of Man is nigh, even at your doors."[22]

The Lord has given us signs so we can be prepared for his coming and the end of the world. Therefore, it is vital that we watch for, and recognize, the signs as they appear. Jesus said,

> Watch ye therefore, and pray always, that ye be accounted worthy to escape all these things that shall come to pass, and to stand before the Son of man. (Luke 21:36)

> And unto you it shall be given to know the signs of the times, and the signs of the coming of the Son of Man. (D&C 68:11)

The apostle James E. Talmage said, "Only through watchfulness and prayer may the signs of the times be correctly interpreted and the imminence of the Lord's appearing be apprehended."[23] And Elder Bruce R. McConkie said in a church conference in 1979 that "there is no promise of safety and no promise of security except for those who love the Lord and who are seeking to do all that he commands. It may be, for instance, that nothing except the power of faith and authority of the priesthood can save individuals and congregations from the atomic holocausts that surely shall be. And so we raise the warning voice and say: Take heed; prepare; watch and be ready."[24]

Notes
1. *The Doctrine and Covenants Student Manual* (Church Educational System manual, 1981), 96.
2. McConkie, *Mormon Doctrine*, 269.
3. "Statistical Report, 2004," *Ensign*, May 2005, 25.
4. Richard M. Smith, ed. "Mormon Moment," *Newsweek*, October 17, 2005, 3.
5. "Statistical Report, 2004," *Ensign*, May 2005, 25.
6. "Two New Missions Created in Africa," *Ensign*, Sept. 2005, 74.
7. Gordon B. Hinckley, "The Church Grows Stronger," *Ensign*, May 2004, 4.
8. Walter Cooley, "Technology Is Spreading the Prophetic Voice," *Ensign*, Aug. 2005, 78.
9. *Doctrine and Covenants Student Manual*, 367.
10. Smith, *Doctrines of Salvation*, 1:86.
11. Joseph Fielding Smith, *Answers to Gospel Questions*, vol. 1 (Salt Lake City: Desert Book, 1966), 110.
12. Smith, *Doctrines of Salvation*, 1:168.
13. Smith, *Teachings of the Prophet Joseph Smith*, 271.
14. Rulon T. Burton, *We Believe* (Salt Lake City: Tabernacle Books, 1994), 1039.
15. *Doctrine and Covenants Student Manual*, 398.
16. James E. Faust, "Voice of the Spirit," *Ensign*, June 2006, 3.
17. Burton, *We Believe*, 493.
18. Milton Lietenburg, "Death in Wars and Conflicts in the 20th Century," Cornell University, 2006, http://www.cissm.umd.edu/papers/files/deathswarsconflicts/june52006.pdf.
19. Smith, *The Signs of the Times*, 118.
20. Ibid., 120.
21. *Stockpile: The Nuclear Menace*, Discovery Channel, Apr. 14, 2005.
22. Smith, *Teachings of the Prophet Joseph Smith*, 160.
23. James E. Talmage, *Jesus the Christ* (Salt Lake City: Deseret Book, 1969), 785.
24. Bruce R. McConkie, "Stand Independent above All Other Creatures," *Ensign*, May 1979, 93.

Four

THE VOICE OF WARNING

Not only are we to watch for the signs of the coming of the Lord, but we are to prepare for that day in order to avoid being swept away with the wicked. Preparation requires living the gospel. That is the reason the Church was restored in these last days.

God does not take pleasure in the destruction of people. He pleads with them, through his latter-day servants, to repent and live the gospel in order to avoid the calamity that awaits them if they do not heed his warning. Therefore, scriptures tell us that "this is a day of warning" (D&C 63:58). "The ax is laid at the root of the tree; and every tree that bringeth not forth good fruit shall be hewn down" (D&C 97:7).

The Lord has declared,

> And the voice of warning shall be unto all people, by the mouths of my disciples, whom I have chosen in these last days. (D&C 1:4)

> The day cometh that they who will not hear the voice of the Lord, neither the voice of his servants, neither give heed to the words of the prophets and apostles, shall be cut off from among the people. (D&C 1:14)

> What I the Lord have spoken, I have spoken . . . whether by mine own voice or by the voice of my servants, it is the same. (D&C 1:38)

The Lord indicated that if people fail to heed the warning voice of his servants, then he will preach his own sermons, which will come in the form of "judgments" such as natural disasters or other calamities. He has told his latter-day servants,

> And after your testimony cometh wrath and indignation upon the people. For after your testimony cometh the testimony of earthquakes, that shall cause groanings in the midst of her, and men shall fall upon the ground and shall not be able to stand. And also cometh the testimony of the voice of thunderings, and the voice of lightnings, and the voice of tempests, and the voice of the waves of the sea heaving themselves beyond their bounds. And all things shall be in commotion; and surely, men's hearts shall fail them; for fear shall come upon all people. (D&C 88:88–91)

President Joseph Fielding Smith also indicated that calamities will follow the testimony of God's servants. He stated, "These things shall follow the testimony of the elders of the Church of Jesus Christ of Latter-day Saints, when the people of the world reject them and drive them from their borders."[1]

Regarding those calamities, President Brigham Young expressed these chilling words:

> Do you think there is calamity abroad now among the people? Not much. All we have seen and all we have experienced is scarcely a preface to the sermon that is going to be preached. When the testimony of the Elders ceases to be given, and the Lord says to them, "Come home; I will now preach my own sermons to the nations of the earth," all you now know can scarcely be called a preface to the sermon that will be preached with fire and sword, tempests, earthquakes, hail, rain, thunders and lightnings, and fearful destruction. What matters the destruction of a few railway cars? You will hear of magnificent cities, now idolized by the people, sinking in the earth, entombing the inhabitants. The sea will heave itself beyond its bounds, engulphing [sic] mighty cities. Famine will spread over the nations, and nation will rise up against nation, kingdom against kingdom, and states against states, in our own country and in foreign lands; and they will destroy each other, caring not for the blood and lives of their neighbors, of their families, or for their own lives....
>
> You may think that the little you hear of now is grievous; yet the faithful of God's people will see days that will cause them to close their eyes because of the sorrow that will come upon the wicked nations. The hearts of the faithful will be filled with pain and anguish for them.[2]

It has been prophesied that the first to feel God's wrath will be those of his own house. The Lord stated,

> Behold, vengeance cometh speedily upon the inhabitants of the earth, a day of wrath, a day of burning, a day of desolation, of weeping, of mourning, and of lamentation; and as a whirlwind it shall come upon all the face of the earth, saith the Lord. And upon my house shall it begin, and from my house shall it go forth, saith the Lord; first among those among you, saith the Lord, who have professed to know my name and have not known me, and have blasphemed against me in the midst of my house, saith the Lord. (D&C 112:24–26)

It is unclear whether the Lord's "house" is the house of Israel, or the Church. However, God said that "the saints also shall hardly escape" (D&C 63:34), indicating that some in the Church might feel the effects of his wrath. President Brigham Young warned,

> The time will come, and is now at hand, when those who profess our faith, if they are guilty of what some of this people are guilty of, will find the axe laid at the root of the tree, and they will be hewn down.[3]

> If the Latter-day Saints do not desist from running after the things of this world, and begin to reform and do the work the Father has given them to do, they will be found wanting, and they, too, will be swept away and counted as unprofitable servants.[4]

President Joseph Fielding Smith pointed out, "All of these things will be withheld while the nations are being punished, if the members of the Church will keep faithfully the commandments. If they will not, then we have received the warning that we, like the rest of the world, shall suffer His wrath in justice."[5]

The apostle Heber C. Kimball taught that the Saints will yet face great tests and trials (some of which may be judgments). He said, "The Saints will be put to the test that will try the very best of them. The pressure will become so great that the righteous among us will cry unto the Lord day and night until deliverance comes. . . . Then is the time to look out for the great sieve, for there will be a great sifting time, and many will fall."[6]

Elder Kimball went on to say,

> We think we are secure here in the chambers of the everlasting hills, where we can close those few doors of the canyons against mobs and persecutors, the wicked and the vile, who have always beset us with violence and robbery, but I want to say to you, my brethren, the time

is coming when we will be mixed up in these peaceful valleys to the extent that it will be difficult to tell the face of a Saint from the face of an enemy to the people of God. Then, brethren, look out for the great sieve, for there will be a great sifting time, and many will fall; for I say unto you there is a *test*, a TEST, a TEST coming, and who will be able to stand? This church has before it many close places through which it will have to pass before the work of God is crowned with victory.[7]

Because most people upon the earth are failing to heed the voice of warning, the Lord informed Joseph Smith in 1832 that angels were then awaiting the command to begin reaping down the wicked. The Lord said,

> Behold, verily I say unto you, the angels are crying unto the Lord day and night, who are ready and waiting to be sent forth to reap down the fields. But the Lord saith unto them, pluck not up the tares while the blade [of wheat] is tender (for verily your faith is weak), lest you destroy the wheat also. Therefore let the wheat and the tares grow together until the harvest is fully ripe; then ye shall first gather out the wheat from among the tares, and after the gathering of the wheat, behold and lo, the tares are bound in bundles, and the field remaineth to be burned. (D&C 86:5–7)

The spiritual gathering of the righteous "wheat" has been continuing for almost two centuries, so now the wicked tares are beginning to be destroyed. In fact, the angel Moroni told the Prophet Joseph Smith that God's judgments would begin to be sent forth "in this generation." Joseph recorded in his history, "He [Moroni] informed me of great judgments which were coming upon the earth, with great desolations by famine, sword, and pestilence; and that these grievous judgments would come on the earth in this generation" (JS—H 1:45).

On June 4, 1894, President Wilford Woodruff announced that the time had come for the "destroying angels" to begin their work of sweeping the wicked from the earth. He said, "God has held the angels of destruction for many years, lest they should reap down the wheat with the tares. But I want to tell you now, that those angels have left the portals of heaven, and they stand over this people and this nation now, and are hovering over the earth waiting to pour out the judgments. And from this very day they shall be poured out."[8]

President Joseph Fielding Smith also testified that the angels have begun their work.

I want to bear testimony to this congregation, and to the heavens and the earth, that the day has come when those angels are privileged to go forth and commence their work. They are laboring in the United States of America; they are laboring among the nations of the earth; and they will continue. We need not marvel or wonder at anything that is transpiring in the earth. . . . The Lord said that the sending forth of these angels was to be at the end of the harvest, and the harvest is the end of the world. Now, that ought to cause us some very serious reflections. . . . We are at the time of the end. This is the time of the harvest. This is the time spoken of which is called the end of the world.[9]

Regarding the harvest, it is clear that there is more than one "grim reaper." In fact, the exact number is four—four angels or four priesthood brethren who have been placed in charge of the judgments. Their identity has not been revealed, but they are referred to as angels in the scriptures because they are sent by God from the other side of the mortal veil. In the seventh chapter of Revelation, the apostle John recorded that he saw the "four angels standing on the four corners of the earth" who were ordered by another angel to "hurt not the earth, neither the sea, nor the trees, till we have sealed the servants of our God in their foreheads" (Revelation 7:1, 3).

The Lord explained to Joseph Smith that those angels "are four angels sent forth from God, to whom is given power over the four parts of the earth, to save life and to destroy: these are they who have the everlasting gospel to commit to every nation, kindred, tongue, and people; having power to shut up the heavens, to seal up unto life, or to cast down to the regions of darkness" (D&C 77:8).

President Joseph Fielding Smith stated that the angels described by John the Revelator and Joseph Smith were similar to those in a well-known parable. President Smith said:

> [These angels] seem to fit the description of the angels spoken of in the parable of the wheat and the tares (Matthew 13:24-43 and D&C 86:7), who plead with the Lord that they might go forth to reap down the fields. They were told to let the wheat and the tares grow together to the time of the end of the harvest, which is the end of the world (Matthew 13:38-39). . . . These angels have been given power over the four parts [quarters] of the earth and they have the power of committing the everlasting gospel to the peoples of the earth . . . power has been given [them] to shut up the heavens, to open them and with power unto life and also unto death and destruction. These are now at work in the earth on their sacred mission.[10]

The prophet Zechariah also recorded that there are "four spirits of the heavens, which go forth from standing before the Lord of all the earth" (Zechariah 6:5). Referring to that scripture, the *Old Testament Student Manual* states, "The Prophet Joseph Smith changed the phrase 'four spirits' (v. 5) to read 'four servants' (JST, Zechariah 6:5). This major change is vital to an understanding of these verses. Servants of the Lord are priesthood holders who labor to bring about the purposes of God. . . . John the Revelator also spoke of the four servants, or angels, who stood at the four corners of the earth (see Revelation 7:1–3)."[11]

In 1894, President Wilford Woodruff indicated that because the angels have been released to begin their work, great changes would be observed in the world. He declared, "Great changes are at our doors. The next 20 years will see mighty changes among the nations of the Earth."[12] Commenting on that statement, Elder Bruce R. McConkie said, "It is interesting to note that almost 20 years later to the day, June 28, 1914, the Archduke Ferdinand of Austria was assassinated, thus initiating the first World War."[13]

Now that the angels have begun their work, natural disasters and other calamities are increasing. President Wilford Woodruff observed, "Calamities and troubles are increasing in the earth, and there is a meaning to these things. Remember this, and reflect upon these matters; if you do your duty, and I do my duty, we'll have protection, and shall pass through the afflictions in peace and safety."[14]

The Lord stated,

> Zion shall escape if she observe to do all things whatsoever I have commanded her. But if she observe not to do whatsoever I have commanded her, I will visit her according to all her works, with sore affliction, with pestilence, with plague, with sword, with vengeance, with devouring fire. (D&C 97:25–26)

> [For] the saints . . . shall hardly escape; nevertheless, I, the Lord, am with them, and will come down in heaven from the presence of my Father and consume the wicked with unquenchable fire. (D&C 63:34)

> And in that day all who are found upon the watch-tower . . . shall be saved. (D&C 101:12)

Joseph Smith taught that "many of the Saints will escape, for the just shall live by faith."[15] So as the world continues to degenerate and self-destruct, the Saints who repent and remove themselves from the ways of the world will likely be spared much of the suffering as God's judgments sweep across the earth. President John Taylor uttered these reassuring words: "We have to pass through some of these things, but it will only be a very little compared with the terrible destruction, the misery, and suffering that will overtake the world."[16]

Notes
1. Smith, *Doctrines of Salvation*, 3:7–8.
2. *Journal of Discourses*, 8:123.
3. Ibid., 4:219.
4. Ibid., 18:262.
5. Joseph Fielding Smith, *The Progress of Man* (Genealogical Society of Utah, 1950), 468.
6. M. Catherine Thomas, *Watch and Be Ready* (Salt Lake City: Deseret Book, 1994), 18.
7. Ibid., 17.
8. *Doctrine and Covenants Student Manual*, 190.
9. Smith, *The Signs of the Times*, 113, 121.
10. *Doctrine and Covenants Student Manual*, 169.
11. *Old Testament: 1 Kings-Malachi Student Manual*, 2nd ed. (Church Education System manual, 1982), 344.
12. McConkie, *Mormon Doctrine*, 728.
13. Ibid., 728.
14. *Doctrine and Covenants Student Manual*, 190–191.
15. Smith, *Teachings of the Prophet Joseph Smith*, 162.
16. Daniel C. Peterson, *The Last Days: Teachings of the Modern Prophets*, vol. 2 (Salt Lake City: Aspen Books, 2000), 357.

Five

GOD'S SERMONS

Because most people are failing to accept and live the gospel, which is being preached by the Lord's servants, God is now beginning to preach his own sermons in the form of natural disasters and other calamities. In 1923 Elder Melvin J. Ballard stated in a general conference of the Church, "[I want] to call the attention of the Latter-day Saints, and indeed if I had the power, the attention of all the world to the fact that God is speaking through the elements. The earthquakes, the sea heaving itself beyond its bounds, bringing such dire destruction as we have seen are the voice of God crying repentance to this generation, a generation that only in part has heeded the warning voice."[1]

Natural disasters have been steadily increasing over the last few decades. According to a report by Professor Debarati Sapir, who works at the Centre for Research on the Epidemiology of Disasters, more than 254 million people were affected by natural disasters, which was 180 percent more than in 1990.[2]

In 1998 Elder Dallin H. Oaks, of the Quorum of the Twelve Apostles, summarized some of the events of the previous decade. He said, "During the past decade there have been many examples of large-scale adversities affecting tens or hundreds of thousands or millions. Only a few can be mentioned. In addition to wars in many nations, we have had earthquakes in Japan, California, China, Armenia, and Mexico; hurricanes or tornadoes in Florida and the central United States; volcanic eruptions in the Philippines; flooding in India and North America; and famine and pestilence in Africa and elsewhere."[3]

In 1952 Elder Joseph Fielding Smith reported the following: "[I]n a book that has been recently published by Robert Gordon Collier, he says this: 'The Bible says the earth is to be visited by earthquakes, dust storms, floods, plagues, and disease. Science reports that from 1914 onwards, there have been more freakish weather, earthquakes, floods, and diseases than any other similar sustained period in history.' "[4]

Elder Smith further remarked,

> The earth suffered greater shaking by earthquakes in 1950 than any other year since 1906, according to Professor L. Don Leet, director of Harvard's seismograph station. The total energy released in the violent movement of the earth in the year 1950 was equal to the explosion of 4,000,000 atomic bombs. Professor Leet explained that a world-wide network of seismograph stations "located" 796 significant earthquakes from the first of January to December 16, including one of the two greatest earthquakes ever recorded (News Dispatch, December 30, 1950). During the year 1951, more than one earthquake a day was recorded; many were with extreme violence, great loss of life and property.[5]

The momentum of destruction appears to have picked up dramatically since the year 2000. An unprecedented tornado struck in downtown Salt Lake City near the turn of the century. Then in 2003, about eighty-three thousand people were killed in an earthquake in Iran. In 2004, we saw four major hurricanes hit Florida within a two-month period. Over seventeen hundred tornadoes were reported in the United States during that year. Then on December 26 of the same year, an enormous earthquake measuring 9.3 on the Richter scale struck in the middle of the Indian Ocean, causing the entire earth to wobble. The massive tremor created a tsunami that swept across the ocean into thirteen different countries, killing over two hundred twenty-five thousand people.[6] In October of 2005, another catastrophic earthquake struck in Pakistan, India, and Afghanistan, killing an estimated eighty-five thousand people, injuring forty-two thousand, and leaving over three million homeless. In August of that same year, a category five hurricane (Katrina) struck the Gulf Coast of the United States, causing disastrous flooding, loss of life, and billions of dollars worth of damage. People who are unfamiliar with the scriptures are now asking, "Why?" These things are coming in fulfillment of prophecy—God's "sermons" have begun.

Still many people will not repent. The Lord declared, "And there shall be earthquakes also in diverse places, and many desolations; yet men will harden their hearts against me" (D&C 45:33). Therefore the disasters we are now seeing "are the beginning of sorrows" (Mark 13:8).

Besides earthquakes, the Lord said that the voice of his servants would be followed by "the voice of the waves of the sea heaving themselves beyond their bounds" (D&C 88:90). "And there shall be signs in the sea . . . the sea and the waves roaring" (Luke 21:25). The prophet Enoch also "saw the sea, that it was troubled" in the last days (Moses 7:66).

The Lord said, "Behold, I the Lord, in the beginning blessed the waters; but in the last days, by the mouth of my servant John, I cursed the waters. Wherefore, the days will come that no flesh shall be safe upon the waters. And it shall be said in days to come that none is able to go up to the land of Zion upon the water, but he that is upright in heart. . . . I, the Lord, have decreed, and the destroyer rideth upon the face thereof, and I revoke not the decree" (D&C 61:14–16, 19).

President Joseph Fielding Smith observed, "While the Lord has spoken of the sea heaving itself beyond its bounds, and the waves roaring, yet we must include the great destruction upon the waters by means of war, and especially by submarine warfare as we have learned of it in recent years."[7]

In addition to earthquakes and troubled seas, global warming is causing dramatic shifts in the weather patterns of the earth, so we are seeing more and more extreme atmospheric conditions. Scientists say that the earth will have changed drastically by the year 2100 if global warming continues at the same rate: "We can expect severe weather to be the norm rather than the exception."[8] This is fulfilling a prophecy of Isaiah, who said to people living in the last days, "Thou shalt be visited . . . with thunder, and with . . . great noise, with storm and tempest" (Isaiah 29:6).

God's sermons are evident in these storms, for the Lord has said,

> And also cometh the testimony of the voice of thunderings, and the voice of lightnings, and the voice of tempests. (D&C 88:90)

> With . . . the thunder of heaven, and the fierce and vivid lightning also, shall the inhabitants of the earth be made to feel the wrath, and indignation, and chastening hand of an Almighty God. (D&C 87:6)

> For . . . what will ye say when the day cometh when the thunders shall utter their voices from the ends of the earth, speaking to the ears of all that live . . . .Yea, and again when the lightnings shall streak forth

from the east unto the west, and shall utter forth their voices unto all that live, and make the ears of all tingle that hear, saying these words—Repent ye, for the great day of the Lord is come? (D&C 43:21–22)

Joseph Smith stated that "there shall [also] be a great hailstorm sent forth to destroy the crops of the earth" (D&C 29:16). Speaking of its effects upon the wicked, he said "All their works [shall] . . . be swept away by the hail, and by the judgments" (D&C 109:30). During Armageddon, an extremely destructive "hail" will fall. John the apostle, who saw it in vision, recorded, "And the temple of God was opened in heaven, and there was seen . . . lightnings . . . and thunderings . . . and great hail" (Revelation 11:19). "And there fell upon men a great hail out of heaven, every stone about the weight of a talent: and men blasphemed God because of the plague of the hail; for the plague thereof was exceeding great" (Revelation 16:21). The Armageddon hailstorm is probably the same as that which Joseph Smith said would destroy the crops of the earth.

Such widespread crop destruction will result in famine, which is another judgment the Lord said he would send upon the earth: "There shall be famines and troubles" (Mark 13:8). "With famine, and plague . . . shall the inhabitants of the earth be made to feel the . . . chastening hand of an Almighty God" (D&C 87:6).

Speaking of the future famines, the Prophet Joseph Smith remarked, "I know not how soon these things will take place . . . How long you will have good crops, and the famine be kept off, I do not know; when the fig tree leaves, know that summer is nigh at hand."[9]

The apostle Heber C. Kimball also warned the Saints about future famines. He said, "When the famines begin upon the earth, we shall be very apt to feel them first. If judgments must need begin at the house of God, and if the righteous scarcely are saved, how will it be with the wicked? Am I looking for famines? Yes, the most terrible and severe that have ever come upon the nations of the earth. These things are right before us, and some of this people are not thinking anything about them."[10]

In response to the warnings regarding famine, modern prophets have urged us to prepare ourselves not only spiritually but temporally as well. We have been encouraged to store wheat and other survival foods to keep us alive for a year or longer. President Wilford Woodruff said, "The Lord makes no mistakes about what is going to transpire. He has decreed the visitation of judgments, and they are certain to take place. President Young has for years repeatedly impressed upon the brethren the necessity of preparing for a period of famine by storing their wheat."[11]

The apostle, Heber C. Kimball, also implored the saints to prepare:

> Wake up, now, wake up, O Israel, and lay up your grain and your stores. I tell you there is trouble coming upon the world.[12]

> Let us go to work and lay up our grain, lay up our wheat, and everything that will and can be preserved; and in so doing, we will save ourselves from sorrow, pain, and anguish . . . This is part of our religion—to lay up stores and provide for ourselves and for the surrounding country; for the day is near when they will come by thousands and by millions, with their fineries, to get a little bread. That time is right by our door . . . The day will come when the people of the United States will come lugging their bundles under their arms, coming to us for bread to eat.[13]

President Wilford Woodruff said that "the Lord is not going to disappoint either Babylon or Zion, with regard to famine . . . Lay up your wheat and other provisions against a day of need, for the day will come when they will be wanted, and no mistake about it. We shall want bread, and the Gentiles will want bread, and if we are wise we shall have something to feed them and ourselves when famine comes."[14]

President Ezra Taft Benson also commented on the need to prepare for future famine. He said, "The revelation to store food may be as essential to our temporal salvation today as boarding the ark was to the people in the days of Noah."[15]

Coupled with famine will be plagues, disease, and pestilence. The Lord has declared through his prophets that "plagues shall go forth, and they shall not be taken from the earth until I have completed my work" (D&C 84:97). These things will be another part of God's "sermons" to the wicked, for the Lord said, "I will plead against him with pestilence and with blood" (Ezekiel 38:22). "Therefore shall . . . plagues come in one day, death, and mourning" (Revelation 18:8).

Even Zion will not escape unless she repents. The Lord warned, "But if she observe not to do whatsoever I have commanded her, I will visit her according to all her works, with sore affliction, with pestilence, with plague, with sword, with vengeance, with devouring fire" (D&C 97:26).

Pestilence includes germs, bacteria, and viruses that can cause epidemics. In the past few years, new strains of some of these things have been discovered, resulting in the emergence of new diseases. One of them is the "Spanish Flu" that killed between twenty and forty million people in 1918.[16] At least forty million others have died from AIDS, and now the Avian Bird Flu and the West Nile Virus have surfaced with the potential to kill millions more. According to the Maine Public Broadcasting Network, even some older diseases are morphing into more deadly forms. It reports that "emerging infectious diseases theaten to kill tens of millions."[17]

Pollutions and contaminantes in our food, water, and air are also contributing to latter-day diseases. The Nephite prophet Mormon saw our day, saying that "there shall be great pollutions upon the face of the earth" (Mormon 8:31). Some pollutants are floating in the air, while others are in the soil and water. A study conducted by the University of California indicated that water contamination in some areas has reached an alarming level. Industrial chemicals and other toxins are seeping into water supplies, making them dangerous for human consumption.[18]

While the human race is advancing scientifically, it is developing many things that contribute to its own destruction. Chemicals are added to our foods as preservatives, and chemicals are sprayed on food crops to produce greater yields. But such foreign elements are toxic to the human body. Toxins can be ingested, inhaled, or absorbed through the pores of the skin, so it is no wonder that chemicals, which are sprayed on or added to many things we are exposed to, are contributing to the increase of disease among us. Cancer is but one example.

Another disease that may be caused by exposure to chemicals is now beginning to affect more people than ever before. It is mental illness in all its forms: depression, panic attacks, obsessive-compulsive disorder, ADD, ADHD, bipolar illness, schizophrenia, and others. When foreign chemicals are combined with the chemicals in the brain, a reaction occurs. The chemical imbalance causes the brain to "short circuit." When drugs, alcohol, and tobacco are added to the brain's chemical store, the brain's capacity to function normally becomes further impaired. According to Fox News in 2006, cigarettes alone contain more than 4,000 chemicals.[19]

All people, righteous and wicked, are susceptible to illness and disease. Therefore we should not assume that a person is wicked if he or she falls prey to mental or physical illness. Joseph Smith taught that in the last days "many of the righteous shall fall a prey to disease, to pestilence, etc., by reason of the weakness of the flesh, and yet be saved in the Kingdom of God. So . . . it is an unhallowed principle to say that such and such have transgressed because they have been preyed upon by disease or death, for all flesh is subject to death; and the Savior has said, 'Judge not, lest ye be judged.' "[20]

It has been prophesied that one latter-day illness will be particularly desolating. Through Joseph Smith, the Lord said,

> In that generation shall the times of the Gentiles be fulfilled. And there shall be men standing in that generation, that shall not pass until they shall see an overflowing scourge; for a desolating sickness shall cover the land. (D&C 45:30–31)
>
> For a desolating scourge shall go forth among the inhabitants of the earth . . . if they repent not, until the earth is empty. (D&C 5:19)
>
> For behold, and lo, vengeance cometh speedily upon the ungodly as a whirlwind; and who shall escape it? The Lord's scourge shall pass over night and day, and the report thereof shall vex all people; yet it shall not be stopped until the Lord come; For the indignation of the Lord is kindled against their abominations and all their wicked works. (D&C 97:22–24)

(That scourge or sickness will be discussed more in connection with the war of Armageddon).

When the scourge begins to sweep the earth, sinners will convince themselves that it will not affect them. The Lord said through the prophet Isaiah,

> Wherefore hear the word of the Lord, ye scornful men. . . . Because ye have said, We have made a covenant with death, and with hell we are at agreement; when the overflowing scourge shall pass through, it shall not come unto us: For we have made lies our refuge, and under falsehood have we hid ourselves. . . .
>
> Judgment also will I lay to the line . . . and the hail shall sweep away the refuge of lies, and the waters shall overflow the hiding place. And your covenant with death shall be disannulled, and your agreement with hell shall not stand; when the overflowing scourge shall pass through, then ye shall be trodden down by it. From the time that it goeth forth it shall take you: for morning by morning shall it pass over, by day and by night: and it shall be a vexation only to understand the report. . . .
>
> Now therefore be ye not mockers . . . for I have heard from the Lord God of hosts a consumption, even determined upon the whole earth. (Isaiah 28:14–15, 17–19, 22)

President Joseph Fielding Smith made the following comment regarding people who choose to disregard God's sermons:

> So many seem to think and say . . . that the world is bound to go on in its present condition for millions of years before the end will come . . . 'We have had worse times,' they say. 'You are wrong in thinking there are more calamities now than in earlier times. There are not more earthquakes, the earth has always been quaking, but now we have facilities for gathering the news which our fathers did not have. These are not signs of the times; things are not different from former times.' And so the people refuse to heed the warning the Lord so kindly gives to them.[21]

Thus, the Lord may have to speak through natural disasters in "louder tones" in order to get people to repent. A few weeks after the eruption of Mount Saint Helens in 1980, the following appeared in the *Church News*:

> A series of most unusual events happened within the past few weeks. Of course the most startling was the Mount St. Helens eruption, with all its damage and toll of human life. But while it was belching forth, a series of tornadoes swept through the middle section of the United States. More than 900 "freak" storms struck America within that month. In a single day 50 tornadoes were counted in six states. The very next day 24 more tornadoes struck Iowa and Nebraska. And during the same period earthquakes shook California . . .
>
> It is important that we look for significance in these upheavals. Can it be that they are signs of the times? Can it be that the Lord is speaking to America by these frightful disasters. . . .
>
> We have a tendency to forget our pains quickly. . . . Little is said even now about the Arizona floods, although the debris and broken bridges remain.
>
> Even the volcano is off the front pages. And the 50 tornadoes in one day? They got only two inches of space on the front page as part of a news summary. Not so much as a headline was given them!
>
> It is possible to become so hardened that we brush aside the warning voice, and even forget our sufferings. . . .
>
> Must the Lord speak in louder tones? Must He send greater disasters before we listen to His warning voice? How much does it take to waken us to a realization that God is real, that there is an end to His patience, and that the only true security in these troubled times is through obedience to the Most High? Why fly in the face of Providence?[22]

In a 1980 General Conference of the Church, President Ezra Taft Benson expressed these words:

> Too often we bask in our comfortable complacency and rationalize that the ravages of war, economic disaster, famine and earthquake cannot happen here. Those who believe this are either not acquainted with the revelations of the Lord, or they do not believe them. Those who smugly think these calamities will not happen, that they somehow will be set aside . . . are deceived and will rue the day they harbored such a delusion.
>
> The Lord has warned and forewarned us against a day of great tribulation, and [has] given us counsel, through His servants, on how we can be prepared for these difficult times. Have we heeded His counsel?[23]

President Gordon B. Hinckley said in 2005,

> Those of us who read and believe the scriptures are aware of the warnings of prophets concerning catastrophes that have come to pass and are yet to come to pass. . . .
>
> What do we do? . . . We can so live that we can call upon the Lord for His protection and guidance. This is a first priority. We cannot expect His help if we are unwilling to keep His commandments. We in this Church have evidence enough of the penalties of disobedience in the examples of both the Jaredite and the Nephite nations. Each went from glory to utter destruction because of wickedness.[24]

President Wilford Woodruff asked,

> Can you tell me where the people are who will be shielded and protected from these great calamities and judgments which are even now at our door? I'll tell you. The priesthood of God who honor their priesthood and who are worthy of their blessings are the only ones who shall have this safety and protection. They are the only mortal beings. No other people have a right to be shielded from these judgments. They are at our very doors; not even this people will escape them entirely.[25]

President Joseph F. Smith said, "We firmly believe that Zion—which is the pure in heart—shall escape, if she observes to do all things whatsoever God has commanded. But, in the opposite event, even Zion will be visited 'with sore affliction, with pestilence, with plague, with sword, with vengeance, and with devouring fire'. . . . All this that her people may be taught to walk in the light of truth and in the way of the God of their salvation."[26]

President Brigham Young remarked, "If we will faithfully mind our own concerns, live our religion, do good to all men, preach the gospel to the nations of the earth, gather up the honest in heart, build up and establish Zion in the earth, and send the Gospel to the House of Israel, and love and serve God in all things, all will be well with us [and] we have no cause to fear in the least."[27]

So as trouble looms on the horizon, the righteous can be confident that, even though they will feel some of the effects of the judgments, the Lord will help them pass through those trials in relative safety. His promise is, "If ye are prepared, ye shall not fear" (D&C 38:30), "for mine elect hear my voice and harden not their hearts" (D&C 29:7).

Notes
1. *Doctrine and Covenants Student Manual,* 400.
2. "Disaster Figures for 2003—Millions Affected, *Platform for the Promotion of Early Warning Newsletter,* 2 December 2004, http://www.unisdr-earlywarning.org.
3. Dallin H. Oaks, "Adversity," *Ensign,* July 1998, 7.
4. Smith, *The Signs of the Times,* 117–18.
5. Ibid., 203.
6. "2004 Indian Ocean Earthquake," Wikipedia, http://en.wikipedia.org/wiki/2004_indian_ocean_earthquake
7. *Doctrine and Covenants Student Manual,* 131.
8. *Global Warming: What You Need to Know with Tom Brokaw,* Discovery Channel, first broadcast 16 July 2006. Directed by Nicolas Brown.
9. Smith, *Teachings of the Prophet Joseph Smith,* 161.
10. *Journal of Discourses,* 5:20.
11. Ibid., 19:136.
12. Ibid., 4:339.
13. Ibid., 5:163, 10.
14. Ibid., 18:121.
15. *The Life and Teachings of Jesus and his Apostles* (Church Educational System Manual, 1979), 279.
16. Molly Billings, "The Influenza Pandemic of 1918," http://virus.stanford.edu/uda/.
17. Maine Public Broadcasting Network, "Pandemic: More Info—New and Re-emerging Infectious Diseases," http://mainepbs.orq/quest/infectdisease.shtml.
18. TV's National Geographic, "Strange Days on Planet Earth," Channel 11, 5-27-05, narrated by Tyrone Hayes.
19. Fox 13 News, KSTU TV, 12 July 2006.

20. Smith, *Teachings of the Prophet Joseph Smith*, 162–63.
21. *Doctrine and Covenants Student Manual*, 96.
22. Ibid., 88–89.
23. Ezra Taft Benson, "Prepare for the Days of Tribulation," *Ensign*, Nov. 1980, 34.
24. Gordon B. Hinckely, "If Ye Are Prepared Ye Shall Not Fear," *Ensign*, Nov. 2005, 61–62.
25. Smith, *The Signs of the Times*, 114–15.
26. Daniel H. Ludlow, *Latter-day Prophets Speak* (Salt Lake City: Bookcraft, 1977), 236.
27. John A. Widtsoe, *Discourses of Brigham Young* (Salt Lake City: Deseret Book, 1976), 270.

Six

AMERICA'S FUTURE

America is not exempt from God's judgments. Through the prophet Ether, the Lord said that the land of America is a "land of promise, which was choice above all other lands, which the Lord God had preserved for a righteous people. And he had sworn in his wrath . . . that whoso should possess the land of promise . . . should serve him the true and only God, or they should be swept off when the fulness of his wrath should come upon them" (Ether 2:7–8).

Many Americans are not serving God as they should, so this country will undoubtedly experience the Lord's wrath. America was established as a "nation under God," but its unrighteous citizens have expelled God from many public places, and they are trampling on many of the Christian principles upon which the country was founded.

One of the greatest evils ever committed in this country was the persecution of God's Saints who simply wanted America's freedom of religion and the other rights that were supposed to be guaranteed them by the U.S. Constitution. Persecution of the Mormons began in the early 1800s and lasted for several decades. Eventually mistreatment of the Saints became so intense that they turned to America's governmental leaders for help. The Lord said that if the judges, governor, and president "heed them not, then will the Lord arise and come forth out of his hiding place, and in his fury vex the nation" (D&C 101:89).

But the Saints' pleas went unheeded. They were driven from their homes, their property was confiscated, the Prophet Joseph Smith and others were brutally killed, and thousands of Saints died from exposure to the elements when they were driven from the United States into Mexican territory (now Utah).

Therefore the Lord said to his people, "Thy brethren have rejected you and your testimony, even the nation that has driven you out; and now cometh the day of their calamity . . . unless they speedily repent. For they killed the prophets and they that were sent unto them; and they have shed innocent blood, which crieth from the ground against them" (D&C 136:34–36).

Before his death, Joseph Smith prophesied about the United States:

> Unless the United States redress the wrongs committed upon the Saints in the State of Missouri and punish the crimes committed by its officers, . . . in a few years the government will be utterly overthrown and wasted, and there will not be so much as a potsherd left for their wickedness in permitting the murder of men, women, and children, and the wholesale plunder and extermination of thousands of her citizens to go unpunished, thereby perpetrating a foul and corroding blot upon the fair fame of this great republic.[1]

The Prophet went on to say, "And now I am prepared to say by the authority of Jesus Christ, that not many years shall pass away before the United States shall present such a scene of bloodshed as has not a parallel in the history of our nation; pestilence, hail, famine, and earthquake will sweep the wicked of this generation from off the face of the land. . . . Repent ye, repent ye, and embrace the everlasting covenant, and flee to Zion, before the overflowing scourge overtake you."[2]

President John Taylor, who personally suffered persecution at the hands of Americans, also testified of this country's fate.

> Do I not know that a nation like that in which we live, a nation which is blessed with the freest, the most enlightened and magnificent government in the world today, with privileges that would exalt people to heaven if lived up to—do I not know that if they do not live up to them, but violate them and trample them under their feet, and discard the sacred principles of liberty by which we ought to be governed—do I not know that their punishment will be commensurate with the enlightenment which they possess? I do. And I know—I cannot help but know—that there are a great many more afflictions yet awaiting this nation.[3]

The Lord prophesied that one of the things that will vex America will be wars. He said,

> Ye hear of wars in far countries, and you say that there will soon be great wars in far countries, but ye know not the hearts of men in your own land. (D&C 38:28–29)

> War shall be poured out upon all nations. . . .
> And it shall come to pass also that the remnants who are left of the land will marshal themselves, and shall become exceedingly angry, and shall vex the Gentiles with a sore vexation. And thus, with the sword and by bloodshed the inhabitants of the earth shall mourn. (D&C 87:3, 5–6)

A short time after that prophecy was given, America's war with Mexico broke out; it was soon followed by the Civil War. The *Doctrine and Covenants Student Manual* states,

> Since the Civil War, the United States has been involved in five major wars: the Spanish-American War, World Wars I and II, and the Korean and Vietnam wars. Nor has war been the only means of vexation. Depressions, natural disasters, and other calamities have plagued the nation. The prophetic promise is that if the people of this nation do not serve the God of the land, who is Jesus Christ, they will be swept off (see Ether 2:10). As yet there has been no nationwide repentance of past and present sins, and so the Lord continues to vex the people of this nation, seeking to bring them to repentance.[4]

The apostle Orson Pratt also prophesied that America will suffer. He warned,

> But what about the American nation? . . . The time is not very far distant in the future, when the Lord God will lay his hand heavily upon that nation.[5]

> This great [civil] war is only a small degree of chastisement, just the beginning; nothing compared to that which God has spoken concerning this nation, if they do not repent. For the Lord has said . . . that if they will not repent, he will throw down all their strongholds, and cut off the cities of the land, and will execute vengeance and fury on the nation, even as upon the heathen, such as they have not heard" (see 3 Nephi 21:21).[6]

President John Taylor remarked,

> This nation and other nations will be overthrown, not because of their virtue, but because of their corruption and iniquity.[7]

Were we surprised when the last terrible [civil] war took place here in the United States? No ... You will see worse things than that, for God will lay his hand upon this nation, and they will feel it more terribly than ever they have done before. There will be more bloodshed, more ruin, more devastation than ever they have seen before. Write it down! You will see it come to pass; it is only just starting in.... There is yet to come a sound of war, trouble and distress, in which brother will be arrayed against brother, father against son, son against father, a scene of desolation and destruction that will permeate our land until it will be a vexation to hear the report thereof.[8]

The day is not far distant when this nation will be shaken from centre to circumference.... And then will be fulfilled that prediction to be found in one of the revelations given through the Prophet Joseph Smith. Those who will not take up their sword to fight against their neighbor must needs flee to Zion for safety.[9] (See D&C 45:68)

Joseph Smith prophesied,

The time is soon coming when no man will have any peace but in Zion and her stakes. I saw [in vision] men hunting the lives of their own sons, and brother murdering brother, women killing their own daughters, and daughters seeking the lives of their mothers. I saw armies arrayed against armies. I saw blood, desolation, fires. The Son of Man has said that the mother shall be against the daughter, and the daughter against the mother. These things are at our doors. They will follow the Saints of God from city to city. Satan will rage, and the spirit of the devil is now enraged. I know not how soon these things will take place; but with a view of them, shall I cry peace? No; I will lift up my voice and testify of them.[10]

President Brigham Young also prophesied of America's future: "Famine will spread over the nations, and nation will rise up against nation, kingdom against kingdom, and states against states, in our country and in foreign lands; and they will destroy each other, caring not for the blood and lives of their neighbors, of their families, or for their own lives.... You may think that the little you hear of now is grievous; yet the faithful of God's people will see days that will cause them to close their eyes because of the sorrow that will come upon the wicked nations."[11]

President Wilford Woodruff also indicated that this nation will suffer because of its wickedness. He remarked, "When I contemplate the condition of our nation and see that wickedness and abominations are increasing ... I ask myself the question, can the American nation escape? The answer comes, No; its destruction, as well as the destruction of the world is sure; . . . sooner or later they will reap the fruits of their own wicked acts and be numbered among the past."[12]

The Lord also declared,

> And thus, with the sword and by bloodshed the inhabitants of the earth shall mourn; and with famine, and plague, and earthquake, and the thunder of heaven, and the fierce and vivid lightning also, shall the inhabitants of the earth be made to feel the wrath, and indignation, and chastening hand of an Almighty God, until the consumption decreed hath made a full end of all nations; That the cry of the saints, and of the blood of the saints, shall cease to come up into the ears of the Lord of Sabbaoth, from the earth, to be avenged of their enemies. (D&C 87:6–7)

Three American cities have been specifically targeted for God's wrath if the people in them fail to repent and live the gospel. In a revelation to the Prophet Joseph Smith, the Lord said, "Let the bishop go unto the city of New York, also to the city of Albany, and also to the city of Boston, and warn the people of those cities with the sound of the gospel, with a loud voice, of the desolation and utter abolishment which await them if they do reject these things. For if they do reject these things the hour of their judgment is nigh, and their house shall be left unto them desolate" (D&C 84:114–115).

In 1863 Elder Wilford Woodruff spoke of those same cities while addressing the youth at a stake conference. He said, "Now, my young friends, I wish you to remember these scenes you are witnessing during the visit of President Young and his brethren . . . the day will come . . . [when] you will . . . stand in the towers of the temple and . . . you will then call to mind this visitation of President Young. . . . You will say: . . . that was before New York was destroyed by an earthquake; it was before Boston was swept into the sea. . . . It was before Albany was destroyed by fire . . . [President Young then stood up and said], What Brother Woodruff has said is revelation and will be fulfilled."[13]

The apostle Orson Pratt prophesied that many other American cities will also be destroyed or left desolate. He said,

> If it be asked, why is America to suffer? The answer is, because they have rejected the kingdom of God, and one of the greatest divine

messages ever sent to man: because they have sanctioned the killing of the Saints, and the martyrdom of the Lord's Prophets, and have suffered his people to be driven from their midst . . . For these great evils, they must suffer; the decrees of Jehovah have gone forth against them; the sword of the Lord has been unsheathed, and will fall with pain upon their devoted heads. The great magnificent cities are to be cut off. New York, Boston, Albany, and numerous other cities will be left desolate . . . [for] by the sword and by pestilence, and by famine, and by the strong arm of the Almighty, shall the inhabitants of that wicked nation be destroyed.[14]

Joseph Smith said that the destruction within the United States during that time will prepare the country for the return of the lost tribes of Israel. He declared, "And now I am prepared to say by the authority of Jesus Christ, that not many years shall pass away before the United States shall present such a scene of bloodshed as has not a parallel in the history of our nation; pestilence, hail, famine, and earthquake will sweep the wicked of this generation from off the face of the land, to open and prepare the way for the return of the lost tribes of Israel from the north country."[15]

According to John Taylor, the Prophet Joseph also indicated that as this nation begins to crumble, its Constitution will "hang by a thread," but it will be preserved among the Saints. President Taylor stated, "The Prophet Joseph said that 'The Constitution of the United States was given by the inspiration of God.' But good, virtuous and holy principles may be perverted by corrupt and wicked men . . . and this nation abounds with traitors who ignore that sacred palladium of liberty and seek to trample it under foot. Joseph Smith said they would do so, and that when deserted by all, the elders of Israel would rally around its shattered fragments and save and preserve it inviolate."[16]

President Brigham Young said that the Constitution will not be completely destroyed. "Will the Constitution be destroyed? No; it will be held inviolate by this people, and, as Joseph Smith said, 'The time will come when the destiny of the nation will hang upon a single thread. At that critical juncture, this people will step forth and save it from the threatened destruction.' It will be so."[17]

Elder George Q. Cannon remarked, "Men everywhere should know that we believe in constitutional principles, and that we expect that it will be our destiny to maintain them . . . [This] republic is . . . leaving the old constitutional landmarks, and . . . the time is not far distant when there will be trouble in consequence of it, when there will be civil broils and strife; and to escape them, we believe men will be compelled to flee to the 'Mormons,' despised as they are now."[18]

President John Taylor also said that as the Saints of Zion sustain the principles of liberty, people will flee to them for safety. He declared,

> Those who will not take up their sword to fight against their neighbor must needs flee to Zion for safety. And they will come, saying, we do not know anything of the principles of your religion, but we perceive that you are an honest community; you administer justice and righteousness, and we want to live with you and receive the protection of your laws, but as for your religion, we will talk about that some other time. Will we protect such people? Yes, all honorable men. When the people shall have torn to shreds the Constitution of the United States, the Elders of Israel will be found holding it up to the nations of the earth and proclaiming liberty and equal rights to all men, and extending the hand of fellowship to the oppressed of all nations.[19]

Notes

1. Ludlow, *Latter-day Prophets Speak*, 229.
2. Smith, *Teachings of the Prophet Joseph Smith*, 17–18.
3. *Journal of Discourses*, 22:141.
4. *Doctrine and Covenants Student Manual*, 352.
5. *Journal of Discourses*, 20:151.
6. Ibid., 12:344.
7. Ibid., 17:4.
8. Ibid., 20:318.
9. Ibid., 21:8.
10. Smith, *Teachings of the Prophet Joseph Smith*, 161.
11. *Journal of Discourses*, 8:123.
12. Ibid., 21:301.
13. *Doctrine and Covenants Student Manual*, 185.
14. Lund, *The Coming of the Lord*, 56.
15. Smith, *Teachings of the Prophet Joseph Smith*, 17.
16. *Journal of Discourses*, 21:31.
17. Ibid., 7:15.
18. Ibid., 18:10.
19. Ibid., 21:8.

Seven

THE MIDDLE EAST CONFLICT

Terrorism is a relatively new form of violence, and it has become more prevalent since 9/11. Terrorism is not only directed against America, but also against Israel. The roots of terrorism against Israel lie not only in latter-day wickedness but also in ancient history. In ancient times, God gave the land of Palestine to the descendants of the prophet Jacob (see Genesis 32:28). Jacob had twelve sons whose descendants became known as the twelve tribes of Israel, or Israelites. Eventually the Israelites fell into a state of wickedness, so the Lord allowed them to be scattered from their God-given promised land into other parts of the world.

Elder Bruce R. McConkie explained that in about 721 BC, ten of the tribes (the northern kingdom of Israel) "were taken captive . . . into Assyria. From thence, in due course, they were led into the north countries, and being lost to the knowledge of men . . . have been designated since as the Lost Tribes. . . . [Then] shortly thereafter [Babylonians] overran Jerusalem, destroyed the [southern] Kingdom of Judah [known as Jews], and carried the remaining remnants of Israel into Babylonian bondage."[1]

Seventy years later under Cyrus, a Persian king, some Jews (from the southern kingdom) were permitted to return to their land and rebuild their temple, which had been destroyed by the conquering invaders. But in AD 70 Jerusalem fell to the Romans, and the temple was again destroyed. *The Doctrine and Covenants Student Manual* states, "More than a million and a half Jews perished, and many were sold into slavery, and thus [were] 'scattered among all nations.' "[2] Hence the Lord's prophetic words were fulfilled: "The children of Israel did evil in the sight of the Lord . . . they forsook the Lord God" (Judges 2:12). "Thus saith the Lord God . . . I have scattered them among the countries" (Ezekiel 11:16).

Joseph Fielding Smith observed, "There were scarcely 8,000 Jews left in Palestine. Jerusalem became a prey, and so did Palestine to the Gentile nations."[3] Later in AD 395 when the Roman Empire split into two empires, Palestine became part of the eastern half (the Byzantine Empire). Then in AD 634, Palestine was conquered by Muslim Arabs, and in AD 691 the Muslims' Islamic mosque called Al-Aqsa Mosque (the Dome of the Rock) was built in Jerusalem on the site of the ancient Jewish temple. For the Muslims, Jerusalem became the third holiest site of Islam (after Mecca and Medina in Saudi Arabia where the Islamic religion originated).

In AD 1096 Christian crusaders began fighting to retake control of the Israelites' Holy Land. They captured Jerusalem in AD 1099 and held it until AD 1187 when Muslims again took control.[4] Later, for a short period in the 1200s, Egyptian Muslims controlled Palestine.

Then in AD 1517, Ottoman Turks (primarily Muslims) captured Jerusalem, and Palestine became part of the Ottoman Empire. So for the next four hundred years, Muslims (Turks and Arabs) inhabited the Israelites' "promised land." Thus the prophecy was fulfilled that "Jerusalem shall be trodden down of the Gentiles [non-Israelites], until the times of the Gentiles be fulfilled" (Luke 21:24).

The times of the Gentiles began to be fulfilled in 1948 when part of Palestine (Israel) was declared by the UN to be the official homeland of the Jews. Just prior to that time, beginning in the late 1800s, oppression of Jews in Europe had set off a mass emigration of Jewish refugees to Palestine. The Jews began a "Zionist" movement to establish a Jewish national homeland in that region. This alarmed the Palestinian Muslims who had declared the land of Palestine to be their own holy land.

But the Lord had promised the Israelites that when they would no more turn aside their hearts against the God of Israel, they would be restored to their land of promise.

> For, lo, the days come, saith the Lord, that I will . . . cause them to return to the land that I gave to their fathers, and they shall possess it. (Jeremiah 30:3)

> [For] when that day cometh . . . that they no more turn aside their hearts against the Holy One of Israel, then will he remember the covenants which he made to their fathers. Yea . . . all of the people who are

of the house of Israel, will I gather in, saith the Lord . . . from the four quarters of the earth. (1 Nephi 19:15–16)

Then shall this covenant which the Father hath covenanted with his people be fulfilled; and then shall Jerusalem be inhabited again with my people, and it shall be the land of their inheritance. (3 Nephi 20:46)

Beginning in the mid-1800s, God began to set the stage for the fulfillment of his promise to restore the Israelites to their land. In 1841, he sent latter-day apostles to dedicate the land for the return of the Jews. President Joseph Fielding Smith stated, "The land of Palestine was dedicated for the return of the Jews, October 24, 1841, by Orson Hyde, but the time had not come then for the return. . . . President George A. Smith again dedicated the land, in March, 1873."[5]

Shortly after that, a spiritual awakening among the Jews began to be observed, especially with regard to their attitude toward Jesus, the Messiah, whom their ancestors had rejected. In 1952, President David O. McKay delivered an address in which he discussed the Jews' change of attitude:

> Mr. Harris Weinstock wrote a book entitled "Jesus, the Jew" . . . This is what he says about the attitude of the Jews when he . . . was a boy. "I recall that on one occasion one of the pupils brought (that would be about 1870) into the religious school a book containing the name of Jesus. I remember how wrought and excited the Rabbi became when he was made aware of its presence in the room. 'Sacrilege! Sacrilege!' he cried indignantly . . . I remember how he delivered an impassioned discourse to his pupils upon the terrible sufferings to which the Jews had been subjected because of Jesus. . . . [But today, Jesus'] wisdom and gentleness, his unselfishness of spirit and his love for humanity . . . are becoming better understood, so that the modern Jew looks upon Jesus as one of the greatest gifts that Israel has given to the world."[6]

As the attitude of Jews began to change, the world scene also began to change. In 1917, during World War I, Great Britain captured Palestine from the Ottoman Turks. The British then issued the Balfour Declaration, which announced Britain's support of a Jewish homeland in Palestine. The Muslim Palestinians strenuously opposed the idea, so in 1947, the United Nations proposed dividing the land between the Jews and the Palestinians.

Subsequently, on May 14, 1948, part of Palestine was given to the Jews, and the nation of Israel was officially created. Thousands of Jews from around the world began returning from their long dispersion to become Israelis in their land of promise. Thus Elder Joseph Fielding Smith said, "Jerusalem is no longer trodden down of Gentiles. . . . On May 14, 1948, England withdrew [from Palestine] and the Republic of Israel came into existence. This is a very significant event which we must not forget. It is a sign to us that the times of the Gentiles are drawing to their close."[7]

Although Jerusalem is no longer "trodden down by Gentiles" today, tensions between the Israeli Jews and their Arab Muslim neighbors have never ceased. In fact, immediately after the republic of Israel was created, surrounding Arab nations attacked the new state, in the first of several Arab-Israeli wars. When the first war ended in 1949, Israel held territories beyond the boundaries set by the UN.[8]

A 1950 article, published in *The Jewish Hope* stated, "It was marvelous what God did for the Jews . . . as the pressure was too great, they were unable to hold the lines any longer and finally decided to give up . . . [but the] Arabs suddenly threw down their arms and surrendered. . . . The Arabs said they saw three persons with long beards and flowing white robes, who warned them not to fight any longer, otherwise they would all be killed."[9]

In spite of that warning, another war broke out in 1956. Then in 1964, the PLO (Palestinian Liberation Organization) was formed by the Arabs to liberate all of Palestine from the Jews. A short time later, in 1967, another war was waged by several Arab nations. But the Israelis again were victorious—in only six days! This Six-day War ended with almost a million Arabs under Israeli rule. The Jews had captured the Palestinians' West Bank, plus Egypt's Gaza Strip and Sinai Penninsula, as well as Syria's Golan Heights.[10]

Israel's occupation of so much territory that the Arabs claimed further inflamed the Palestinians and other Muslims. In 1973 the Yom Kippur War was waged on Israel by Syria and Egypt, but to no avail for the Muslims. Finally, "in 1978, Israel and Egypt signed the Camp David Accords, an agreement designed to settle their disputes. [And] Israel withdrew from the Sinai Penninsula."[11]

However, other Arab nations did not support a compromise with the Israelis. In 1981, after signing the peace treaty with Israel, Egypt's president, Anwar Sadat, was assassinated. (A few years later, Israel's prime minister, Yitzhak Rabin, was also assassinated.) And today terrorist attacks against Israel are almost a daily occurrence. The former Palestinian leader, Yasser Arafat, was even heard to say that the nation of Israel should be annihiliated.

This struggle over the land of Israel will undoubtedly be the catalyst that will ignite the war of Armageddon, for there is a continuing escalation of hostilities toward the Jews in Israel. In fact, the president of Iran recently vowed to "wipe Israel off the map."[12] That threat should not be taken lightly. According to prophecy, Iran (called Persia in the Bible) will be one of the countries that will come against Israel in the war of Armageddon (see Ezekiel 38:5). And Iran is currently engaged in a nuclear program.

So far, with God's help, the tiny nation of Israel has been able to defeat every opposing army. The Lord has promised, "No weapon that is formed against thee shall prosper" (Isaiah 54:17). That does not mean, however, that the republic will not be attacked. At some point in the near future, prophecies regarding the Armageddon siege of Israel will be fulfilled.

Notes
1. McConkie, *Mormon Doctrine*, 418.
2. *Doctrine and Covenants Student Manual*, 93.
3. Smith, *The Signs of the Times*, 64.
4. See *World Book Encyclopedia*, 1991, 15:104–105.
5. Smith, *The Signs of the Times*, 67.
6. LeGrand Richard, *Israel! Do You Know?* (Salt Lake City: Deseret Book, 1954), 237.
7. Smith, *Doctrines of Salvation*, 3:261.
8. *World Book Encyclopedia*, 1991, 15:105.
9. LeGrand Richards, *Israel! Do You Know?* 230.
10. *World Book Encyclopedia*, 1991, 15:105.
11. Ibid., 15:105.
12. *The Hal Lindsey Report*, July 23, 2006.

Eight

ISLAMIC JIHAD

The land of Israel (and its capital city, Jerusalem) will be the target of Armageddon. The Lord declared, "I will gather all nations against Jerusalem to battle" (Zechariah 14:2). "For my determination is to gather the nations, that I may . . . pour upon the mine indignation, even all my fierce anger" (Zephaniah 3:8).

Israel is already surrounded by hostile nations, which are likely to become part of the enormous army which will wage the final world war. These nations are inhabited primarily by Muslim Arabs who claim the land of Israel as one of their holy lands. Some Muslims have a radical view of their religion, Islam. These Islamic fundamentalists believe that infidels (non-Muslims) should be removed from all Muslim holy lands. They also believe that one day the entire world will become Islamic. (Muslims also claim Saudi Arabia as a holy land. It is the home of Islam's two holiest cities, Mecca and Medina. Jerusalem is their third holiest city.)

The extremist fundamentalist Muslims are now engaging in a Jihad (holy war) to remove infidels from those lands. As they do so, they believe they are preparing for the day when their own savior (Mahdi) will appear to help them militarily defeat all non-Muslims and bring the entire world into the Islamic religion.[1] On May 13, 2005, a Muslim sheik, Ibrahim Mudeiris, of the PA (Palestinian Authority), said this on PA television: "We have ruled the world before [during the Persian and Ottoman Empire eras], and by Allah, the day will come when we will rule the entire world again."[2]

The radical Muslims' belief in Jihad stems from their interpretation of the Islamic book of scripture, the Koran. They believe it teaches that all non-Muslims must be converted to Islam or be killed. A former Jihadist, Walid Shoebat, describes how some Koran scriptures can be interpreted in this manner. For instance, Koran 9:29 allegedly states, "Make war upon such of those whom the Scriptures have been given as believe not in Allah or the last day."[3] Other Koran references include:

> Koran 9:5—When the sacred months are passed, kill those who join other gods with Allah [Islam's god], or the last day.
>
> Koran 9:123—Make war on the infidels who dwell around you and let them see how harsh you can be.
>
> Koran 8:12–13—Cast terror into the hearts of the infidels. Strike off their heads, strike off the very tips of their fingers.
>
> Koran 8:60—Muster against them all the men and cavalry at your command, so that you may strike terror into the enemy of Allah and your enemy. . . . All that you give in the cause of Allah shall be repaid to you.[4]

Islamic Jihadists believe that when their Mahdi comes (about the time of Jesus' return), Muslims are to target and assassinate non-Muslims, especially Jews. "Trees and boulders will speak to the Muslims informing of any Jew seeking shelter and protection by them. . . . Others who choose to disbelieve, will [also] be put to death. Thereafter the entire world will be ruled by Muslims."[5]

Militant Muslims are not waiting for the appearance of the Mahdi to begin their killings because they believe that infidels have encroached upon their holy lands. Fighting began shortly after Palestine was divided between Muslims and Jews in 1948. The Muslims do not recognize the Jews' right to the land.

As Palestinian Muslims attempt to remove Jews from Israel, the Jews are, for the most part, trying to exercise restraint. An example is their permitting of the Muslims' Dome of the Rock mosque to remain on the Jews' sacred temple mount. The Jews have even given some land back to the Palestinians (land which they captured during the Six-day War) in an attempt to bring peace to the region. In 1978 Israel relinquished the Sinai Penninsula, and in August of 2005, it gave up the Gaza strip. But terrorism still persists. It clearly does little good to give Jihadists a token portion of land for peace. They want it all, and Jews will never relinquish it completely, so a stalemate exists. Presently the Israeli Jews are preventing a total domination of Islam in the Middle East.

The Lord also appears to be against giving up any of the land of Israel. He said, "I will also gather all nations down into the valley of Jehoshaphat [during Armageddon], and will plead with them there for my people . . . whom they have scattered . . . and parted my land" (Joel 3:2).

It is difficult to believe that a major world religion would pose such a threat against Israel, even though we see evidence of it almost daily in the news. Muslim terrorist activities against Israel are a frequent occurence, and it appears that very little can be done to stop them. It has become clear that land of peace will not work, and peace treaties will have no lasting effect, because neither the Israelis nor the Muslims will relinquish their holy land.

Terrorist organizations include Hamas, Hezbollah, and Al Qaeda, among others. Hezbollah now claims to have chemical and biological weapons that can reach Israel.[6] And in January 2006, Hamas gained control of the Palestinian government. Its charter calles for the destruction of Israel.[7]

Al Qaeda, which is led by Osama Bin Laden, is probably the most well-known because of its attack on the United States on 9/11. Islamic terrorist hit lists include America for three reasons: first, it is non-Muslim; second, it supports Israel; and third, it too has "encroached" upon Muslim holy lands. During the Gulf War in the late 1900s, the United States conducted much of its military campaign from Saudi Arabia. That enraged many Muslims (including Osama Bin Laden), although the Saudi government had given permission for the United States to enter the country. To Jihadists, America is the greatest infidel on earth, "the Great Satan." Militant Muslims believe that Americans must be expelled from all Muslim countries.

Because of America's support of the Israeli Jews, one Muslim leader, Mufti Ikrima Sabri, said, "Oh, Allah, destroy America for it is controlled by Zionist Jews."[8]

And according to Shoebat, "The following exerpt is from a sermon delivered over live Palestinian TV: 'Wherever you are, kill the Jews, the Americans, who are like them, and those who stand by them. They are all in one accord against the Muslims.' . . . [And] on June 8, 2001, Sheikh Ibrahim Madhi used a 'sermon' to issue the following warning over Palestinian television: 'Allah is willing for the unjust state of Israel to be erased.

The unjust state, the United States, will be erased. The unjust state, Britain, will be erased.' "[9]

Mr. Shoebat also stated that "with Islamism, only those who adhere to militant radical fundamentalism are safe; the rest of the world are infidels who must be converted or destroyed. [The Jihadists] . . . plan first to destroy the Saturday [worshippers], the Jews, and then the Sunday [worshippers], the Christians."[10]

He went on to say that the second-best deed a Muslim can do is "to participate in Jihad in Allah's cause [the first-best thing is to worship Allah]. . . . In the Quran and in the mosques, it is openly preached from the pulpits that it is every Muslim's duty to take part in [J]ihad, which is directed at the 'infidels' i.e. the West and Israel, especially Israel."[11]

Thus it is clear that the killing of Jews and Christians is a religious obligation for fundamentalist Muslims. To them such killings are considered "righteous killings." In fact, many Islamic schools today are training centers for Jihad. Muslim children are taught to hate the Jews in Israel and to participate in Jihad. On Sepetember 24, 2005, *Jewish Voice Today* aired a television program in which Muslim children were shown reciting threats of death and violence against Jews in Israel.

While just a teenager, Mr. Shoebat was initiated into Yasser Arafat's Fatah terror group in Palestine and threw his first bomb when he was only sixteen. He said, "I felt I had to be a martyr, to kill Jews in order to go to heaven. . . . I vowed to fight my Jewish enemy, believing that I was doing God's will on earth."[12] Interestingly, the true God of Israel knew that this day of Jihad would come. He said, "Yea, the time cometh, that whosoever killeth you [Jews] will think that he doeth God service" (John 16:2).

Only the devil would convince people that violence should be an important part of religion. There will be no lasting peace on earth until Satan and all his Jihadist-type followers are removed. Until that day comes, violence will continue to escalate until it erupts into the war of Armageddon. That war is probably not too far away. On July, 27, 2006, Al-Qaeda's second in command, Al-Zawahiri, called for a worldwide Jihad against Israel and her allies. A few days later, Venezuela's president, Hugo Chavez, met with Iran's anti-Israel president, and then called for worldwide support for Iran in order "to save humanity and end the American empire."[13] Thus the stage is being set for Armageddon.

Notes
1. Stone, *Unleashing the Beast*, 65.
2. *Jewish Voice Today*, "Is Peace at Hand? Glad You Asked!" July/August 2005, 16.
3. Walid Shoebat, *Why I Left Jihad* (United States: Top Executive Media, 2005), 52–54.
4. Ibid., 52–54
5. Ibid., 226.
6. *The Lindsey Report*, Channel 262, 23 July 2006.
7. *Fox News*, 19 February 2006.
8. Shoebat, *Why I Left Jihad*, 110.
9. Ibid., 396–97.
10. Ibid., 396.
11. Ibid., 95, 300.
12. Ibid., 15–16.
13. *Fox News*, 30 July 2006.

Nine

THE NEW JERUSALEM

Sometime before or during Armageddon, the initial building of the New Jerusalem will take place before the Lord comes. Bruce R. McConkie stated, "The latter days are to see the initial building of a New Jerusalem on the American continent."¹ The student manual for the Doctrine and Covenants states, "The Lord has decreed that Israel will be gathered and the New Jerusalem will be built in preparation for his coming."² President Lorenzo Snow also declared, "He is coming soon. . . . But we will not hear his voice until we build up Jackson County."³

Evidence suggests that the city will be built near the end of the war of Armageddon, or at least after a time of great destruction. Joseph Fielding Smith taught, "Zion [the New Jerusalem] on this continent will be built according to the promise. . . . The land will first be cleansed of its evil before that day can come. The word of the Lord shall not fail. . . . There are indications in the revelations that Zion is not to be built up or redeemed, until the indignation of the Lord shall be poured out without measure upon all nations; and 'This will be when the cup of their iniquity is full' (D&C 101)."⁴

President Heber C. Kimball was quoted in a general conference as saying, "The western boundaries of the State of Missouri [where the city is to be built] will be swept so clean of its inhabitants that as President Young tells us, 'when we return to that place, there will not be so much as a yellow dog to wag its tail.' "⁵

Joseph Fielding Smith also indicated that the Saints will return to redeem the land about the time when the Lord will take vengeance on the wicked (a large part of which will occur during Armageddon). Elder Smith said, "This redemption will come, but inferences in the revelations point to that redemption when the Lord comes to take vengeance on the wicked and fulfill his promise made to Enoch, to cleanse the earth."[6]

President Joseph F. Smith described how he pictured the return to Jackson County:

> Let me picture to you how some of us may be gathered and led to Jackson County. I think I see two or three hundred thousand people wending their way across the great plains enduring the nameless hardships of the journey, herding and guarding their cattle by day and by night, and defending themselves and little ones from foes on the right hand and on the left, as when they came here [to Utah]. They will find the journey back to Jackson County will be as real as when they came here. Now, mark it. And though you may be led by God 'with a stretched out arm,' it will not be more manifest than the leading the people out here. They will think there are a great many hardships to endure in this manifestation of the power of God. . . .
>
> Some might ask, what will become of the railroads? I fear that the sifting process would be insufficient were we to travel by railroads. We are apt to overlook the manifestations of the power of God to us because we are participators in them, and regard them as commonplace events. But when it is written in history—as it will be written—it will be shown forth to future generations as one of the most marvelous, unexampled and unprecedented accomplishments that has ever been known to history.[7]

The Lord taught that a man "like as Moses" will lead the Saints in their return. "Behold, I say unto you, the redemption of Zion must needs come by power; Therefore, I will raise up unto my people a man, who shall lead them like as Moses led the children of Israel. For ye are the children of Israel, and of the seed of Abraham, and ye must needs be led out of bondage by power, and with a stretched-out arm. And as your fathers were led at the first, even so shall the redemption of Zion be" (D&C 103:15–18).

Many people have speculated about the identity of the man "like as Moses." Elder John A. Widtsoe said,

> There have been many conjectures concerning this statement. There have been many misguided men who have declared themselves to be this man "like as Moses."

Yet, the meaning as set forth in the scriptures is very simple. In modern revelation the President of the Church is frequently compared to Moses. Soon after the organization of the Church, the Lord said, "no one shall be appointed to receive commandments and revelations in this church excepting my servant Joseph Smith, Jun., for he receiveth them even as Moses" (D&C 28:2). In one of the great revelations upon Priesthood, this is more specifically expressed: "the duty of the President of the office of the High Priesthood is to preside over the whole church, and to be like unto Moses" (D&C 107:91). . . .

The man like unto Moses in the church is the President of the Church.[8]

Elder Harold B. Lee pointed out, "The Lord has placed the responsibility for directing the work of gathering in the hands of the leaders of the Church to whom he will reveal his will where and when such gatherings would take place in the future."[9]

Until the day comes for the redemption of Zion, the Saints must continue to prepare for that event. Brigham Young remarked,

> Just as soon as the Latter-day Saints are ready and prepared to return to Independence, Jackson County . . . the voice of the Lord [will] be heard, 'Arise now, Israel, and make your way to the center Stake of Zion'. . . . Do you believe that we, as Latter-day Saints, are preparing our own hearts, our own lives . . . as fast as the Lord is preparing to cleanse the land from those ungodly persons who dwell there? . . . If we are not very careful, the earth will be cleansed from wickedness before we are prepared to take possession of it. We must be prepared to build up Zion, [the New Jerusalem].[10]

Brigham Young also indicated that not all the Saints will return:

> Are we going back to Jackson County? Yes. When? As soon as the way opens up. Are we all going? O no! Of course not. The country is not large enough to hold our present numbers.[11]

> A portion of the Priesthood will go and redeem and build up the centre Stake of Zion.[12]

> When Joseph [Smith] first revealed the land where the Saints should gather, a woman in Canada asked if we thought that Jackson County would be large enough to gather all the people that would want to go to Zion. I will answer the question really as it is. Zion will extend, eventually, all over the earth.[13]

The land of Joseph is the land of Zion; and it takes North and South America to make the land of Joseph.[14]

When the resurrected Lord appeared to his "other sheep" in ancient America, he told them that in the last days, their posterity (and others of the house of Israel) would be assisted by Gentile saints in building the American New Jerusalem. He declared, "And behold this people will I establish in this land, unto the fulfilling of the covenant which I made with your father Jacob; and it shall be a New Jerusalem" (3 Nephi 20:22). "And they [Gentiles] shall assist my people, the remnant of Jacob, and also as many of the house of Israel as shall come, that they may build a city, which shall be called the New Jerusalem" (3 Nephi 31:23).

The preceding scripture has led some people to believe that the Lamanites, who are a remnant of Jacob, will take the lead in building the New Jerusalem. But President Joseph Fielding Smith said,

> I fail to find any single passage which indicates that this is to be the order of things when these great events are to be fulfilled. . . . The remnant of Jacob . . . is Israel. . . . Ephraimites [stand] at the head to guide and bless the whole house of Israel. . . . The keys are with Ephraim. It is Ephraim who is to be endowed with power to bless and give to the other tribes, including the Lamanites, their blessings. . . . And the great work of this restoration, the building of the temple and the City of Zion, or New Jerusalem, will fall to the descendants of Joseph [which includes Lamanites], but it is Ephraim who will stand at the head and direct the work.[15]

(And, of course, it is the President of the Church who holds the keys for governing all the affairs of the Church, including the building of the New Jerusalem.)

During the millennial era, the New Jerusalem and the Jerusalem in Israel will both be capital cities from which Jesus will reign. The spiritual word of the Lord will go forth from Jerusalem, while constitutional law will go forth from the New Jerusalem. The prophet Isaiah said, "For out of Zion shall go forth the law, and the word of the Lord from Jerusalem" (Isaiah 2:3; see also Micah 4:2). "He that is left in Zion, and he that remaineth in Jerusalem, shall be called holy" (Isaiah 4:3–4).

The prophet Zechariah, while discussing the four destroying "angels" who will reap down the wicked, described them as riding in four chariots between the two world capitals which he called mountains. "And

I turned, and lifted up mine eyes, and looked, and behold, there came four chariots out from between two mountains; and the mountains were mountains of brass," firm and strong (Zechariah 6:1). The *Old Testament Student Manual* states, "The servants came from between two mountains (two places where the Lord will judge the nations) which were made of brass, a symbol of firmness."[16]

It is not known if the New Jerusalem will be completely finished before the Lord comes. However, a significant portion of the city and its temple will be completed. Elder George Q. Cannon stated, "We expect to go back to Jackson County, Missouri, and to lay the foundation of a temple, and to build a great city to be called the centre stake of Zion."[17]

The temple must be built before the Lord comes, for he will appear to the Saints there before he steps on the Mount of Olives in the old Jerusalem. President Brigham Young taught, "When he comes again, he will not . . . appear first at Jerusalem . . . but he will appear first on the land where he commenced his work in the beginnning . . . and that was done in the land of America."[18]

The *Doctrine and Covenants Student Manual* manual points out that "the Lord shall come, without a doubt to His temple [in the New Jerusalem]. . . . This appearing will be separate and distinct from the great coming in the clouds of heaven, when He will appear with power and great glory (Matt. 24:30). . . . This coming will be for the blessing and benefit of the most faithful of His saints."[19]

The Lord himself said that he will appear in the New Jerusalem temple.

> Verily this is the word of the Lord, that the city New Jerusalem shall be built by the gathering of the saints, beginning at this place, even the place of the temple, which temple shall be reared in this generation. For verily this generation shall not all pass away until an house shall be built unto the Lord, and a cloud shall rest upon it, which cloud shall be even the glory of the Lord. (D&C 84:4–5)

> And I will suddenly come to my temple. (D&C 36:8)

> Yea . . . my presence shall be there, for I will come into it, and all the pure in heart that shall come into it shall see God. (D&C 97:16)

Why must the Lord come to a temple instead of some other place? Temples are representative of heaven where God dwells. Whenever the Lord visits the earth, a little bit of heaven must be provided for him in which to dwell, for he cannot abide in the evil that exists on the earth. A temple is, therefore, not just a beautiful building. Nor is it an ordinary house of worship. It is literally God's house on earth, his sacred and holy home away from his heavenly home. Brigham Young explained, "He requires his servants to build him a house that he can come to and where he can make known his will."[20] Thus, when the Lord appears to the Saints at his Second Coming, he will come to his house in the New Jerusalem.

Because temples are literally houses of God, they belong to him and must be constructed with his divine approval and by those whom he authorizes. Any so-called temple that has not been authorized by him is simply an edifice built by the hands of men, and "God . . . dwelleth not in temples made with hands" (Acts 17:24). Thus, the rebuilding of the ancient Jewish temple must be authorized by God, or it will not be considered by him to be his holy house.

It is true that a temple will be built in old Jerusalem, but by whom? President Wilford Woodruff said, "[The Lord] will never come until the Jews are gathered home and have rebuilt their temple and city and the Gentiles have gone up there to battle against them."[21] It appears from this statement that Jews will build the temple, but further evidence indicates that they will probably be Jewish members of the Church who will be authorized by God to build it. During Armageddon, righteous Jews will be warned to flee to the "mountains of the Lord's house" in Jerusalem. The Lord said, "Let them who be of Judah flee unto Jerusalem, unto the mountains of the Lord's house" (D&C 133:13).

Elder Erastus Snow explained that "the mountain of the Lord's house" is "a peculiar phrase, and was probably used by the prophet [Micah] because it was a common mode of expression in Israel in the days of David and many of the prophets several hundred years after him, for, in speaking of Mount Moriah, on which the Temple of Solomon was built, they spoke of it as the mountain of the Lord's house."[22]

Most people have assumed that the Jerusalem temple will be rebuilt on the same site as the ancient Jewish temple, but a Muslim mosque (Dome of the Rock) now occupies that spot. For that reason, the Lord may choose another location for his temple. On the other hand, it is possible that the Muslim mosque might be destroyed by natural or man-made causes. However, if the Jews were to rush in to remove the rubble and build their own sacred edifice there, things would likely get worse for them.

Interestingly, the site for the New Jerusalem temple is also claimed and occupied by other churches. Their unauthorized edifices will either be destroyed during the time when God cleanses the area of Jackson County, or the buildings will simply be abandoned or sold to the Lord's church, for prophecy must be fulfilled that a temple of God will be built there. Both temples must be built in preparation for the millennium, for they will serve as world capitals during that thousand-year era.

Notes
1. McConkie, *Mormon Doctrine*, 532.
2. *Doctrine and Covenants Student Manual*, 239.
3. Burton, *We Believe*, 1135.
4. Smith, *The Signs of the Times*, p. 194, 196.
5. Thomas, *Watch and Be Ready*, 18.
6. Smith, *The Signs of the Times*, 245.
7. *Journal of Discourses*, 24:156–57.
8. *Doctrine and Covenants Student Manual*, 250
9. Ibid., 286.
10. *Journal of Discourses*, 9:137.
11. Ibid., 18:355.
12. Ibid., 11:16.
13. Ibid., 9:138.
14. Ibid., 6:296.
15. Smith, *Doctrines of Salvation*, 2:247–48, 251.
16. *Old Testament Student Manual*, 2:344.
17. *Journal of Discourses*, 15:154.
18. Widtsoe, *Discourses of Brigham Young*, 122.
19. *Doctrine and Covenants Student Manual*, 336.
20. Widtsow, *Discourses of Brigham Young*, 394.
21. *Journal of Discourses*, 18:111.
22. Ibid., 16:202.

Ten

MUSTERING FOR ARMAGEDDON

The world today is sitting on a bomb of its own making. Wickedness and violence are increasing so rapidly that the world will soon be plunged into a war of such catastrophic proportions that all other wars will pale in comparison. That final world conflict will be the war of Armageddon. "The kings of the earth and of the whole world [will be gathered] to the battle of that great day of God Almighty . . . into a place called in the Hebrew tongue Armageddon" (Revelation 16:14, 16).

The destruction of human life during that time will be so extensive and devastating that millions of people will pass from this life into eternity (see Revelation 9:18).

> For then shall be great tribulation, such as was not since the beginning of the world to this time, no, nor ever shall be. (Matthew 24:21)

> And the slain of the Lord shall be at that day from one end of the earth even unto the other. (Jeremiah 25:33)

> [And thus] he shall make even a speedy riddance of all them that dwell in the land. (Zephaniah 1:18)

The Lord said,

> I will gather all nations against Jerusalem to battle. (Zechariah 14:2)

> For my determination is to gather the nations that I may assemble the kingdoms, to pour upon them mine indignation, even all my fierce anger. (Zephaniah 3:8)

The great day of the Lord is near, it is near. . . . That day is a day of wrath, a day of trouble and distress . . . a day of clouds and thick darkness, a day of the trumpet and alarm against the fenced cities and against the high towers. And I will bring distress upon men, that they shall walk like blind men, because they have sinned against the Lord: and their blood shall be poured out as dust, and their flesh as the dung. Neither their silver nor their gold shall be able to deliver them in the day of the Lord's wrath; but the whole land shall be devoured. (Zephaniah 1:14–18)

Much of the battle is described in the ninth chapter of the book of Revelation. The Lord told Joseph Smith that the things described in that chapter would "be accomplished after the opening of the seventh seal, before the coming of Christ" (D&C 77:1–3).

The instigator of the war will, of course, be Satan, the great "dragon" (see Revelation 13:2). He, who has been ruling the earth now for over six thousand years, knows that the rightful ruler and king of the earth, Jesus Christ, is about to return and take control of his usurped kingdom. Thus the devil, knowing he has only a short time left, will unleash all of his wrath in its full strength and fury during that final war. The scriptures warn, "Woe to the inhabiters of the earth and of the sea! For the devil is come down unto you, having great wrath, because he knoweth that he hath but a short time" (Revelation 12:12). And "behold, at that day shall he rage in the hearts of the children of men" (2 Nephi 28:20).

The war of Armageddon will be part of Satan's continuing war with God (which began in our pre-earth life). The devil undoubtedly believes the spiritual and physical destruction of millions of God's children, in these last days, will be a crushing blow to the Lord's great plan of salvation. Therefore Satan will wreak as much havoc as possible during Armageddon, knowing that soon his reign of tyranny will come to an end, he will be stripped of his power, and he will be bound for "a thousand years" (Revelation 20:2), putting an end to his conquest and destruction of humanity.

The devil began his war with God in the premortal world in order to exalt himself above God. The prophet Isaiah wrote of Satan, "For thou hast said in thine heart, I will ascend into heaven, I will exalt my throne above the stars of God: I will sit also upon the mount of the congregation, in the sides of the north: I will ascend above the heights of the clouds; I will be like the most High" (Isaiah 14:13–14).

Satan (who was known as Lucifer in our pre-earth life) not only wanted to be exalted above God, but he also wanted higher prominence than Jesus, the favored Son of God. So he sought to replace Jesus as the Redeemer of mankind. He said to Heavenly Father, "Behold, here am I, send me, I will be thy son, and I will redeem all mankind, that one soul shall not be lost, and surely I will do it; wherefore give me thine honor" (Moses 4:1).

Lucifer's plan was to eliminate freedom of choice, which would give him great power over others. Therefore God, in his infinite wisdom, rejected Satan and chose Jesus. Lucifer was so outraged over the Father's decision that he persuaded one-third of the host of heaven to join him in a rebellion against the Lord and his Beloved Son. From that time on, Lucifer became known as the devil, or Satan. Several scriptures also refer to him as the "dragon." The apostle John recorded, "And there appeared another wonder in heaven; and behold a great red dragon. . . . And his tail drew the third part of the stars of heaven. . . . And there was war in heaven: Michael and his angels fought against the dragon; and the dragon fought and his angels" (Revelation 12:3–4, 7).

Eventually Satan and his angels "prevailed not; neither was their place found any more in heaven. And the great dragon was cast out, that old serpent, called the Devil, and Satan, which deceiveth the whole world: he was cast out to the earth, and his angels were cast out with him. . . . A loud voice [was heard] saying in heaven, Now is come salvation, and strength, and the kingdom of our God, and the power of his Christ: for the accuser of our brethren is cast down, which accused them before our God day and night. . . . Therefore rejoice, ye heavens, and ye that dwell in them" (Revelation 12:8–10, 12).

Isaiah lamented that Lucifer, who had been the son of the morning, had fallen so low. "How art thou fallen from heaven, O Lucifer, son of the morning! How art thou cut down to the ground, which didst weaken the nations!" (Isaiah 14:12).

God is now allowing Satan and his angels to exert their influence upon mankind so that people can have a choice between good and evil. Ironically, Satan is now unwittingly playing an important role in the exercise of agency, the very thing which he had sought to eliminate from the plan of salvation. The Lord said, "And it must needs be that the devil should tempt the children of men, or they could not be agents unto themselves; for if they never should know the bitter they could not know the sweet" (D&C 29:39).

Jesus was rewarded for his loyalty to God and his unselfish willingness to redeem mankind with his own life. He was given his own kingdom—this earth and its inhabitants. Daniel recorded, "There was given him dominion, and glory, and a kingdom, that all people, nations, and languages, should serve him" (Daniel 7:14).

Now the devil, who failed to take control of God's heavenly kingdom, is attempting to take control of Jesus' earthly kingdom. The evil anti-Christ can only achieve that by destroying God's children spiritually and physically. Satan knows their spiritual destruction will ultimately lead to their physical destruction. Thus,

> Satan goeth up and down, to and fro in the earth, seeking to destroy the souls of men. (D&C 10:27)

> Satan hath come among the children of men, and tempteth them to worship him; and men have become carnal, sensual, and devilish. (Moses 6:49)

> [Therefore,] the wicked shall slay the wicked. (D&C 63:33)

Thus the "dragon" is the most deadly and evil of all beings. His influence is manifest in the world through all organizations, governmental powers, and people whose philosophies or activities run counter to the righteous principles and acts which God espouses. All those devil-inspired groups and individuals are collectively called the church of the devil or the great and abominable church. It is in opposition to the Church of Jesus Christ. Therefore, people who reject Jesus and his Church automatically become part of Satan's church.

The prophet Nephi spoke of the two churches:

> Behold, there are save two churches only; the one is the church of the Lamb of God, and the other is the church of the devil; wherefore, whoso belongeth not to the church of the Lamb of God belongeth to that great church, which is the mother of abominations, and she is the whore of all the earth. (1 Nephi 14:10)

> And it came to pass that I beheld the great and abominable church; and I saw the devil that he was the founder of it. (1 Nephi 13:6)

Satan's "church" not only leads people into paths of sin and away from God, but it also attempts to enslave people, depriving them of agency. Elder George Q. Morris stated that through communism alone, Satan has successfully "subjugated about one billion people of the world, and by a dire, sanguinary, and deadly philosophy has brought death to millions."[1]

John the Revelator depicted the true church as a woman whom the devil persecutes. He recorded,

> When the dragon saw that he was cast unto the earth, he persecuted the woman. . . . And the dragon was wroth with the woman, and went to make war with the remnant of her seed, which keep the commandments of God, and have the testimony of Jesus Christ. (Revelation 12:13, 17)

> Wherefore, he [Satan] maketh war with the saints of God, and encompasseth them round about. (D&C 76:29)

> For Satan seeketh to destroy. (D&C 132:57)

Besides his desire to destroy Jesus' church and the Saints who belong to it, the devil also desires to destroy God's chosen people, the Israelites, who were foreordained to hold the priesthood, God's ruling power over the church (see Abraham 3:22–23; Exodus 19:5–6). Anyone favored by God is targeted by Satan. Thus Jews have been persecuted for centuries, and the nation of Israel will be a major focus of Satan's wrath during Armageddon.

The devil has already succeeded in turning many people against Israel (as well as America because of its support of Israel). Muslim fundamentalists today have a particular hatred of Jews and Americans. Satan is using them to accomplish his evil designs. Hence they are part of his "church." They have allied themselves with the devil in an attempt to annihilate the nation of Israel. The Psalmist declared, "They have said, Come, and let us cut them off from being a nation; that the name of Israel may be no more in remembrance"(Psalm 83:4).

Because neither Muslims nor Jews will vacate the land of Israel, the war of Armageddon is inevitable. The battlefield will be in that locale, near the ancient city of Megiddo, which in Hebrew means "the place of troops."[2] It is strategically located near Israel's capital city of Jerusalem. The LDS Bible dictionary states that the name Armageddon is a "Greek transliteration from the Hebrew *Har Megiddon*, or Mountain of Megiddo. The valley of Megiddo is in the western portion of the plain of Esdraelon 50 miles north of Jerusalem. . . . [And] the battle of Armageddon . . . will be fought in the same locale and will be decisive."[3]

The Armageddon armies will also fight in the valley of Jehoshaphat, an area east of Jerusalem, between the city and the Mount of Olives.[4] The

Lord said through the prophet Joel,

> For, behold, in those days . . . I will also gather all nations, and will bring them down into the valley of Jehoshaphat, and will plead with them there for my people and for my heritage Israel, whom they have scattered among the nations, and parted my land. . . .
> Proclaim ye this among the Gentiles: Prepare war. . . .
> Assemble yourselves, and come, all ye heathen [non-Christian]. . . . Let the heathen be wakened, and come up to the valley of Jehoshaphat: for there will I sit to judge all the heathen round about . . . the harvest is ripe . . . their wickedness is great. Multitudes, multitudes in the valley of decision: for the day of the Lord is near. (Joel 3:1–2, 9, 11–14)

What must happen to cause the present turmoil in the Middle East to erupt into the war of Armageddon? Apostle Charles W. Penrose stated that some nations (possibly Muslim) will first become bankrupt: "The bankrupt nations, envying the wealth of the sons of Judah, will seek a pretext to make war upon them, and will invade the 'holy land' to 'take a prey and a spoil.' "[5]

The more the Muslim nations fight against Israel, the more bankrupt they become. The West Bank and Gaza, where many Muslim Palestinians reside, are two good examples. Israel, on the other hand, will be prospering before Armageddon begins. The prophet Ezekiel said that nations will invade Israel "to take a spoil and to take a prey [from] . . . the people that are gathered out of the nations, which have gotten cattle and goods" (Ezekekiel 38:12).

Another thing that must happen is the appearance of the man known as Gog in the scriptures (see chapter 12 of this book) who, under Satan's influence, will lead Armageddon's evil army into battle. Perhaps that man is already waiting in the wings for his chance to become the future leader of the nations which will comprise the world's largest and most powerful army. Clearly the signs of the approaching war of Armageddon are already looming on the horizon. Satan is mustering his army and drawing the nations of the earth into the conflict which will one day erupt into the most horrific war this earth has ever seen.

Notes

1. *Old Testament Student Manual,* 2:292.
2. Ibid., 2:291.
3. Bible Dictionary, "Armageddon," 614.
4. See Bible Dictionary, p. 614.
5. *Old Testament Student Manual,* 2:295.

Eleven

AN EVIL ALLIANCE

In the book of Revelation, the apostle John mentions two beasts in connection with the war of Armageddon. The beasts are man-made governments or kingdoms. They are depicted as beasts in the scriptures because, unlike God's kingdom, they are full of wickedness and violence. The Prophet Joseph Smith taught, "When God made use of the figure of a beast in visions to the prophets, He did it to represent those kingdoms which had degenerated and become corrupt, savage and beast-like in their disposition. . . . You there see that the beasts are spoken of to represent the kingdoms of the world, the inhabitants whereof were beastly and abominable characters."[1]

The two Armageddon beasts seem to be two separate governmental kingdoms, but the second may simply be a combination of the first beast and other kingdoms that will unite with it to fight against Israel. The apostle John recorded, "And I saw the beast and the kings of the earth, and their armies, gathered together to make war" (Revelation 19:19).

We do not have enough information to determine definitively which earthly kingdom or kingdoms are represented by the first beast. However, we do know that it is not, as some people have suggested, merely a symbolic representation of the devil, for the devil will give the beast its power. John recorded, "And the beast which I saw . . . the dragon gave him his power, and his seat, and great authority" (Revelation 13:2). Nor is the "beast" a symbolic representation of the world. John said that "the world wondered after the beast" (Revelation 13:3). "The beast . . . shall ascend out of the bottomless pit . . . and they that dwell on the earth shall wonder"

(Revelation 17:8). The Prophet Joseph Smith remarked, "And if the beast was all the world, how could the world wonder after the beast? It must have been a wonderful beast to cause all human beings to wonder after it; and I will venture to say that when God allows the devil to give power to the beast to destroy the inhabitants of the earth, all will wonder."[2]

The apostle John also recorded that when the beastly government comes to power, the wicked world will honor it to the extent of worship. "And [the world] worshipped the beast, saying, Who is like unto the beast? Who is able to make war with him. . . . And all that dwell upon the earth shall worship him, whose names are not written in the book of life of the Lamb" (Revelation 13:4, 8).

Thus the beast will apparently be a very powerful government or kingdom. And it will have great authority over people during Armageddon, for the "dragon gave him his power, and his seat, and great authority" (Revelation 13:2). It seems that it will not only be the major player in the war of Armageddon, but it will be the major player in the world—a world super power. Elder Bruce R. McConkie said, "The kingdom (or kingdoms) involved will be a world power (or powers)."[3]

John the Revelator said that the beast will have power over every nation. He recorded, "And . . . power was given [the beast] over all kindreds, and tongues, and nations" (Revelation 13:7). The prophet Daniel recorded that "the beast . . . shall devour the whole earth, and shall tread it down, and break it in pieces" (Daniel 7:23). And it shall be "dreadful and terrible, and strong exceedingly" (Daniel 7:7).

Scriptures tell us that the beastly government or kingdom will be different from all other kingdoms that had existed before it. The prophet Daniel wrote that "it was diverse from all the beasts that were before it" (Daniel 7:7). Its difference is significant, for it will apparently be a league of nations, rather than a single nation. John the Revelator recorded that several nations "shall give their power and strength . . . and . . . their kingdom unto the beast" (Revelation 17:13, 17).

It could be a league of nations similar to the UN (United Nations) which is empowered to govern all nations to an extent through the UDHR (Universal Declaration of Human Rights). However, the UN has member nations from all over the world, while the Armageddon league will probably receive its members and power from the nations of Europe. How do we know this? The beast had ten horns that appear to represent the nations of Europe and their leaders. The prophet Daniel stated that the beast "had ten horns. . . . And the ten horns . . . are ten kings that shall arise" (Daniel 7:7, 24; see also Revelation 13:1). The *Old Testament Student* manual published by the church says, "The ten horns are the kingdoms [of Europe] into which the Roman Empire was afterwards divided. They are similar to the ten toes of the great image described in Daniel 2."[4]

The Church student manuals are not as authoritative as scripture, but the conclusions they draw are quite reasonable. It is probably true that the ten horns are similar to the ten toes that Daniel described, and therefore they likely represent the nations of Europe (and their kings) that emerged after the fall of the Roman Empire. Some evidence of that will be given later in this book.

If it is true that the ten horns represent modern Europe, those nations will unite with the beast, giving it authority and power to rule over them. An angel explained to John the Revelator, "The ten horns which thou sawest are ten kings, which have received no kingdom as yet [at the time of John's revelation]; but [later] receive power as kings one hour with the beast. These have one mind, and shall give their power and strength unto the beast. . . . For God hath put in their hearts to fulfil his will, and to agree, and give their kingdom unto the beast" (Revelation 17:12–13, 17).

The beast will probably be a revised version of an ancient empire, perhaps the ancient beastly kingdom of John's day—the Roman Empire. We can draw this conclusion because the beast "was, and is not, and yet is" (Revelation 17:8). Something that "was" is something that existed in the past. But when it "is not," it no longer exists. The Roman Empire which existed anciently collapsed in AD 476,[5] but John's revelation indicates that the beast "yet is." That probably means that the ancient beastly kingdom will revive.

An angel said to John, "The beast that thou sawest was, and is not . . . and they that dwell on the earth shall wonder . . . when they behold the beast that was, and is not, and yet is" (Revelation 17:8). The ancient beast was "wounded to death; and his deadly wound was healed: and all the world wondered after the beast . . . the beast which had the wound by a sword and [yet] did live" (Revelation 13:3, 14).

Scriptures can often have dual meaning or application, so the same passages in the book of Revelation, which seem to be describing the ancient Roman Empire, also appear to be describing the revived latter-day empire or beast. Therefore many of the characteristics of the ancient empire will probably be characteristics of the modern beastly empire or government. One difference is that modern nations (likely in Europe) will give their strength, power, and kingdoms to the modern beast.

Writings of the apostle John seem to indicate that the latter-day "beast" will arise from the modern remnant of one of seven ancient kingdoms which were historically connected to the Roman Empire. Those seven kingdoms are described as seven "heads" on the ancient Roman "beast." John said, "And I . . . saw a beast rising up out of the sea, having seven heads and ten horns, and upon his horns ten crowns, and upon his heads the name of blasphemy. . . . And I saw one of his heads as it were wounded to death; and his deadly wound was healed" (Revelation 13:1, 3).

John then explained, "The seven heads are seven mountains. . . . And there are seven kings, five are fallen [no longer exist], and one is [in existence at the time of John's revelation], and the other is not yet come . . . And the beast that was, and is not, even he is the eighth, and is of the seven" (Revelation 17:9–11). Thus it seems that the eighth (the latter-day beast) will emerge from one of the seven ancient heads or kingdoms. That particular ancient kingdom will apparently revive, for the scriptures say it was "wounded to death; and his deadly wound was healed" (Revelation 13:3).

The five heads or empires which had already fallen (by the time John wrote about the beast) could include: Egypt, Babylon, Assyria, Persia, and Greece. The sixth kingdom that "is" (meaning still in existence) was probably the Roman Empire which was at the height of its power in John's day. Later, in AD 395, the Roman Empire split into an east and a west division. The eastern half became the Byzantine Empire which, at its height, covered all of eastern Europe and part of Asia. The kingdom that had "not yet come" might be the Ottoman Empire which in 1453 took control of the eastern Byzantine Empire.[6] The Ottoman Empire became one of the world's most powerful and wealthy empires, ruling over southeast Europe, Asia Minor (Turkey), the Balkan countries west of Turkey, parts of northern Africa, Egypt, present-day Iran, Saudi Arabia, and Syria. The empire was inhabited primarily by Muslims who spread their Islamic religion throughout the Empire before it came to an end in 1922. It was defeated by the British in World War I.[7]

It is therefore possible that the Ottoman Empire was the head that was wounded by a sword and yet did live (if it revives to become the future beast). The parts of Europe and the Middle East, which are remnants of the Ottoman Empire, are still inhabited by Muslims, and many of those people are now hostile toward the Jews in Israel (Armageddon's target). According to a former Muslim who converted to Christianity, Walid Shoebat, many Islamists are trying to revive the Ottoman Empire right now.[8]

The latter-day beast's military leader will come from the north, an area that was inhabited by ancient Scythians, and which today is probably Russia, or a country that used to be part of the former USSR (Union of Soviet Socialist Republics) (see next chapter). Could that leader influence Muslim nations to become part of his evil "league of nations," and fight against Israel in the war of Armageddon? That is certainly possible in light of the number of Muslims who already hate the Jews in Israel. Could Muslim nations qualify as the ten horns or ten kingdoms of Europe? Most Muslim nations today are in the Middle East, which is not considered part of Europe. However, the former Ottoman Empire covered southeast Europe, and it emerged from the Roman Empire which covered most of Europe.[9]

We do not know if the ten European horns (kings and their kingdoms) are representative of exactly ten nations, or if they merely symbolize all of the European nations that will be involved (which could be more or less than ten). The ten horns might even represent nations outside of Europe that emerged from Europe.

And we do not know how the beast's military leader from the north will persuade the ten kings to give him their power. If he becomes the leader of the EU (European Union), most of Europe would fall under his leadership. The EU's function is similar to that of the U.S. federal government—the nations of Europe have their own separate governments but many now come under the umbrella of the larger government, the EU. They have voluntarily given much of their "power and strength . . . and . . . their kingdom" to the EU, just as the "ten horns" will give to the beast (see Revelation 17:13).

Through the EU, the European nations cooperate in political, economic, and military matters. The EU also attempts to manage world trade and to deal with military matters throughout the world. In 1993 the EU organized with twelve member nations.[10] Three more were added in 1994, and ten more in 2004. Croatia and Turkey are now negotiating for membership. And Fox news reported on April 10, 2005, that Bulgaria and Romania will be added by 2007.

Currently the EU has more people in it than the United States. It even has its own bank, the European Central Bank, and its own currency—the euro.[11] Because the EU is expanding, it has the potential to grow into a world super power, which could replace the United States as the most powerful kingdom in the world.

It has been rumored that the EU has proposed a ten-kingdom administration, but apparently that has not yet been established. Or, if it is in existence, it could be the secret combination that the Lord said would arise in the last days. Through the prophet Ether, the Lord warned,

> Wherefore, the Lord commandeth you, when ye shall see these things come among you that ye shall awake to a sense of your awful situation, because of this secret combination which shall be among you; or wo be unto it, because of the blood of them who have been slain; for they cry from the dust for vengeance upon it, and also upon those who built it up. For it cometh to pass that whoso buildeth it up seeketh to overthrow the freedom of all lands, nations, and countries; and it bringeth to pass the destruction of all people, for it is built up by the devil. (Ether 8:24–25)

The EU's common system of law and government resembles that of the ancient Roman Empire. However, unlike the Roman Empire, which persecuted and killed Christians, the EU has so far shown no tendency for violence. Whatever government becomes the evil latter-day beast, it will eventually seek to control the world, and it will turn on the nation of Israel, as well as the Lord and his saints.

The apostle John stated,

> And I saw the beast and the kings of the earth, and their armies, gathered together to make war against him on the white horse [Jesus]. (Revelation 19:19)

> And [the beast] opened his mouth in blasphemy against God, to blaspheme his name, and his tabernacle, and them that dwell in heaven.... And it was given unto him to make war with the saints and to overcome them. (Revelation 13:6, 7)

> And the ten horns which ... are ten kings.... [These] shall give their power and strength unto the beast. These shall make war with the Lamb. (Revelation 17:12–14)

The Psalmist might have been referring to the evil latter-day league when he wrote, "They have taken crafty counsel against thy people, and consulted against thy hidden ones. . . . For they have consulted together with one consent: they are confederate against thee" (Psalm 83:3–5).

During the war of Armageddon, the beast will tread down Jerusalem for three and a half years. John recorded, "And . . . who is like unto the beast? Who is able to make war with him? And there was given unto him a mouth speaking great things and blasphemies; and power was given unto him to continue forty and two months" (Revelation 13:4–5). And "the holy city shall they tread under foot forty and two months" (Revelation 11:2).

During that time two "witnesses" (prophets in Jerusalem) will hold the beast at bay for three and one-half years until they are finally killed by it. The Lord said of them, "And I will give power unto my two witnesses, and they shall prophesy a thousand two hundred and threescore days [three and one-half years]" (Revelation 11:3). "And when [the two witnesses] have finished their testimony, the beast that ascendeth out of the bottomless pit shall make war against them, and shall overcome them, and kill them" (Revelation 11:7).

That prophecy, as well as all other prophecies regarding the beast, will be fulfilled when the ten-horned kingdom emerges to the world scene and wages the final world war. Until then, the actual identity of the beast, and how it will gain its enormous power, will probably remain unknown.

Had the former Soviet Union not collapsed in 1991, it would have been a prime candidate for the beast. The USSR had ten republics (horns), and its communistic form of government set it apart from all other kingdoms. Perhaps communism, which no longer appears to be a world threat, will revive. This is very possible in light of the fact that a remnant of the former communistic Soviet Union will likely be involved in the Armageddon war (see next chapter). "Elder George Q. Morris of the Quorum of the Twelve stated that an important part of the evil coalition of the last days will be communism: 'Another sign of great importance was the rise of an evil power. Brother [Ezra Taft] Benson had already very impressively referred to it—communism.'"[12]

The EU does not appear to be influenced by communism today, but there is always the possibility it could be in the future. However, there is still the possibility that the beastly confederacy will be an organization or kingdom other than the EU. Another strong contender is the radical Islamic Movement which many Muslims are now joining. Those Muslim fundamentalists are not communists, but they practice a form of subjugation and violence which is very similar to that of communism.

Although it is unlikely the UN will be the beast, it might give its support to the beast. For by the time Jerusalem is besieged, all nations will likely be involved, either directly or indirectly. The Lord said, "I will bring all nations down into the valley of Jehoshaphat, and will plead with them there for my people and for my heritage Israel" (Joel 3:2).

"For I will gather all nations against Jerusalem to battle" (Zechariah 14:2). However, the phrase, "all nations," might refer only to the remnants of nations which were known to exist anciently. Or it might simply be symbolic of the many nations which will be involved in the war.

The scriptures also refer to the first beast as "the northern army" (Joel 2:20). Speaking of the leader of the northern army, the Lord said,

> Thou shalt come from thy place out of the north parts, thou and many people with thee. (Ezekiel 38:15)

> And I will . . . cause thee to come up from the north parts, and will bring thee upon the mountains of Israel. (Ezekiel 39:2)

> For I will bring evil from the north, and a great destruction . . . and thy cities shall be laid waste without an inhabitant. (Jeremiah 4:6–7)

> Therefore hear, ye nations . . . thus saith the Lord, Behold, a people cometh from the north country, and a great nation shall be raised from the sides of the earth" (Jeremiah 6:18, 22).

The nations north of Israel today not only include Muslim nations such as Lebanon, Syria, and Turkey, but also Russia. Russia is in Europe and was once strongly communistic. It is not part of the EU, but it could be in the future. Or it could persuade European nations (ten kings) to form a coalition similar to the EU, with Russia at its head, for the scripture quoted above says, "And a great nation shall be raised." The Lord also mentioned that particular nation in the writings of Joel: "For a nation is come up upon my land, strong, and without number" (Joel 1:6).

The strongest indication that Russia (or another country which was part of the former USSR) will be involved is the fact that the leader of the northern army (Gog) will come from Magog, an area north of Israel between the Black Sea and the Caspian Sea, which area was inhabited anciently by Scythians, and today is probably within the area of Russia or the former Soviet Union (see LDS Bible dictionary and map #11). (Gog will be discussed more in the next chapter.)

The apostle Orson Pratt also indicated that part of the northern army will come from Russia. He said, "When you see the nations of the earth, especially the heathen nations, and also those north of Jerusalem—the great nation of Russia and other nations on the continent of Asia, together with many in Europe, gather up against Jerusalem . . . then you may look for the Lord to come. . . . The children of Israel . . . will know that they cannot stand without the aid of the Lord against all those from the north quarters—Gog and Magog, all the hosts of Russia and of the various nations round about."[13]

The prophet Daniel said that the beast will prevail until the "Ancient of days" (Adam) will sit at the meeting of Adam ondi-Ahman. He recorded, "After this I saw in the night visions, and behold a . . . beast . . . and it had ten horns. . . . I beheld till the thrones were cast down, and the Ancient of days did sit. . . . I beheld . . . until the Ancient of days came, and judgment was given to the saints of the most High" (Daniel 7:7, 9, 21–22).

The beast, and those who align themselves with it, will be destroyed at the Second Coming of Jesus. The scriptures tell us, "Then will the Lord be jealous for his land, and pity his people. Yea, the Lord will answer and say unto his people, Behold . . . I will remove far off from you the northern army, and will drive him into a land barren and desolate, with his face toward the east sea, and his hinder part toward the utmost sea, and his stink shall come up. . . . Fear not, O land; be glad and rejoice for the Lord will do great things" (Joel 2:18–21).

We will not be able to prevent the evil league from forming, but we do not have to be part of it. We, as individuals and as a nation, should refrain from affiliating with any organization that promotes philosophies or conduct which run counter to the gospel of Jesus Christ. Voting for righteous people to run our government is one of the best ways to guarantee America will not become part of the beastly confederacy. The Church declared about governments: "We believe that governments were instituted of God for the benefit of man; and that he holds men accountable for their acts in relation to them . . . such [men] as will administer the law in equity and justice should be sought for and upheld by the voice of the people" (D&C 134:1–3).

Righteous leaders will realize that it is dangerous for the United States to join any world organization or alliance that will limit its power. President J. Reuben Clark said, "Every alliance requires a surrender of rights, since mutual aid, in strictly non-sovereign interests, is the purpose of the alliance."[14]

Even our membership in the UN is dangerous according to President Clark. He said, "We have lost the sovereign power to adjust our own international difficulties—a power which has enabled us to live as the most peace-loving nation in the world.... We have surrendered, by the Charter terms at least... the power to declare war... the power to decide against whom we shall make war, the power to conduct war, and the power to make peace and to determine its terms."[15]

President Ezra Taft Benson expressed a similar belief. He quoted Dan Smoot as saying, "United States membership in the United Nations has caused a perversion of our fundamental concepts of government.... We cannot have an American policy, either foreign or domestic; we cannot re-establish America as a free and independent constitutional republic—until we withdraw from the United Nations."[16]

Remaining neutral in world conflicts confines the United States in as narrow a space as possible. However, there are conditions when entrance into war is necessary and justifiable—all national governments have an obligation to protect the lives of their citizens. The prophet Alma said that "except ye do bestir yourselves in the defense of your country and your little ones, the sword of justice doth hang over you" (Alma 60:29).

In the event that the United States will become involved in the war of Armageddon (or any other war), President Brigham Young said we should be prepared militarily. He taught, "The Lord requires us to be quite as willing to fight our own battles as to have Him fight them for us. If we are not ready for an enemy when he comes upon us, we have not lived up to the requirements of Him who guides the ship."[17]

However, we are to strive to be peacemakers as much as possible, not only internationally, but individually. Peacemakers will avoid allying themselves with the destroyers of peace—Satan and his "beast."

Notes
1. Smith, *Teachings of the Prophet Joseph Smith*, 289.
2. Ibid., 293.
3. McConkie, *Doctrinal New Testament Commentary*, vol. III, 522.
4 *Old Testament Student Manual*, 2:304.
5. *World Book Encyclopedia*, 16:448.
6. Ibid., 2:770.
7. Ibid., 14:883–85.
8. Shoebat, *Why I Left Jihad*, 41.
9. *World Book Encyclopedia*, 6:421.
10. Ibid., 6:418–20.

11. Ibid.
12. *Old Testament Student Manual*, 2:292.
13. *Journal of Discourses*, 15:337.
14. Newquist, *Prophets, Principles and National Survival*, 438.
15. Ibid., 456.
16. Ibid., 460–61.
17. *Journal of Discourses*, 11:131.

Twelve

GOG AND MAGOG

The leader of the northern army will be someone who the scriptures refer to as *Gog*. The *Old Testament Student Manual* states, "Gog is a symbolic name for the leader . . . of this great evil power that will arise in the last days."[1] He is called the "little horn" by the prophet Daniel, who indicates that among the ten horns of the beast, another horn will arise, which will possibly be another king (and kingdom) within the European area. And it is the little horn who will lead the beast into battle.

At some point, either during or before the war begins, that king will subdue three of the other ten kings. Daniel writes,

> And the ten horns . . . are ten kings that shall arise: and another shall rise after them; and he shall be diverse from the first, and he shall subdue three kings. (Daniel 7:24)
>
> I considered the horns, and behold, there came up among them [the] little horn, before whom there were three of the first horns plucked up by the roots: and behold, in this horn were eyes like the eyes of a man, and a mouth speaking great things. . . .
>
> Then I would to know the truth of the . . beast . . . And of the ten horns that were in his head, and of the other which came up, and before whom three fell, even of that horn that had eyes, and a mouth that spake very great things, whose look was more stout than his fellows. (Daniel 7:8, 19–20)

Daniel also referred to the little horn as "a king of fierce countenance." He recorded, "And in the latter times of their kingdom, when the transgressors are come to the full, a king of fierce countenance, and understanding dark sentences, shall stand up. And his power shall be mighty, but not by his own power, and he shall destroy wonderfully and shall prosper, and practice, and shall destroy the mighty and the holy people. And through his policy also he shall cause craft to prosper in his hand; and he shall magnify himself in his heart, and shall . . . destroy many" (Daniel 8:23–25; see also the chapter heading).

The prophet Nahum refers to Gog as a wicked counselor. He wrote, "There is one come out of thee, that imagineth evil against the Lord, a wicked counselor. . . . Though [the people] be quiet, and likewise many, yet thus shall they be cut down, when he shall pass through" (Nahum 1:11–12).

The Lord said through the prophet Daniel that the "little horn" will arise very near the end of the world before Jesus comes: "Understand, O son of man: at the time of the end shall be the vision. . . . Behold, I will make thee know what shall be in the last end of the indignation: for at the time appointed the end shall be" (Daniel 8:17, 19). The student manual quoted earlier also states, "The little horn represented a notable anti-Christ power that was to be raised up after the time of the Roman Empire, and it was to be different from the other ten kingdoms mentioned after the Roman kingdom. Daniel said that this horn would have power to make war with and hinder the Saints until the time of Christ's second coming (see Daniel 7:20–27)."[2]

Like Satan and the beast, the little horn will eventually focus on conquering the land of Israel and destroying God's people. Daniel recorded,

> I beheld, and the same horn made war with the saints, and prevailed against them; until the Ancient of Days came [at Adam ondi-Ahman]. (Daniel 7:21-22)

> And he shall destroy wonderfully, and shall prosper, and practice, and shall destroy the mighty and the holy people. . . . He shall also stand up against the Prince of princes. (Daniel 8:24-25)

> And he shall speak great words against the most High, and shall wear out the saints of the most High, and think to change times and laws: and they shall be given into his hand until a time and times and the dividing of time. (Daniel 7:25)

A "time" equals one year or one period of time; the plural of "time" is "times"—two years; and "the dividing of time" is one-half of one year. Thus the Saints "shall be given into his hand" for three and one-half years.

Gog (the little horn) will apparently be the mouth of the beast. John the Revelator said,

> And there was given [the beast] a mouth speaking great things and blasphemies; and power was given unto him to continue forty and two months [three and one-half years]. And he opened his mouth in blasphemy against God, to blaspheme his name, and his tabernacle, and them that dwell in heaven. And it was given unto him to make war with the saints and to overcome them: and power was given him over all kindreds, and tongues, and nations. And all that dwell upon the earth shall worship him whose names are not written in the book of life. (Revelation 13:5–8)

The little horn will most likely arise from the area or estate that was, in ancient times, controlled by one of Alexander the Great's four generals. Daniel prophesied that "out of one of [the estates] came forth a little horn, which waxed exceedingly great, toward the south, and toward the east, and toward the pleasant land. And it waxed great, even to the host of heaven; and it cast down some of the host and of the stars to the ground, and stamped upon them" (Daniel 8:9–10).

Alexander's generals were Ptolemy, who received the southern part of Alexander's empire (Egypt and surrounding area); Cassander, who received the western part (Greece, Macedonia, and so forth); Seleucus, who received the eastern part (Babylon, Syria, Iran, and Iraq); and Lysimachus, who received the northern part of the empire (Turkey, Thrace, and so forth).[3] One of those regions contains an area which, in ancient times, was called Magog. Gog will come from Magog. He will also be the chief prince of Meshech and Tubal.

The Lord speaks of Gog from Magog in the book of Ezekiel: "Son of man, set thy face against Gog [from] the land of Magog, the chief prince of Meshech and Tubal, and prophesy against him, and say, Thus saith the Lord God; Behold, I am against thee, O Gog, the chief prince of Meshech and Tubal" (Ezekiel 38:2–3).

The names *Gog* and *Magog* are sometimes misunderstood. The *Old Testament Student Manual* states that "Gog is a name of a person and Magog the land from which he comes. Technically, 'Gog of Magog' is the correct way to say it."[4]

The student manual quoted above is not scripture, but it has been designed by the Church to give us useful background information, as well as interpretive and prophetic commentary on the scriptures.[5] As we study the commentary, along with the scriptures, and draw upon the Spirit of the Lord, we can gain insights and a greater understanding of the scriptures. With that in mind, let us consider additional information provided by the study guide.

> Meshech and Tubal were ancient countries occupying lands presently found, for the most part, in the [former] USSR or its satellites.[6]

> The people of Meshech were anciently called the Mushki. Some linguists think they gave their name to Moscow. . . . This area was also in the territory [once] under the control of the USSR. Both Meshech and Tubal, like Magog, were descendants of Japeth (see Genesis 10:2), and the three are usually associated. They seem to have had close geographical and other ties. Tubal [by] association is assumed to have been close to Meshech, very likely in the area around the Black Sea in Georgia and Turkey.[7]

The commentary quoted above also indicates that Magog includes "the areas north and east of the Black Sea and the Crimea, territories occupied by the [former] USSR or her satellites. Magog was inhabited anciently by the Scythians, a fierce barbaric people who were masters of swift and brutal warfare. Thus Magog becomes a symbol, or type, suggesting the warlike nature of these people."[8] The LDS Bible Dictionary also says that Magog is "a country or people near the Black Sea, and is equivalent to Scythian."[9]

Daniel implies that Magog is somewhere north of Israel, for he refers to the little horn (Gog from Magog) as the king of the north. That reference is found in the eleventh chapter of Daniel. The heading to that chapter reads, "Daniel sees the successive kings and their wars, leagues, and conflicts which lead up to the Second Coming of Christ." Joseph Fielding Smith also stated that chapter eleven of Daniel discusses events which lead up to the Second Coming of Christ. He wrote, "The opening of this chapter 11 of the book of Daniel begins in the days of the Medes and Persians. . . . These chapters contain history from that day down to the coming of the Son of God."[10]

The reference to Gog likely begins with verse twenty-one of that chapter: "And in [the general's] estate shall stand up a vile person to whom they shall not give the honor of the kingdom: but he shall come in peaceably and obtain the kingdom by flatteries" (Daniel 11:21). And "by peace [he] shall destroy many" (Daniel 8:25). This could mean that he will appear to be striving for peace. He might step forward and pledge to restore peace between Israel and the Muslims. Or he might sign a peace treaty to temporarily pacify people and gain their confidence. Daniel continues, "And after the league [agreement] made with him, he shall work deceitfully: for he shall come up, and shall become strong with a small people. He shall enter peaceably even upon the fattest places of the province . . . and he shall forecast his devices against the strongholds, even for a time" (Daniel 11:23–24).

Because Gog will be a little horn or king (probably meaning an insignificant king or leader), he might come from a little country which used to be part of the former USSR. Daniel tells us that he "shall become strong with a small people" (Daniel 11:23). There are presently three small countries north and east of the Black Sea which used to be part of the Soviet Union. They are Armenia, Azerbaijan, and Georgia. The area which they occupy appears to be in or near the area which has been identified as Magog.

However, the little horn might be an insignificant leader within Russia itself and will begin working with a small number of people there. Although Gog will begin "with a small people," he will eventually build his army into a very large and powerful one. The Lord declared, "I will bring thee forth, and all thine army . . . even a great company. . . . And thou shalt come from thy place out of the north parts, thou, and many people with thee . . . a great company, and a mighty army" (Ezekiel 38:4, 15).

The scriptures also indicate that other kings will join with him.

> Behold, a people shall come from the north, and a great nation, and many kings shall be raised up from the coasts of the earth. (Jeremiah 50:41)

> The noise of the multitude in the mountains, like as of a great people; a tumultuous noise of the kingdoms of nations gathered together: the Lord of Hosts mustereth the hosts of the battle. They come from a far country, from the end of heaven, even the Lord, and the weapons of his indignation, to destroy the whole land. Howl ye; for the day of the Lord is at hand; it shall come as a destruction from the Almighty. (Isaiah 13:4–6)

If the latter part of Daniel's eleventh chapter is referring to Gog, then he will overthrow many countries before he invades Israel. Daniel states that he will subdue three of the horns of Europe (see Daniel 7:8, 24), and "he shall stretch forth his hand also upon [other] countries: and the land of Egypt shall not escape. . . . And the Libyans and the Ethiopians shall be at his steps. . . . He shall enter also into the glorious land, and many countries shall be overthrown: but these shall escape out of his hand, even Edom and Moab, and the chief of the children of Ammon" (Daniel 11:42–43, 41). (These last-mentioned areas are in present-day Jordan— see Bible Dictionary).

Daniel indicates that the king of the north will not regard any god except the "god of forces"; neither will he regard the desire of women.

> And the king shall do according to his will; and he shall exalt himself, and magnify himself above every god, and shall speak marvelous things against the God of gods. . . .
>
> Neither shall he regard the God of his fathers, nor the desire of women, nor regard any god; for he shall magnify himself above all. But in his estate shall he honour the God of forces: and a god whom his fathers knew not shall he honor with gold, and silver, and with precious stones, and pleasant things. Thus shall he do in the most strong holds with a strange god, whom he shall acknowledge and increase with glory: and he shall cause [his army] to rule over many, and shall divide the land for gain. . . .
>
> And with the arms of a flood shall [the people] be overflown from before him and shall be broken. (Daniel 11:36–39, 22)
>
> Though they be quiet, and likewise many, yet thus shall they be cut down, when he shall pass through. (Nahum 1:12)

If Gog is the "king of the north," one of his battles will be with a king from the south whose identity is not given. It could be a future leader of Egypt, for "Egypt shall not escape" (Daniel 11:42). Daniel stated,

> And at the time of the end shall the king of the south push at [the king of the north]: and the king of the north shall come against him like a whirlwind, with chariots, and with horsemen, and with many ships; and he shall enter into the countries, and shall overflow and pass over. (Daniel 11:40)
>
> And he shall stir up his power and his courage against the king of the south with a great army; and the king of the south shall be stirred up to battle with a very great and mighty army; but he [king of the south] shall not stand: for they shall forecast devices against

him. Yea, they that feed of the portion of his meat shall destroy him, and his army shall overflow: and many shall fall down slain. And both these kings' hearts shall be to do mischief and they shall speak lies at one table; but it shall not prosper: for yet the end shall be at the time appointed. (Daniel 11:25–27)

Daniel informs us that after those initial battles, Gog will apparently return to his own country with great riches before he proceeds to invade Israel.

> Then shall he return into his land with great riches . . . he shall do exploits, and return to his own land . . . [and] he shall have power over the treasures of gold and of silver, and over all the precious things of Egypt. (Daniel 11:28, 43)

> He shall . . . do that which his fathers have not done, nor his fathers' fathers; he shall scatter among [his army] the prey, and spoil, and riches: yea, and he shall forecast his devices against the strong holds, even for a time. (Daniel 11:24)

The conquest of Israel will be Gog's final goal. The Lord declared,

> Therefore, son of man, prophesy and say unto Gog, Thus saith the Lord God: In that day when my people of Israel dwelleth safely . . . thou shalt come up against my people Israel. . . .
> And it shall come to pass at the same time when Gog shall come against the land of Israel, saith the Lord God, that my fury shall come up in my face. (Ezekiel 38:14, 16, 18)

> My determination is to gather the nations, that I may assemble the kingdoms, to pour upon them mine indignation, even all my fierce anger. (Zephaniah 3:8)

> I will bring thee [Gog] forth, and all thine army . . . even a great company . . . Persia, Ethiopia, and Libya with them . . . Gomer, and all his bands; the house of Togarmah of the north quarters, and all his bands: and many people with thee . . . In the latter years thou shalt come into the land that is brought back from the sword, and is gathered out of many people, against the mountains of Israel. (Ezekiel 38:4–6, 8)

The *Old Testament Student Manual* states that the modern equivalent of Persia is Iran. Ehiopia is "the southern part of the continent of Africa." Libya is "the northern African countries . . . areas now occupied by Libya, Tunisia, Morocco, and Algeria." Gomer is "most of modern Europe and parts of Asia Minor." Togarmah is Asia Minor (Turkey and the area between the Black Sea and the Mediterranean). Anciently "Togarmah was a son of Gomer (see Genesis 10:3), and the Armenians claim to be his descendants . . . Armenia used to include . . . part of southern USSR, Turkey, and Syria."[11]

The prophet Daniel pointed out that at some point in Gog's future war, "tidings out of the east and out of the north shall trouble him: therefore he shall go forth with a great fury to destroy, and utterly to make away many" (Daniel 11:44). The scriptures do not indicate what the tidings from the east and north will be. However, "kings of the east" will unite with Gog in his war against Israel (Revelation 16:12–16).

East of Israel are Muslim countries (Iraq, Iran, Pakistan, Afghanistan, and Saudi Arabia). North Korea and China are also east of Israel. North Korea is an ally of Iran, one of the participants in the war, according to scripture (see Ezekiel 38:5). The scriptures indicate that Gog will be "great toward the east" (Daniel 8:9). "Behold, these shall come from far: and, lo, these from the north and from the west; and these from the land of Sinim" (Isaiah 49:12). Sinim is possibly China, according to the LDS Bible dictionary: "It is uncertain what country is meant, but it must have been one of the most distant lands known to the writer of the prophecy. China has been suggested, but the identification is uncertain."[12]

The apostle John said the kings of the east will enter the war after the river Euphrates is dried up (possibly from drought). He recorded,

> And the sixth angel poured out his vial upon the great river Euphrates: and the water was dried up, that the way of the kings of the east might be prepared. And I saw three unclean spirits come out of the mouth of the dragon [Satan], and out of the mouth of the beast, and out of the mouth of the false prophet [probably Gog] . . . which go forth unto the kings of the earth and of the whole world, to gather them to the battle of that great day of God Almighty . . . into a place called in the Hebrew tongue Armageddon. (Revelation 16:12–14, 16)

Gog's combined forces will equal 200 million people. John stated, "And the number of the army of the horsemen were two hundred thousand thousand" (Revelation 9:16). The Lord said of them,

> For a nation is come up upon my land, strong, and without number. (Joel 1:6)

A great people and a strong; there hath not been ever the like, neither shall be any more after it. (Joel 2:2)

Proclaim ye this among the Gentiles: Prepare war, wake up the mighty men, let all the men of war draw near; let them come up: Beat your plowshares into swords, and your pruninghooks into spears: let the weak say, I am strong. . . .

Multitudes, multitudes in the valley of decision: for the day of the Lord is near in the valley of decision. (Joel 3:9–10, 14)

The likes of those who will put their trust in Gog are already being seen in the Middle East. On October 26, 2005, Iran's president, Mahmoud Ahmadinejad, said, "Israel must be wiped off the map."[13] He also indicated that he is now ready to share his nuclear technology with other Muslim nations.[14] The former Muslim who was referred to previously, Walid Shoebat, says, "There are [also] suspicions that Pakistan has sold nuclear weapons to Libya, Iran and North Korea."[15] Thus it is becoming clear that the initial fires of Armageddon are already beginning to smolder.

Notes
1. *Old Testament Student Manual,* 2:292.
2. Ibid., 2:304–305.
3. See Perry Stone, *Unleashing the Beast,* 46.
4. *Old Testament Student Manual,* 2:285.
5. See preface to the manual, p. vi.
6. *Old Testament Student Manual,* 2:292.
7. Ibid., 2:286.
8. Ibid., 2:286.
9. Bible Dictionary, "Magog," 728.
10. Smith, *The Signs of the Times,* 156.
11. *Old Testament Student Manual,* 2:286.
12. Bible Dictionary, "Sinim, Land of," 775.
13. *Fox News,* 13 November 2005.
14. *Fox News,* 15 September 2005.
15. Shoebat, *Why I Left Jihad,* 312.

Thirteen

THE SECOND BEAST

In addition to the beast that Gog will lead (the northern army), a second beast will also be involved in the war of Armageddon. It will likely be an expanded version of the first beast. After Gog returns from the north, following his initial battles, "kings of the east" and many nations (prossibly Muslim) will unite with him to fight against Israel.

The second beast will be somewhat religious in nature, whereas the first appears to be more political. The apostle John wrote, "And I beheld another beast coming up out of the earth; and he had two horns like a lamb, and he spake as a dragon" (Revelation 13:11). The "two horns like a lamb" might be two leaders or organizations that will make the beast appear to be harmless or even religious. However, it will be extremely dangerous and unholy, for unlike the true Lamb of God, it will be influenced by Satan who is bent on the destruction of God's children.

To solidify its claim to be religious, the unholy beast will use counterfeit miracles to deceive people. The apostle John recorded, "And he doeth great wonders, so that he maketh fire come down from heaven on the earth in the sight of men, and deceiveth them that dwell on the earth by the means of those miracles which he had power to do in the sight of the [first] beast" (Revelation 13:13–14).

Satan will help the beast to perform his false miracles. He may influence astrologers, fortune tellers, psychics, or others to assist in these miracles. Referring to the evil powers that will be used by the beast, the apostle John remarked, "For by thy sorceries were all nations deceived" (Revelation 18:23). But none of those false miracles or powers will save the beast from the Lord's wrath when he comes, for he declared, "Let now the astrologers, the stargazers, the monthly prognosticators, stand up, and save thee from these things that shall come upon thee. Behold they shall be as stubble; the fire shall burn them up; they shall not deliver themselves from the power of the flame. . . . Thus shall they be unto thee with whom thou hast labored. . . . None shall save thee" (Isaiah 47:13–15).

Using false miracles, the second beast will attempt to establish a type of world religion. He will persuade the people of the world to worship the first beast, as well as an "image" of it. The apostle John recorded,

> And he exerciseth all the power of the first beast before him, and causeth the earth and them which dwell therein to worship the first beast, whose deadly wound was healed. . . .
>
> He had power to do [miracles] in the sight of the beast; saying to them that dwell on the earth, that they should make an image to the [first] beast, which had the wound by a sword and did live. And he had power to give life unto the image of the beast, that the image of the beast should both speak, and cause that as many as would not worship the image of the beast should be killed. (Revelation 13:12, 14–15)

It is not clear what the image will be. An image is usually something that resembles something else. The first beast appears to be a league of nations resembling an ancient empire. The second beast could be another league resembling the first beast or its ancient counterpart.

The Revelator continued his description of the second beast, saying that "he causeth all, both small and great, rich and poor, free and bond, to receive a mark in their right hand, or in their foreheads" (Revelation 13:16). The mark of the beast could be some kind of literal mark which will distinguish the followers of the beast from those who reject him.

The mark of the beast could also be symbolic rather than literal. Those who worship the devil, or accept his false religious systems, are spiritually "sealed" to him, receiving his mark of damnation upon them. Use of a literal forehead mark could be the devil's attempt to imitate God who seals the righteous to him when their "calling and election" is made sure; they are symbolically "sealed . . . in their foreheads" (Revelation 7:3). Thus those who are sealed to God will not receive the mark of the beast; that is, they will not be sealed to the devil.

John the Revelator also recorded "that no man might buy or sell, save he that had the mark, or the name of the beast, or the number of his name" (Revelation 13:11). Thus the beast will attempt to control world trade between countries, as well as commerce within countries. The result will undoubtedly be a global economic crisis. (Perhaps this is one reason we have been warned to store emergency food and supplies.) We can only speculate as to how the beast will be able to control buying and selling—perhaps through a world monetary system or through control of the world's oil supply. If the oil supply stopped, the transportation of goods would also stop, for vehicles are dependent on oil for fuel. Perhaps that is why the Lord said, "And it shall come to pass in that day, that I will cut off thy horses out of the midst of thee, and I will destroy thy chariots" (Micah 5:10). However, it appears from John's revelation that people with the mark of the beast will somehow still buy and sell goods.

Many people have speculated about the number of the beast. John recorded, "Here is wisdom. Let him that hath understanding count the number of the beast: for it is the number of a man; and his number is Six hundred threescore and six [666]" (Revelation 13:18). The meaning of the number has not been revealed. When, through the apostle John, the Lord mentioned the beast's number, he may have simply been showing the similarity between the latter-day beast and the beast of John's day, which was the Roman Empire. Basic Roman numerals add up to 666: I=1; V=5; X=10; L=50; C=100; and D=500. However, John's Revelation states that the number 666 is "the number of a man." So it is unlikely that the beast's number is merely a reference to the Roman Empire.

Because it appears this number will identify a particular man, we should resist the temptation to speculate that the man will be a pope simply because popes reside in Rome and are religious. A more likely candidate would be Gog, the man who will muster the second beastly army when he persuades many nations to join his northern army. If Gog is the man with the number 666, he is probably the false prophet referred to in John's Revelation. The apostle recorded, "And I saw three unclean spirits like frogs come out of the mouth of the dragon, and out of the mouth of the beast, and out of the mouth of the false prophet. For they are the spirits of devils, working miracles, which go forth unto the kings of the earth and of the whole world, to gather them to the battle of that great day of God Almighty" (Revelation 16:13).

It is unclear why the man has been identified by a number rather than a name. However, the Lord may have given a clue to help "him with understanding" determine the name. The scripture seems to suggest that if we "count the number of the beast" or count "the number of his name," the name will be revealed to "him that hath understanding." The apostle who wrote about the man was Hebrew, and Hebrews traditionally assigned numbers to letters of their alphabet so they could be counted. The letters in the man's name could add up to 666. According to Jack Zimmerman of Jewish Voice Ministries International, the Hebrew letters which add up to 666 are *tav, resh, samech,* and *vov* or *vav*.[1] Those letters are respectively transliterated into English as *t, r, s,* and *v* or *w*. Without vowels, the letters make little sense, so it is obvious that more information is needed before the man's name can be determined (and remember that the Bible does not say that the number is "six, six, six"—it says "six hundred threescore and six").

Because the beast will make it impossible for anyone to buy or sell without the number of his name, or his mark, it has been suggested that he might require the use of a credit card or identification card containing the number 666 (as well as his name and mark).

People without the beast's identification will be targeted for death. Among those singled out will be the Saints, for scriptures tell us, "And it was given unto [the beast] to make war with the saints and to overcome them" (Revelation 13:7). However, most of the righteous will escape, for the Lord has promised that he "will preserve the righteous by his power . . . even unto the destruction of their enemies by fire" (1 Nephi 22:17).

The apostle John wrote about the eventual destruction of the beast. He recorded, "And the beast was taken, and with him the false prophet that wrought miracles before him, with which he deceived them that had received the mark of the beast, and them that worshipped his image. These both were cast alive into a lake of fire burning with brimstone" (Revelation 19:20).

Not only will the Lord destroy the beast and its false prophet, he will also destroy their supporters, those who receive the mark of the beast. The Revelator wrote,

> If any man worship the beast and his image, and receive his mark in his forehead, or in his hand, the same shall drink of the wine of the wrath of God, which is poured out without mixture into the cup of his indignation; and he shall be tormented with fire and brimstone in the presence of the holy angels, and in the presence of the Lamb. And the smoke of their torment ascendeth up for ever and ever: and they have no rest day nor night, who worship the beast and his image, and whosoever receiveth the mark of his name. (Revelation 14:9–11).

The Islamic Jihad movement seems to partially fit the description of the Armageddon beast. First of all, Jihadists are attempting to establish a world religion through violence and killings. The beast will also "cause that as many as would not worship the image of the [first] beast should be killed" (Revelation 13:15).

Second, Jihadists promote the destruction of Jews and Christians. Gog and his beast will "destroy the mighty and the holy people" (Daniel 8:24), and "it was given unto [the beast] to make war with the saints and to overcome them" (Revelation 13:7).

Third, the Muslim Jihad "kingdom" is different from all other kingdoms or governments. And Gog's beastly kingdom will be "diverse from all the beasts [governments] that were before it" (Daniel 7:7).

Fourth, Jihadists "honor the God of forces" (military strength) just as Gog will do (see Daniel 11:38). They even believe that a person, whom they call "Mahdi," will soon come to militarily defeat non-Muslims and bring the entire world into the Islamic religion.[2] Gog will likely be accepted as the Mahdi when he appears on the scene. Then he and his beast will militarily "devour the whole earth, and shall tread it down, and break it in pieces" (Daniel 7:23).

Fifth, Islam uses Sharia law which has changed the calendar system "from AD to AH, based on the Muslim calendar of Hijra," and acceptance of the Hijra calendar "marks the beginning of Islam's ascendance as a world religion."[3] The prophet Daniel recorded that "the little horn" (Gog) will also "think to change times and laws" (Daniel 7:25).

Sixth, Jihadists who behead infidels today are like Gog and his soldiers who will behead people during the war of Armageddon. The apostle John wrote, "I saw the souls of them that were beheaded for the witness of Jesus, and for the word of God, and which had not worshipped the beast, neither his image, neither had received his mark upon their foreheads" (Revelation 20:4). According to Walid Shoebat, Islam's Sharia law requires beheadings for specified offences, and in the last few years, Jihadists have carried out beheadings in several countries. He said, "Wall Street Journal reporter, Daniel Pearl, was beheaded [in 2002] simply because he was Jewish."[4]

And last, according to scripture, heathens and Gentiles will wage the war of Armageddon. Heathens are non-Christian, and Gentiles are non-Jewish or non-Israelite. The prophet Joel wrote, "Proclaim ye this among the Gentiles; Prepare war . . . Assemble yourselves, and come, all ye heathen . . . Let the heathen be wakened, and come up to the valley of Jehoshaphat.... Multitudes, multitudes in the valley of decision: for the day of the Lord is near" (Joel 3:9, 11–12, 14). Muslims are both non-Israelite and non-Christian—they do not descend from Jacob, the father of the Israelites, and they do not accept Jesus as the Christ.

We clearly do not have enough information to determine with certainty what the "beast" will be, but whatever or whoever it will be, we know that it will assuredly be a dangerous power to be reckoned with. Therefore we need to watch for it in order to avoid its deceptive and dangerous tentacles. We are already beginning to see the formation of beastly powers on the earth, but the full identity of the future beast will remain unknown until the war of Armageddon begins. Elder Bruce R. McConkie remarked that it will be interesting someday to discover who or what the beast will be: "It will be interesting—interesting? Nay, fascinating!—to see what the future holds as the full meaning of this passage unfolds and the identity of the actual 'beast' is revealed."[5]

To avoid being deceived by the beast's false prophet and his deceptive powers, we must live righteously and follow the true prophet. Elder Harold B. Lee said, "We have a mouthpiece to whom God does and is revealing his mind and will. God will never permit him to lead us astray."[6]

Elder George Q. Cannon also expressed his testimony about following the true prophet: "Now, the only safe course for you and all mankind to pursue is to obey the Priesthood, to listen to the teachings of the servants of God and never murmur against them. Then God's power will increase with you . . . when false prophets arise and wonderful works are performed by them through the power of the evil one, you will not be deceived; for you will know that they are not of God. Though they may call down fire from Heaven, you will still cling to the Priesthood of God."[7]

Notes
1. This information was obtained from personal correspondence with Mr. Zimmerman.
2. Stone, *Unleashing the Beast*, 65.
3. Shoebat, *Why I Left Jihad*, 369.
4. Ibid., 376.
5. McConkie, *Doctrinal New Testament Commentary*, 3:524.
6. Burton, *We Believe*, 763.
7. Ibid., 507.

Fourteen

The Destruction of Babylon

According to scripture, the first beast carried on its back a woman representing the devil's kingdom. His kingdom is depicted as a harlot because of its spiritual adultery (its unfaithfulness to God). Having abandoned righteousness, the harlot prostitutes herself to evil. The *Life and Teachings of Jesus and His Apostles Student Manual* states, "The kingdom of Satan, in all its opulent and wicked splendor, is depicted as a harlot, lavishly dressed and riding on a beast."[1] In his vision, the apostle John saw the harlot enticing the nations of the earth to commit spiritual fornication with her: "I saw a woman sit upon a scarlet coloured beast, full of names of blasphemy. . . . And the woman was arrayed in purple and scarlet colour, and decked with gold and precious stones and pearls, having a golden cup in her hand full of abominations and filthiness of her fornication" (Revelation 17:3–4). And "all nations have drunk of the wine of the wrath of her fornication, and the kings of the earth have committed fornication with her, and the merchants of the earth are waxed rich through the abundance of her delicacies" (Revelation 18:3).

Satan's kingdom, the world with all its evil, is also compared to the ancient city of Babylon, which, in its day, was known as the center of wickedness. Elder Bruce R. McConkie stated,

> As the seat of the world empire, Babylon was the persistent persecutor and enemy of the Lord's people. . . . To the Lord's people . . . Babylon was known as the center of iniquity, carnality, and worldliness. Everything connected with it was in opposition to all righteousness and had the effect of leading men downward to the destruction of their

souls. It was natural, therefore, for the apostles and inspired men of New Testament times to apply the name Babylon to the forces organized to spread confusion and darkness in the realm of spiritual things. . . . In a general sense, the wickedness of the world generally is Babylon.[2]

An angel explained to John the Revelator that "the woman which thou sawest is that great city [Babylon], which reigneth over the kings of the earth" (Revelation 17:18). She is

> The great whore that sitteth upon many waters: With whom the kings of the earth have committed fornication, and the inhabitants of the earth have been made drunk with the wine of her fornication. . . . And the waters . . . where the whore sitteth, are peoples, and multitudes, and nations, and tongues. (Revelation 17:1–2, 15)

> And upon her forehead was a name written, MYSTERY, BABYLON THE GREAT, THE MOTHER OF HARLOTS AND ABOMINATIONS OF THE EARTH. (Revelation 17:5)

John added,

> And I saw the woman drunken with the blood of the saints, and with the blood of the martyrs of Jesus. (Revelation 17:6)

> And in her was found the blood of prophets, and of saints, and of all that were slain upon the earth. (Revelation 18:24)

The woman also represents Satan's apostate church system, the "great and abominable church" which is the competitor of God's true church and kingdom. God's kingdom, Zion, is "the pure in heart," while the devil's church and kingdom, Babylon, is the impure in heart. So the representation of the harlot, "lavishly dressed and riding on a beast," is that of impurity, worldliness, and evil.

The devil's church consists of all churches, organizations, philosophies, and people who reject or oppose God and his true church. The student manual quoted earlier states, "The titles *church of the devil* and *great and abominable church* are used to identify all churches or organizations . . . which are designed to take men on a course that leads away from God."[3] Thus Zion and Babylon are opposites. The Lord said, "He that is not with me is against me" (Matthew 12:30). "And now if ye are not the sheep of the good shepherd, of what fold are ye? Behold, I say unto you, that the devil is your shepherd, and ye are of his fold" (Alma 5:39). There are then just two basic churches as Nephi taught (see 1 Nephi 14:9–12), one being the church of God, and the other the church of the devil.

Not only did John see the great and abominable church of the devil in vision, but he also saw God's church. It too was depicted as a woman, but a very different type of woman. She was trying to bring forth the heavenly kingdom of Zion, which will replace Satan's Babylon during the Millennium. The apostle John compared the bringing forth of God's kingdom to the delivery of a baby. He saw the true church "clothed with the sun, and the moon under her feet, and upon her head a crown of twelve stars: And she being with child cried, travailing in birth, and pained to be delivered . . . and the dragon stood before the woman which was ready to be delivered, for to devour her child as soon as it was born. And she brought forth a man child, who was to rule all nations . . . and her child was caught up to God, and to his throne" (Revelation 12:1–2, 4–5).

Although the "man child" is presumed by some people to be Jesus Christ, it is not. Rather it is the kingdom over which he will reign. The church could not produce Jesus—Jesus produced the church. Therefore, the millennial kingdom will be a product of the church. Elder McConkie confirmed this when he said, "A woman ('the church of God'!) gives birth to a man child ('the kingdom of our God and his Christ') which shall hold sway during the Millennial Era."[4]

Because Jesus, when he comes, plans to banish Satan and replace Babylon with his own millennial kingdom (the man child), Satan, the dragon, is attacking the true church to prevent it from producing the future kingdom. The Revelator recorded, "And when the dragon saw that he was cast down unto the earth, he persecuted the woman [church] which brought forth the man child . . . And the dragon was wroth with the woman, and went to make war with the remnant of her seed, which keep the commandments of God, and have the testimony of Jesus Christ" (Revelation 12:13, 17).

Satan, of course, will fail. Much of his own kingdom will be destroyed during the war of Armageddon when "the wicked shall slay the wicked" (D&C 63:33). An angel told the apostle John that during the war, Babylon, the whore of the earth, will be desolated and burned. The angelic messenger said, "And the ten horns which thou sawest upon the beast, these shall hate the whore, and shall make her desolate and naked, and shall eat her flesh, and burn her with fire" (Revelation 17:16).

Nephi also prophesied of the destruction of Babylon during Armageddon:

The blood of the great and abominable church, which is the whore of all the earth, shall turn upon their own heads for they shall war among themselves, and the sword of their own hands shall fall upon their own heads . . . And every nation which shall war against thee, O house of Israel, shall be turned one against another. . . .

And all that fight against Zion shall be destroyed, and that great whore, who hath perverted the right ways of the Lord, yea, that great and abominable church, shall tumble to the dust and great shall be the fall of it. (1 Nephi 22:13–14)

And that great pit which hath been digged for [the righteous] by that great and abominable church, which was founded by the devil and his children, that he might lead away the souls of men down to hell—yea, that great pit which hath been digged for the destruction of man shall be filled by those who digged it, unto their utter destruction" (1 Nephi 14:3)

The Lord declared,

He that fighteth against Zion, both Jew and Gentile . . . shall perish; for they are they who are the whore of all the earth; for they who are not for me are against me, saith our God. (2 Nephi 10:16)

Every one that is joined to the wicked shall fall by the sword. . . .
And Babylon, the glory of the kingdoms . . . shall be as when God overthrew Sodom and Gomorrah. (2 Nephi 23:15, 19)

As Babylon hath caused the slain of Israel to fall, so at Babylon shall fall the slain of all the earth. (Jeremiah 51:49)

Therefore shall her plagues come in one day, death, and mourning, and famine. (Revelation 18:8)

And the great and abominable church, which is the whore of all the earth, shall be cast down by devouring fire . . . for abominations shall not reign. (D&C 29:21)

Thus with violence shall that great city Babylon be thrown down, and shall be found no more at all. (Revelation 18:21)

Just as ancient Babylon's destroyers came from the north, so will the latter-day destroyers. Armageddon's northern army, the European "beast," will assist in destroying much of Satan's Babylon. The Lord declared,

Set ye up a standard in the land, blow the trumpet among the

nations, prepare the nations against her [Babylon]. . . .
For the spoilers shall come unto her from the north, saith the Lord. (Jeremiah 51:27, 48)

Declare ye among the nations. . . . Babylon is taken. . . .
For out of the north there cometh up a nation against her, which shall make her land desolate, and none shall dwell therein. . . .
Remove out of the midst of Babylon . . . for, lo, I will raise and cause to come up against Babylon an assembly of great nations from the north country: and they shall set themselves in array against her; from thence she shall be taken. . . .
The hindermost of the nations shall be a wilderness, a dry land, and a desert. Because of the wrath of the Lord it shall not be inhabited, but shall be wholly desolate: everyone that goeth by Babylon shall be astonished, and hiss at all her plagues. . . .
Her walls are thrown down: for it is the vengeance of the Lord. (Jeremiah 50:2–3, 8–9, 12–13, 15)

Scriptures indicate that the destroyers of Babylon will be like the "noise of a multitude in the mountains, like as of a great people; a tumultuous noise of the kingdoms of nations gathered together. . . . They come from a far country, from the end of heaven, even the Lord, and the weapons of his indignation, to destroy the whole land. Howl ye: for the day of the Lord is at hand; it shall come as a destruction from the Almighty. . . . He shall destroy the sinners out of it" (Isaiah 13:4–6, 9). For the "ten horns . . . shall . . . burn her [Babylon] with fire" (Revelation 17:16).

That last statement implies that Armageddon's fire might be the same as, or the beginning of, the final world conflagration which will burn the wicked. The Lord said,

For after today cometh the burning . . . and I will not spare any that remain in Babylon. (D&C 64:24)

For . . . the day soon cometh that all the proud and they who do wickedly shall be as stubble; and the day cometh that they must be burned. (1 Nephi 22:15)

[But] the righteous need not fear, for they are those who shall not be confounded. But it is the kingdom of the devil, which shall be built up among the children of men. . . .
All churches which are built up to get gain . . . to get power . . . to become popular . . . who seek the lusts of the flesh and the things of the world, and to do all manner of iniquity, yea, in fine, all those who

belong to the kingdom of the devil . . . they are those who must be consumed as stubble. (1 Nephi 22:22–23)

The Lord gives another reason for Babylon's destruction: "For they have strayed from mine ordinances, and have broken mine everlasting covenant; they seek not the Lord to establish his righteousness, but every man walketh in his own way, and after the image of his own god, whose image is in the likeness of the world, and whose substance is that of an idol, which waxeth old and shall perish in Babylon, even Babylon the great, which shall fall" (D&C 1:15–16).

The destruction of Babylon will prepare the earth for the reign of Jesus Christ, the Bridegroom, who will take the righteous woman (the true church and kingdom) as his bride, to be united to him forever. Thus the scriptures teach,

> Wherefore, be faithful, praying always, having your lamps trimmed and burning, and oil with you, that you may be ready at the coming of the Bridegroom. (D&C 33:17)

> Be prepared for the days to come [when] the Son of man shall come . . . to meet the kingdom of God which is set up on the earth. Wherefore, may the kingdom of God go forth, that the kingdom of heaven [Zion] may come. (D&C 65:5–6)

Only people who have removed themselves from Babylon will be part of Jesus' heavenly kingdom (his bride). Therefore prophets plead with us to "come unto Christ," for every step we take toward Jesus Christ leads us out of Babylon, Satan's realm of evil. The Lord declared,

> The time has come when the voice of the Lord is unto you: Go ye out of Babylon. . . .
> Go ye out from among the nations, even from Babylon, from the midst of wickedness, which is spiritual Babylon. (D&C 133:7, 14)

> Come out of her, my people, that ye be not partakers of her sins, and that ye receive not of her plagues. (Revelation 18:4)

> Flee out of the midst of Babylon, and deliver every man his soul: be not cut off in her iniquity; for this is the time of the Lord's vengeance. (Jeremiah 51:6)

President Marion G. Romney observed,

> We must not permit our minds to become surfeited with the interests,

things, and practices of the world about us. To do so is tantamount to adopting a going along with them, for the experience of the race sustains the conclusion of him who said that—

Vice is a monster of so frightful mien,
As to be hated needs to be seen;
Yet seen too oft, familiar with her face,
We first endure, then pity, and then embrace.

If we would avoid adopting the evils of the world, we must pursue a course which will daily feed our minds with . . . the things of the Spirit.[5]

Following such a spiritual course will ensure our place in God's Zion kingdom and not in Babylon.

Notes
1. *The Life and Teachings of Jesus and His Apostles*, 464.
2. McConkie, *Mormon Doctrine*, 69.
3. *The Life and Teachings of Jesus and His Apostles*, 464.
4. McConkie, *Doctrinal New Testament Commentary*, 3:516.
5. Romney, "Gosepl Classics: Book of Mormon," *Ensign*, Aug. 2005, 10.

Fifteen

THE INVASION OF ISRAEL

One of the purposes of Gog's invasion of Israel appears to be the taking of spoil, or wealth, from the prosperous country. The Lord said through the prophet Ezekiel,

> Thus saith the Lord God: It shall also come to pass, that at the same time shall things come into thy [Gog's] mind, and thou shalt think an evil thought: And thou shalt say, I will go up to the land of unwalled villages; I will go to them that are at rest, that dwell safely. . . .
>
> To take a spoil, and to take a prey; to turn thine hand upon the desolate places that are now inhabited, and upon the people that are gathered out of the nations, which have gotten cattle and goods, that dwell in the midst of the land. . . .
>
> Therefore, son of man, prophesy and say unto Gog, Thus saith the Lord God; In that day when my people of Israel dwelleth safely, shalt thou not know it? (Ezekiel 38:10–12, 14)

Other people, referred to as "watchers" in the scriptures, will be in favor of Gog's invasion of Israel (the watchers could be news reporters or ambassadors). The prophet Jeremiah declared, "Make ye mention to the nations; behold, publish against Jerusalem, that the watchers come from a far country, and give out their voice against the cities of Judah" (Jeremiah 4:16).

Therefore, after Gog's initial conquests and his return to his own land in the north, he will come back toward the south. Daniel prophesied,

> He shall enter also into the glorious land. (Daniel 11:41)

> He shall . . . return, and have indignation against the holy covenant: so shall he do; he shall even return and have intelligence with them that forsake the holy covenant. . . . [This seems to indicate that there will be traitors within Israel or the church.]
>
> And such as do wickedly against the covenant shall he corrupt by flatteries: but the people that do know their God shall be strong, and do exploits. And they that understand among the people shall instruct many. (Daniel 11:30, 32–33)

When Gog begins his invasion of Israel, heathen "kings of the east" will join his beastly army. The Psalmist wrote, "O God . . . they have taken crafty counsel against thy people, and consulted against thy hidden ones. They have said, Come, and let us cut them off from being a nation; that the name of Israel may be no more in remembrance" (Psalm 83:1, 3–4).

The Lord declared he will allow the evil armies to gather so they can be destroyed, and he can be "sanctified" before the heathens.

> O Gog, the chief prince of Meshech and Tubal . . . I will turn thee back, and put hooks into thy jaws, and I will bring thee forth, and all thine army, horses and horsemen, all of them clothed with all sorts of armour, even a great company with bucklers and shields, all of them handling swords . . . and many people with thee. (Ezekiel 38:3–6)
>
> In the latter years thou shalt come into the land that is brought back from the sword, and is gathered out of many people, against the mountains of Israel, which have been always waste: but it is brought forth out of the nations. . . . Thou shalt ascend and come like a storm, thou shalt be like a cloud to cover the land, thou, and all thy bands, and many people with thee. (Ezekiel 38:8–9)
>
> And thou shalt come from thy place out of the north parts, thou, and many people with thee, all of them riding upon horses, a great company, and a mighty army: And thou shalt come up against my people of Israel, as a cloud to cover the land; it shall be in the latter days, and I will bring thee against my land, that the heathen may know me, when I shall be sanctified in thee, O Gog, before their eyes. (Ezekiel 38:15–16)

Gog will have the advantage of having a much larger army than the small country of Israel will have, for "arms shall stand on his part" (Daniel 11:31). "And the number of the army of the horsemen were two hundred thousand thousand [200 million]" (Revelation 9:16). "Multitudes, multitudes in the valley of decision: for the day of the Lord is near in the valley of decision" (Joel 3:14).

Isaiah prophesied, "The noise of a multitude in the mountains, like as of a great people; a tumultuous noise of the kingdoms of nations gathered together: the Lord of hosts mustereth the host of the battle. They come from a far country, from the end of heaven, even the Lord, and the weapons of his indignation, to destroy the whole land. Howl ye, for the day of the Lord is at hand; it shall come as a destruction from the Almighty. . . . Their faces shall be as flames" (Isaiah 13:4–5).

The prophet Joel described the day when Gog's army will enter the land of Israel:

> A day of darkness and of gloominess, a day of clouds and of thick darkness, as the morning spread upon the mountains: a great people and a strong; there hath not been ever the like, neither shall be any more after it, even to the years of many generations. A fire devoureth before them; and behind them a flame burneth: the land is as the garden of Eden before them, and behind them a desolate wilderness. (Joel 2:2–3)

The Lord indicated through the prophet Joel that the army's size will make it appear to be invincible. He said,

> A nation is come up upon my land, strong, and without number. (Joel 1:6)

> They shall run like mighty men; they shall climb the wall like men of war; and they shall march every one on his ways, and they shall not break their ranks. . . . Neither shall one thrust another; they shall walk every one in his path: and when they fall upon the sword, they shall not be wounded. (Joel 2:7–8)

When the biblical prophets Joel and John attempted to describe the attacking army, they were unfamiliar with modern military weapons, vehicles, and armament, so they appear to have described them in terms that people of their day understood. Referring to their imagery, Elder Bruce R. McConkie remarked, "It is not improbable that these ancient prophets were seeing such things as men wearing or protected by armor; as troops of cavalry and companies of tanks and flame throwers; as airplanes and airborne missiles which explode, fire shells and drop bombs; and even other weapons yet to be devised in an age when warfare is the desire and love of wicked men."[1]

John described locusts engaged in battle, some of which appear to be using biological or chemical weapons that will not hurt grass or trees:

> And there came out of the smoke locusts upon the earth: and unto them was given power, as the scorpions of the earth have power.
> And it was commanded them that they should not hurt the grass of the earth, neither any green thing, neither any tree; but only those men which have not the seal of God in their foreheads.
> And to them it was given that they should not kill them, but that they should be tormented five months: and their torment was as the torment of a scorpion when he striketh a man.
> And in those days shall men seek death, and shall not find it; and shall desire to die, and death shall flee from them.
> And the shapes of the locusts were like unto horses prepared unto battle. (Revelation 9:3–7)

> And they had breastplates, as it were breastplates of iron; and the sound of their wings was as the sound of chariots of many horses running to battle.
> And they had tails like unto scorpions and there were stings in their tails: and their power was to hurt men five months. (Revelation 9:9–10)

To conquer the land of Israel, Gog must attack and capture its capital city, Jerusalem. For that phase of the battle, the armies will assemble in the valley of Jehoshaphat which is east of Jerusalem. The Lord said,

> I will gather all nations against Jerusalem to battle. (Zechariah 14:2)

> Proclaim ye this among the Gentiles; Prepare war . . . Beat your plowshares into swords, and your pruninghooks into spears. . . .
> Let the heathen be wakened, and come up to the valley of Jehoshaphat: for there will I sit to judge all the heathen round about. (Joel 3:9–10, 12)

> And it shall come to pass in that day, saith the Lord, that there shall be the noise of a cry from the fish gate, and an howling from the second, and a great crashing from the hills. . . .
> The great day of the Lord is near, it is near, and hasteth greatly, even the voice of the day of the Lord: the mighty men shall cry there bitterly. That day is a day of wrath, a day of trouble and distress, a day of wasteness and desolation, a day of darkness and gloominess, a day of

clouds and thick darkness, a day of the trumpet and alarm. (Zephaniah 1:10, 14–16)

> Like the noise of chariots on the tops of mountains shall they leap, like the noise of a flame of fire that devoureth the stubble, as a strong people set in battle array. Before their face the people shall be much pained: all faces shall gather blackness. (Joel 2:5–6)

The prophet Daniel indicated that Gog will "scatter the power of the holy people" (Daniel 12:7).

> And his power shall be mighty . . . and he . . . shall destroy the mighty and the holy people. And through his policy . . . shall destroy many. (Daniel 8:24–25)

> And they that understand among the people shall instruct many: yet they shall fall by the sword, and by flame, by captivity, and by spoil, many days.
> Now when they shall fall, they shall be holpen with a little help: but many shall cleave to them with flatteries.
> And some of them of understanding shall fall, to try them, and to purge, and to make them white, even to the time of the end: because it is yet for a time appointed. (Daniel 11:33–35)

Isaiah also declared, "Howl, O gate; cry, O city; thou whole Palestina, art dissolved: for there shall come from the north a smoke. . . . What shall one then answer the messengers of the nations?" (Isaiah 14:31–32).

Gog's army will succeed in capturing at least part of Jerusalem, for the Revelator records, "The holy city shall they tread underfoot forty and two months [three and one-half years]" (Revelation 11:2; 13:5). But during that time, they will be hindered from completely overthrowing the city, for two prophets, boldly defying Gog, will hold his massive army at bay for three and one-half years. Elder Parley P. Pratt remarked that "the Gentiles will tread [Jerusalem] under foot forty and two months [three and one-half years] during which time there will be two prophets continually prophesying and working miracles. And it seems that the Gentile army shall be hindered from utterly destroying and overthrowing the city, while these two prophets continue."[2]

The apostle John discussed the miraculous powers that will enable the two prophets to prevent Gog's enormous army from completely annihilating the city: "These have power to shut heaven, that it rain not in the days of their prophecy; and [they] have power over waters to turn them to blood, and to smite the earth with all plagues, as often as they will" (Revelation 11:6).

The Lord revealed to Joseph Smith that the two prophets will "be raised up to the Jewish nation in the last days, at the time of the restoration, and to prophesy to the Jews after they are gathered and have built the city of Jerusalem in the land of their fathers" (D&C 77:15). The apostle LeGrand Richards observed, "No doubt these prophets will be called and ordained and sent by the First Presidency of the Church of Jesus Christ of Latter-day Saints, for the Lord's house is a house of order, and true prophets are never self-sent—they must be called and sent of God."[3]

The Lord said of his two prophets,

> When the enemy shall come in like a flood, the Spirit of the Lord shall lift up a standard against him. (Isaiah 59:19)

> And I will give power unto my two witnesses, and they shall prophesy a thousand two hundred and threescore days [three and one-half years], clothed in sackcloth. These are the two olive trees, and the two candlesticks standing before the God of the earth. And if any man will hurt them, fire proceedeth out of their mouth, and devoureth their enemies: and if any man will hurt them, he must in this manner be killed. (Revelation 11:3–5)

> [And these] two shall put their tens of thousands to flight" (D&C 133:58)

People who do not believe in latter-day prophets will surely take notice of these two men of God when they begin "smiting the earth" with plagues, famine, and fire!

Notes
1. McConkie, *Doctrinal New Testament Commentary*, 3:503.
2. Parley P. Pratt, *A Voice of Warning* (Salt Lake City: Deseret Book, 1978), 33.
3. Richards, *Israel! Do You Know?*, 197.

Sixteen

THE ABOMINATION OF DESOLATION

When Gog and his army begin to tread down Jerusalem, it appears they will, for awhile at least, be prevented from getting inside the temple, but "the court which is without the temple . . . is given unto the Gentiles; and the holy city shall they tread under foot" (Revelation 11:2). Eventually though, they will probably succeed in desecrating the Lord's house. That act (or some other abominable act which Gog will commit) is called "the abomination of desolation" (Matthew 24:15). Such abominable acts bring the Lord's desolation upon those who commit them.

Speaking of Gog and his evil army, the prophet Daniel declared, "They shall pollute the sanctuary of strength, and shall take away the daily sacrifice, and they shall place the abomination that maketh desolate. . . . And the king [Gog] shall do according to his will; and he shall exalt himself, and magnify himself above every god" (Daniel 11:31, 36).

Gog's abominable behavior will resemble that of Satan, himself, "who opposeth and exalteth himself above all that is called God, or that is worshipped; so that he as God sitteth in the temple of God, shewing himself that he is God" (2 Thessalonians 2:4).

The prophet Joel was referring to Gog's abominable act when he said,

> The meat offering and the drink offering is cut off from the house of the Lord; the priests, the Lord's ministers mourn. . . . Gird yourselves, and lament, ye priests: howl ye ministers of the altar: come, lie all night in sackcloth ye ministers of my God: for the meat offering and the drink offering is withholden from the house of your God. (Joel 1:9, 13)

> Let the priests, the ministers of the Lord, weep between the porch and the altar, and let them say, Spare thy people, O Lord, and give not thine heritage to reproach, that the heathen should rule over them. (Joel 2:17)

Jeremiah may also have been prophesying of Gog's abomination when he said, "Strangers are come into the sanctuaries of the Lord's house" (Jeremiah 51:51), and destruction will come upon them because of "the vengeance of the Lord, the vengeance of his temple" (Jeremiah 51:11).

The scriptures are not clear as to how long the Lord's sanctuary will be polluted. In one reference, Daniel wrote, "How long shall be the vision concerning the daily sacrifice, and the transgression of desolation, to give both the sanctuary and the host to be trodden under foot? And he said unto me, Unto two thousand and three hundred days [about six and one-third years]; then shall the sanctuary be cleansed. . . . At the time of the end shall be the vision . . . in the last end of the indignation: for at the time appointed shall the end be" (Daniel 8:13–14, 17, 19).

In another reference Daniel recorded,

> How long shall it be to the end of these wonders? And I heard the man clothed in linen . . . sware by him that liveth for ever that it should be for a time, times, and an half [three and one-half years] and when he [Gog] shall have accomplished to scatter the power of the holy people, all these things shall be finished. . . .
>
> And from the time that the daily sacrifice shall be taken away, and the abomination that maketh desolate set up, there shall be a thousand two hundred and ninety days [about three and one-half years].
>
> Blessed is he that waiteth, and cometh to the thousand three hundred and five and thirty days [45 days later]. But go thy way till the end be. (Daniel 12:6–7, 11–13)

Jesus warned that once the abomination is "set up," people should flee the area, for the Lord's "desolation" will soon follow. He said,

> When ye shall see the abomination of desolation spoken of by Daniel the prophet, stand where it ought not (let him that readeth understand), then let them that be in Judea flee to the mountains. (Mark 13:14)

> [For] when ye shall see Jerusalem compassed with armies, then know that desolation is nigh. Then let them which are in Judea . . . depart out. . . .

> For these be the days of vengeance . . . for there shall be great distress in the land, and wrath upon this people. (Luke 21:20–23)
>
> When ye therefore shall see the abomination of desolation . . .
> Let him which is on the housetop not come down to take anything out of his house:
> Neither let him which is in the field return back to take his clothes. And woe to them that are with child, and to those that give suck in those days!
> But pray that your flight be not in winter. . . .
> For then shall be great tribulation, such as was not since the beginning of the world to this time, no, nor ever shall be. (Matthew 24:15, 17–21)

Much of the Lord's desolation upon the wicked will come from the sinners themselves (most likely from a nuclear bomb or bombs). The Lord declared,

> And it shall come to pass at the same time when Gog shall come against the land of Israel, saith the Lord God, that my fury shall come up in my face. For in my jealousy and in the fire of my wrath have I spoken. Surely in that day there shall be a great shaking in the land of Israel. . . .
> And I will call for a sword against him throughout all my mountains, saith the Lord God: every man's sword shall be against his brother. (Ezekiel 38:18–19, 21)

> The wicked shall slay the wicked. (D&C 63:33)

> I will overthrow the chariots and those that ride in them and their riders shall come down, every one by the sword of his brother. (Haggai 2:22)

> And the blood of that great and abominable church, which is the whore of all the earth, shall turn upon their own heads; for they shall war among themselves, and the sword of their own hands shall fall upon their own heads, and they shall be drunken with their own blood. (1 Nephi 22:13)

The Lord also said,

> Behold, I will make Jerusalem a cup of trembling unto all the people round about, when they shall be in the siege both against Judah and against Jerusalem.

And in that day will I make Jerusalem a burdensome stone for all people: all that burden themselves with it shall be cut in pieces though all the people of the earth be gathered together against it. . . .

In that day will I make the governors of Judah like an hearth of fire among the wood, and like a torch of fire in a sheaf; and they shall devour all thy people round about" (Zechariah 12:2–3, 6).

The preceding scripture seems to indicate that Judah (Israel) will prevail, either initially or ultimately. Perhaps that tiny nation will be the first to detonate a nuclear bomb. And that might be the event which will cause Gog's soldiers to become confused or so stressed that they will turn on each other. The prophet Zechariah tells us, "And it shall come to pass in that day, that a great tumult [disorderly commotion or confusion] from the Lord shall be among them; and they shall lay hold every one on the hand of his neighbor, and his hand shall rise up against the hand of his neighbor, and Judah also shall fight at Jerusalem" (Zechariah 14:13–14). The Lord said that "every man's sword shall be against his brother. And I will plead against him with pestilence and with blood; and I will rain upon him, and upon his bands, and upon the many people that are with him, an overflowing rain, and great hailstones, fire, and brimstone" (Ezekiel 38:21–22).

The *Old Testament Student Manaual* indicates that the "hailstones, fire, and brimstone" may be descriptive of atomic warfare: "A great rain of fire and hail will shower down upon the army. . . . fire will also be sent against the land of Magog (see Ezekiel 39:6). The account by Ezekiel could easily be a description of atomic warfare."[1] That theory is not conclusive, but it is certainly possible in light of scriptural descriptions of the effects and aftermath of the war (those will be discussed later).

John the Revelator also described what appears to be atomic or nuclear warfare. It is possible that because he had never seen bombs before, he described them as "hail," a term with which he was familiar. He said, "And there followed hail and fire mingled with blood, and they were cast upon the earth: and the third part of the trees was burnt up, and all green grass was burnt up" (Revelation 8:7). "And there fell upon men a great hail out of heaven, every stone about the weight of a talent:[2] and men blasphemed God because of the plague of the hail; for the plague thereof was exceeding great" (Revelation 16:21).

In addition to hail, the brimstone that John mentioned is also likely associated with atomic or nuclear warfare. Brimstone is sulfur[3] and the *World Book Encyclopedia* explains,

> Sulfur is a very reactive element. At 250 [degrees] C, it ignites with air . . . [and it has been] important as one of the main ingredients of gun powder. . . . As it burns, it combines with oxygen to form sulfur dioxide, a colorless [poisonous] gas. . . .
>
> This gas has been associated with respiratory diseases, damage to buildings, and a type of precipitation called acid rain. . . .
>
> [Sulfur dioxide is used to produce] sulfuric acid [which] is used . . . in the production of . . . explosives. . . .
>
> Water and concentrated sulfuric acid react violently when they are combined.[4]

Chemical weapons, such as the VX nerve agent, contain sulfur.[5] And sulfur is found near Israel.

The apostle John indicated that fire, smoke, and brimstone (sulfur) will be responsible for the death of a "third part of men." He said,

> And the winepress was trodden without the city, and blood came out of the winepress, even unto the horses bridles, by the space of a thousand and six hundred furlongs [200 miles]. (Revelation 14:20)
>
> And thus I [John] saw the horses in the vision, and them that sat on them, having breastplates of fire, and of jacinth, and brimstone: and the heads of the horses were as the heads of lions; and out of their mouths issued fire and smoke and brimstone.
>
> By these three was the third part of men killed, by the fire, and by the smoke, and by the brimstone, which issued out of their mouths.
>
> For their power is in their mouth, and in their tails: for their tails were like unto serpents, and had heads, and with them they do hurt.
>
> And the rest of the men which were not killed by these plagues yet repented not of the works of their hands. (Revelation 9:17–20)

The Lord described the effects of the some weapons upon the Armageddon armies.

> In that day, saith the Lord, I will smite every horse with astonishment, and his rider with madness: and I will open mine eyes upon the house of Judah and will smite every horse of the people with blindness. (Zechariah 12:4)
>
> And so shall be the plague of the horse . . . and of all the beasts that shall be in these tents. (Zechariah 14:15)
>
> Therefore shall all hands be faint, every man's heart shall melt; and they shall be afraid; pangs and sorrows shall take hold of them; they

shall be amazed one at another; their faces shall be as flames. (2 Nephi 23:7–8)

And this shall be the plague wherewith the Lord will smite all the people that have fought against Jerusalem; Their flesh shall consume away while they stand upon their feet, and their eyes shall consume away in their holes, and their tongue shall consume away in their mouth. (Zechariah 14:12)

And their tongues shall be stayed that they shall not utter against me [saith the Lord]; and their flesh shall fall from off their bones, and their eyes from their sockets. And it shall come to pass that the beasts of the forest and the fowls of the air shall devour them up. (D&C 29:19)

Not only will beasts and birds flock to the deadly scene, but flies and maggots will also take hold of the dead and wounded (and possibly even many uninjured survivors). The Lord said,

Wherefore I the Lord God will send flies upon the face of the earth, which shall take hold of the inhabitants thereof, and shall cause maggots to come in upon them. (D&C 29:18)

[For] thy men shall fall by the sword, and thy mighty in the war. (Isaiah 3:25)

And the hail shall sweep away the refuge of lies . . . a consumption [is] even determined upon the whole earth. (Isaiah 28:17, 22)

And men's hearts will be "failing them for fear, and for looking after those things which are coming on the earth: for the powers of heaven shall be shaken" (Luke 21:26). (It is no wonder that people shudder at the word *Armageddon*.)

The worldwide death toll could be over 2 billion people, for "the third part of men" which shall die (Revelation 9:18) could be a third of the 6.5 billion people who are on the earth today. Two-thirds will die in and around the land of Israel.

And it shall come to pass, that in all the land, saith the Lord, two parts therein shall be cut off and die; but the third shall be left therein. (Zechariah 13:8)

And in that day seven women shall take hold of one man, saying: We will eat our own bread, and wear our own apparel: only let us be called by thy name, to take away our reproach. (Isaiah 4:1)

Egypt [also] shall be a desolation, and Edom [southeast of Israel] shall be a desolate wilderness, for the violence against the children of Judah, because they have shed innocent blood in their land. (Joel 3:19)

Behold, Damascus [in Syria] is taken away from being a city, and it shall be a ruinous heap. (Isaiah 17:1)

There shalt not be any remaining of the house of Esau. [The house of Esau was Edomites, southeast of Israel.] (Obadiah 1:18)

And the slain of the Lord shall be at that day from one end of the earth even unto the other. (Jeremiah 25:33)

And thus the Lord will punish the world for its evil, as he prophesied: "I will punish the world for their evil. . . . Every one that is found shall be thrust through; and every one that is joined unto them shall fall by the sword. . . . I will stir up the Medes [Iran] against them. . . . And Babylon . . . shall be as when God overthrew Sodom and Gomorrah. It shall never be inhabited [again]" (Isaiah 13:11, 15, 17, 19–20). (According to the LDS Bible Dictionary and Bible Map #2, the Medes are modern Iran, "the country between the Caspian Sea and Elam." Elam is southern Iran, "east of Babylonia." Babylonia is modern Iraq, with "the Persian Gulf on the south and southeast.")

Notes
1. *Old Testament Student Manual*, 2:295.
2. A talent is about 75 pounds—see *Old Testament Student Manual* 2:295.
3. See *American Heritage Dictionary*, 166.
4. *World Book Encyclopedia*, 18:966–968.
5. "VX (nerve agent)," Wikipedia, http://en.wikipedia.org/wiki/VX_nerve_agent.

Seventeen

UNUSUAL PHENOMENA

The scriptures tell us that some unusual phenomena will be seen, heard, and felt during the war of Armageddon. One of them will be a great noise which will be heard "to the ends of the earth." "And when that day shall come they shall be visited of the Lord of hosts, with . . . a great noise" (2 Nephi 27:2). "A noise shall come even to the ends of the earth; for the Lord hath a controversy with the nations" (Jeremiah 25:31). A nuclear explosion could account for at least part of the noise.

The noise is associated with "a grievous sore," another phenomenon. The scriptures say, "And there fell a noisome and grievous sore upon the men which had the mark of the beast, and upon them which worshipped his image. . . . And they gnawed their tongues for pain, and blasphemed the God of heaven because of their pains, and their sores, and repented not of their deeds" (Revelation 16:2, 10–11). The sore could also result from a nuclear explosion. Because such explosions produce a mushroom-shaped cloud filled with radiation, which can burn and kill, the sore could be caused by radioactive "fallout" from the blast.

Fallout is explained in the *World Book Encyclopedia*:

> All nuclear explosions produce a giant fireball of intensely hot gases. . . . The fireball vaporizes soil, vegetation, and buildings. It then begins to rise [into a mushroom-shaped cloud], carrying the vaporized material with it. . . .
>
> Much of this debris may be lifted up through the atmosphere along with the fireball. . . .
>
> These radioisotopes eventually return to the earth as fallout. . . .

> Distant fallout consists of fine radioactive material that may be scattered by winds to any part of the world.[1]
>
> Thermal radiation consists of ultraviolet, visible, and infrared radiation given off by the fireball. . . .
> The visible and infrared radiation can cause . . . burns called flash burns.[2]

The scriptures also mention "an overflowing scourge" and "a desolating sickness." The Lord said, "There shall be men standing in that generation, that shall not pass until they shall see an overflowing scourge; for a desolating sickness shall cover the land. But my disciples shall stand in holy places, and shall not be moved; but among the wicked, men shall lift up their voices and curse God and die" (D&C 45:31–32).

The sickness could result from chemical or biological weapons, or from nuclear radiation. The encyclopedia tells us,

> Radiation sickness is the term for a variety of symptoms that follow a person's exposure to damaging amounts of certain types of radiation. The radiation may come from nuclear explosions and the resulting fallout.[3]
>
> Exposure to large amounts of radiation can result in immediate sickness and even death. . . . A serious accident in a nuclear reactor can release the same radioisotopes that occur in fallout. In 1986, an explosion and fire at the Chernobyl nuclear power plant in the Soviet Union released radioisotopes that scattered across the Western Hemisphere.[4]

The Lord said that when the "overflowing scourge" begins to spread, the wicked will not believe it will overtake them. But the Lord warned they will not escape it. He declared, "Ye have said . . . when the overflowing scourge shall pass through, it shall not come unto us: for we have made lies our refuge [but] . . . your agreement with hell shall not stand; when the overflowing scourge shall pass through, then ye shall be trodden down by it . . . for morning by morning shall it pass over, by day and by night: and it shall be a vexation only to understand the report" (Isaiah 28:15, 18–19).

It is possible that the "desolating scourge" will be carried around the earth in a great wind, another phenomenon of the war. The encyclopedia tells us, "Radioactive material . . . may be scattered by winds to any part of the world."[5] The Lord also said,

> Behold, I will raise up against Babylon, and against them that dwell in the midst of them that rise up against me, a destroying wind. (Jeremiah 51:1)
>
> Behold, the whirlwind of the Lord goeth forth with fury, a continuing whirlwind: it shall fall with pain upon the head of the wicked. (Jeremiah 30:23)
>
> A great whirlwind shall be raised up from the coasts of the earth. And the slain of the Lord shall be at that day from one end of the earth even unto the other end of the earth: they shall not be lamented, neither gathered, nor buried; they shall be dung upon the ground. (Jeremiah 25:32–33)
>
> For behold, and lo, vengeance cometh speedily upon the ungodly as a whirlwind; and who shall escape it? The Lord's scourge shall pass over by night and by day, and the report thereof shall vex all people. (D&C 97:22)

Another phenomenon associated with Armageddon will be a large amount of fire. In the scriptures, the fire is usually associated with smoke and brimstone. There we read,

> By these three was the third part of men killed, by the fire, and by the smoke, and by the brimstone. (Revelation 9:17–18)
>
> And . . . power was given . . . to scorch men with fire. And men were scorched with great heat, and blasphemed the name of God, which hath power over these plagues. (Revelation 16:7–9)
>
> [For] the wicked shall be tormented with fire and brimstone. (Revelation 14:10)
>
> [And] all faces shall gather blackness. (Joel 2:6)
>
> [Even] the third part of trees [will be] burnt up, and all green grass. (Revelation 8:7)
>
> [All] these things must shortly come; yea, even blood, and fire, and vapor of smoke must come; and it must needs be upon the face of this earth. (1 Nephi 22:18)

A nuclear explosion "begins with the formation of a fireball which consists of a cloud of dust and of extremely hot gases under very high pressure. A fraction of a second after the explosion, the gases begin to expand and form a blast wave, also called a shock wave. This wave moves rapidly away from the fireball like a moving wall of highly compressed air. . . . Thermal radiation also can ignite such highly flammable materials as newspapers and dry leaves. The burning of these materials can lead to large fires."[6]

Very little of the land around Israel shall escape Armageddon's fire-producing weapons. In fact, the prophet Joel says that nothing shall escape them. "A fire devoureth before them; and behind them a flame burneth: the land is as the garden of Eden before them, and behind them a desolate wilderness; yea, and nothing shall escape them" (Joel 2:3).

Armageddon's fires could be the beginning of the inferno which will burn the wicked at the end of the world. The Lord said,

> All the proud and they that do wickedly shall be as stubble; and I will burn them up, for I am the Lord of Hosts; and I will not spare any that remain in Babylon. (D&C 64:24)

> Behold, vengeance cometh speedily upon the inhabitants of the earth, a day of wrath, a day of burning . . . and as a whirlwind it shall come upon all the face of the earth. (D&C 112:24)

The apostle John also stated, "And the ten horns . . . shall hate the whore [Babylon], and shall make her desolate and naked, and shall eat her flesh, and burn her with fire" (Revelation 17:16). "Therefore . . . she shall be utterly burned with fire" (Revelation 18:8).

The scriptures inform us that so many people will be killed in Babylon at that time that "many houses shall be desolate . . . without inhabitant" (Isaiah 5:9), for "the third part of men [shall be] killed" (Revelation 9:18).

> The spoilers are come . . . for the sword of the Lord shall devour from the one end of the land even to the other end of the land. (Jeremiah 12:12)

> Your country is desolate, your cities are burned with fire: your land, strangers devour it in your presence, and it is desolate, as overthrown by strangers. (Isaiah 1:7)

> And the house of Jacob shall be a fire, and the house of Joseph a flame, and the house of Esau for stubble, and they shall kindle them, and devour them. (Obadiah 1:18)

The Lord also said, "I will send a fire on Magog, and among them that dwell carelessly in the isles" (Ezekiel 39:6). "The broad walls of

Babylon shall be utterly broken, and her high gates shall be burned with fire" (Jeremiah 51:58).

The incredible destruction which will occur during the war of Armageddon will produce another unusual phenomenon. The massive explosions of fire-producing weapons and bombs (some of which may not have even been invented yet) will fill the skies with extreme amounts of smoke, ash, and gas. These will likely obscure the sun and cause changes in the atmosphere. Joel stated, "The sun and the moon, shall be dark, and the stars shall withdraw their shining" (Joel 2:10).

Other prophets have written,

> Immediately after the tribulation of those days shall the sun be darkened, and the moon shall not give her light . . . and the powers of the heavens shall be shaken. (Matthew 24:29)

> And there arose a smoke . . . as the smoke of a great furnace; and the sun and the air were darkened by reason of the smoke. (Revelation 9:2)

> That day is a day of wrath, a day of trouble and distress, a day of wasteness and desolation, a day of darkness and gloominess, a day of clouds and thick darkness. (Zephaniah 1:15)

> [Therefore] the stars of heaven and the constellations thereof shall not give their light; the sun shall be darkened in his going forth, and the moon shall not cause her light to shine. (Isaiah 13:10)

The Revelator stated, "The third part of the sun was smitten, and the third part of the moon, and the third part of the stars; so as the third part of them was darkened, and the sun shone not for the third part of it, and the night likewise" (Revelation 8:12).

Another interesting phenomenon will also occur at that time, probably as a result of the extreme amount of smoke, dust, and gas in the atmosphere. The moon will become the color of blood. Scriptures tell us, "They shall behold blood, and fire, and vapors of smoke. And before the day of the Lord shall come, the sun shall be darkened, and the moon be turned to blood" (D&C 45:41–42). "The sun shall be turned into darkness, and the moon into blood, before the great and terrible day of the Lord come" (Joel 2:31). The apostle John recorded, "And the sun became black as sackcloth of hair, and the moon became blood" (Revelation 6:12).

During the war, water will also become as blood. This time the blood may be more literal than metaphorical, for death will accompany it.

> A great mountain burning with fire was cast into the sea: and the third part of the sea became blood; and the third part of the creatures which were in the sea, and had life, died; and the third part of the ships were destroyed. . . . and many men died of the waters, because they were made bitter. (Revelation 8:8–9, 11)

> And the streams thereof shall be turned into pitch and the dust thereof into brimstone, and the land thereof shall become burning pitch. It shall not be quenched night nor day. (Isaiah 34:9)

The "mountain" could be something like a volcano or an asteroid, but it is also possible that it could be a man-made object produced for warfare.

Another phenomenon which will occur during that time will be "lightnings [which] shall streak forth from the east unto the west" (D&C 43:22). "With . . . the fierce and vivid lightning also, shall the inhabitants of the earth be made to feel the wrath . . . of an Almighty God" (D&C 87:6). Armageddon's sulfur weapons might assist in causing the lightning, if the sulfuric atmosphere is just right (sulfur can produce lightning around some erupting volcanoes).

Another phenomenon seen during Armageddon will be "falling stars." The Lord said,

> But, behold, I say unto you that before this great day [of Jesus' Second Coming] shall come . . . the stars shall fall from heaven, and there shall be greater signs in heaven above and in the earth beneath; and there shall be weeping and wailing among the hosts of men. (D&C 29:14–15)

> And the moon shall withhold its light, and the stars shall be hurled from their places. (D&C 13:49)

> And the stars shall become exceedingly angry, and shall cast themselves down as a fig that falleth from off a fig-tree. (D&C 88:87)

The stars might be real falling stars, or they could be military missiles. Missiles fired during the 1991 Gulf War greatly resembled falling stars as they were fired over Iraq.

John described one particular "star" which will hit the earth: "There fell a great star from heaven, burning as it were a lamp, and it fell upon the third part of the rivers, and upon the fountains of water; and the name of the star is called Wormwood: and the third part of the waters became wormwood; and many men died of the waters, because they were made bitter" (Revelation 8:10–11).

Although the wormwood star could be an actual star, it is not beyond the realm of possibility that it could be a highly explosive weapon which will appear to burn as it falls. And it is conceivable that such a weapon could make waters bitter, not only from toxic debris, but also from radioactive fallout or dangerous chemical or biological substances.

However, if it is a real falling star, it will likely be a meteor, asteroid, or comet. For several years, the famous astronomer Eugene Shoemaker warned that an impact of an asteroid or comet upon the earth would, sooner or later, be inevitable. Such a possibility was ridiculed until a comet was observed striking the planet, Jupiter, on July 16, 1994.[7]

Asteroids have chaotic orbits, so a collision with the earth is possible. In fact our planet is already pocked with many impact craters. It is estimated that there are 750,000 asteroids larger than three-fifths of a mile (1 kilometer) in the asteroid belt between the orbits of Mars and Jupiter, and there are millions of smaller ones.[8] One of the largest to ever come near the earth was discovered in 1898. The Eros asteroid is 21 miles long and 7 miles wide.[9] The impact of such a large asteroid could cause a cosmic disaster. It would produce a super-heated wind, molten rock, and a darkened sun, resulting from extreme amounts of dust and debris forced into the atmosphere at the time of impact. Global famine would also result.

Another asteroid near the earth was discovered in June 2004. It is so close that, according to scientists, it will barely miss the earth in 2029. But they warn that it could return in subsequent orbits to hit the planet a few years later.[10] One report reads:

> On April 13th—Friday the 13th—2029, millions of people are going to go outside, look up and marvel at their good luck. A point of light will be gliding across the sky, faster than many satellites, brighter than most stars. What's so lucky about that? It's asteroid 2004 MN4 . . . not hitting Earth. For awhile astronomers thought it might. On Christmas Eve 2004, Paul Chodas, Steve Chesley and Don Yeomans at NASA's Near Earth Objects Program office calculated a 1-in-60 chance that 2004 MN4 would collide with Earth. Impact date: April 13, 2029. The asteroid is about 320 meters wide. "That's big enough to punch through Earth's atmosphere, devastating a region the size of, say, Texas, if it hit land, or causing widespread tsunamis if it hit ocean," says Chodas.[11]

For now, most scientists say they aren't losing sleep over the possibility of an impact. Rather, they're gearing up for a good show when the asteroid passes within 23,000 miles of Earth's surface—closer than the distance between the Earth and the moon . . . "Certainly, asteroids have made close encounters in the past and some have hit Earth. But in recent history, this is probably the biggest, closest asteroid that we know about," said Bill Bottke, a space studies scientist at the Southwest Research Institute.[12]

The other "falling stars" could also be asteroids, meteors, or comets. However, another possible explanation for the falling stars could be the movement of the earth itself, rather than the stars. The Lord said, "For not many days hence and the earth shall tremble and reel to and fro as a drunken man" (D&C 88:87). A massive earthquake could cause the earth to shake violently, making the stars appear to move. In December of 2004, the earthquake that caused the enormous Indonesian tsunami caused the earth to wobble on its axis. The blast of a powerful nuclear bomb might also cause the entire earth to shake, perhaps even more violently than the tsumani earthquake. If the atomic bomb, which was dropped on Hiroshima during World War II, had the potential to crack the earth's crust,[13] one wonders what a larger more modern bomb could do.

There is also the possibility that when Jesus comes, or maybe just before, the earth will move to another location in the universe, a millennial location. Such a movement could make stars look as if they were falling. Joseph Smith taught that when the earth becomes a celestial planet at the end of the Millennium, it will move to a location in closer proximity to God's dwelling place.[14] Thus it is reasonable to assume that when the earth becomes a terrestrial planet for Jesus' Millennial reign, it will move to a terrestrial location. The scriptures imply that will be the case. They say that "the earth shall remove out of her place" (2 Nephi 23:13), and there will be "new heavens" (Isaiah 65:17).

Another phenomenon associated with Armageddon will be a worldwide famine. Because the sun will be darkened, crops will not grow. The *World Book Encyclopedia* tells us,

> A [nuclear] war could bring on nuclear winter by causing disastrous changes in the earth's atmosphere . . . Nuclear winter could develop from city fires created by the extreme heat of nuclear explosions. Large amounts of smoke from these fires could spread and cover at least half of the earth's surface. The smoke could prevent most sunlight from

reaching the ground. Temperatures could drop substantially, and rainfall could be reduced. These conditions might last for several months or years. With greatly reduced sunlight, less rain, and lower temperatures, farming could stop, and worldwide famine could result.[15]

Joel prophesied of Armageddon's famine.

> Awake, ye drunkards, and weep; and howl, all ye drinkers of wine, because of the new wine; for it is cut off from your mouth. . . .
>
> The field is wasted, the land mourneth . . . howl, O ye vinedressers, for the wheat and for the barley; because the harvest of the field is perished. The vine is dried up . . . even all the trees of the field, are withered. . . .
>
> Is not the meat [food] cut off before our eyes. . . . The seed is rotten under their clods, the garners are laid desolate, the barns are broken down; for the corn is withered. How do the beasts groan! The herds of cattle are perplexed, because they have no pasture . . . for the fire hath devoured the pastures . . . and the flame hath burned all the trees of the field. The beasts of the field cry also unto thee: for the rivers of waters are dried up, and the fire hath devoured the pastures of the wilderness. (Joel 1:5, 10–12, 16–20)

The famine will probably occur during the final year of the war, the same year the Lord will come. Joseph Smith prophesied that during that year, no rainbow will be seen; the lack of a rainbow is an indication of lack of rain. The Prophet said,

> The Lord hath set the bow in the cloud for a sign that while it shall be seen, seed time and harvest, summer and winter shall not fail; but when it shall disappear, woe to that generation, for behold the end cometh quickly. . . . In any year that the bow should be seen the Lord would not come . . . but whenever you see the bow withdrawn, it shall be a token that there shall be famine, pestilence, and great distress among the nations, and that the coming of the Messiah is not far distant.[16]

The Lord pointed out that hail will also be responsible for the destruction of the earth's crops. He said, "And there shall be a great hailstorm sent forth to destroy the crops of the earth" (D&C 29:16). The unusual hailstorm is another phenomenon of Armageddon. (It was mentioned previously that the hail could be bombs.) Scriptures tell us,

> Hail and fire mingled with blood . . . were cast upon the earth. (Revelation 8:7)

And there fell upon men a great hail . . . and men blasphemed God because of the plague of the hail; for the plague thereof was exceeding great. (Revelation 16:21)

[And] the hail shall sweep away the refuge of lies . . . when the overflowing scourge shall pass through. (Isaiah 28:17–18)

That all their [evil] works may be brought to naught, and be swept away by the hail. (D&C 109:30)

And thus with the sword and by bloodshed . . . and with famine, and plagues . . . shall the inhabitants of the earth be made to feel the wrath, and indignation, and chastening hand of an Almighty God, until the consumption decreed hath made a full end of all nations. (D&C 87:6)

The extraordinary phenomena that will assist in bringing an end to all nations cannot be easily imagined now. But the day will come when they will be perceived by everyone as that stage of the world's history opens before us.

Notes
1. *World Book Encyclopedia*, 7:17.
2. Ibid., 14:604.
3. Ibid., 16:78.
4. Ibid., 7:17.
5. Ibid., 7:17.
6. Ibid., 14:604–5.
7. "Comet Shoemaker-Levy 9," Wikipedia, http://en.wikipedia.org/wiki/Comet_Shoemaker-Levy_9.
8. *World Book Encyclopedia*, 2006 ed., 1:823.
9. Ibid., 6:354–55.
10. www.dailyrecord.co.uk, 6-29-05.
11. www.unexplained-mysteries.com, 6-29-05.
12. www.wired.com, 6-29-05.
13. Deke Parson, "Second World War: Hiroshima," http://www.spartacus.schoolnet.co.uk/2WWhiroshima.htm.
14. Smith, *Teachings of the Prophet Joseph Smith*, 181.
15. *World Book Encyclopedia*, 14:608.
16. Smith, *Teachings of the Prophet Joseph Smith*, 305, 340–41.

Eighteen

GATHERING FOR SAFETY

The righteous will not be caught off guard and unprepared when the "desolation" comes upon the wicked. The apostle Paul taught, "Sudden destruction cometh upon [the wicked] . . . and they shall not escape. But ye, brethren, are not in darkness, that that day should overtake you as a thief" (1 Thessalonians 5:3–4).

How will the righteous avoid being overtaken? First of all, they will heed the warning to flee from Babylon, the world of evil. The Lord said, "Yea, verily, I say unto you . . . the time has come when the voice of the Lord is unto you: Go ye out from Babylon; gather ye out from among the nations, from the four winds, from one end of heaven to the other" (D&C 133:7). "My people, go ye out of the midst of her, and deliver ye every man his soul from the fierce anger of the Lord" (Jeremiah 51:45).

Second, the righteous will gather to holy places for safety. The Lord has instructed, "Behold, it is my will, that all they who call on my name, and worship me according to mine everlasting gospel, should gather together, and stand in holy places; And prepare for . . . when . . . all flesh shall see me" (D&C 101:22–23). "My disciples shall stand in holy places, and shall not be moved; but among the wicked, men shall lift up their voices and curse God and die" (D&C 45:32).

President Harold B. Lee indicated where the holy places are: "The Lord has told us where these 'holy places' are: 'And it shall come to pass among the wicked, that every man that will not take his sword against his neighbor must needs flee unto Zion for safety' (D&C 45:68)."[1]

The *Doctrine and Covenants Student Manual* also states that Zion is a holy place of safety: "The tribulations and judgments that will be poured out upon the world prior to the Second Coming will be so extensive and devastating that if the Lord did not prepare a means of preservation, his people too would perish. But he has prepared a means for his people to escape those terrible times; that means is Zion."[2]

The Prophet Joseph Smith taught,

> Without Zion, and a place of deliverance, we must fall; because the time is near when the sun will be darkened, and the moon turn to blood, and the stars fall from heaven, and the earth reel to and fro. Then, if this is the case, and if we are not sanctified and gathered to the places God has appointed, with all our former professions and our great love for the Bible, we must fall; we cannot stand; we cannot be saved; for God will gather out his Saints from the Gentiles, and then comes desolation and destruction, and none can escape except the pure in heart who are gathered.[3]

The Lord also declared, "The gathering together upon the land of Zion and upon her stakes, may be for a defense, and for a refuge from the storm and from wrath when it shall be poured out without mixture upon the whole earth" (D&C 115:6).

Because Zion is to be a place of safety, Joseph Smith gave the following admonition:

> We ought to have the building up of Zion as our greatest object. When wars come, we shall have to flee to Zion. The cry is to make haste. The . . . revelation says, Ye shall not have time to have gone over the earth, until these things come. . . . The time is soon coming when no man will have any peace but in Zion and her stakes. I saw [in vision] men hunting the lives of their own sons, and brother murdering brother, women killing their own daughters, and daughters seeking the lives of their mothers. I saw armies arrayed against armies. I saw blood, desolation, fires. The Son of Man has said that the mother shall be against the daughter, and the daughter against the mother. These things are at our doors.[4]

In his dedication of the Kirtland Temple, the Prophet prayed that the righteous would be gathered to Zion before God's judgments fall upon the cities of the earth: "And whatsoever city thy servants shall enter, and the people of that city receive their testimony, let thy peace and thy salvation be upon that city; that they may gather out of that city the righteous, that they may come forth to Zion, or to her stakes, the places of thine appointment, with songs of everlasting joy. And until this be accomplished, let not thy judgments fall upon that city" (D&C 109:39–40).

President John Taylor indicated that thousands of people will flock to Zion when the desolation comes. He said,

> All those who are not fond of blood and carnage and desolation, if they want to be preserved will flee to Zion. Have we not got a Zion for them to flee to? Yes . . . we want to organize in such a way and advocate and maintain such correct principles, that they will become the admiration of all honest men, who feel that they can be protected and find safety and an asylum in Zion.[5]

> You will see them flocking to Zion by thousands and tens of thousands; and they will say . . . we want to put ourselves under your protection, for we cannot feel safe anywhere else.[6]

The stakes of Utah will be among the stakes of Zion to which people will flee. In 1856 President Heber C. Kimball prophesied of the future gathering to Utah:

> Two companies have come through [to Utah] safe and sound. Is this the end of it? No; there will be millions on millions that will come much in the same way, only they will not have hand carts, for they will take their bundles under their arms, and their children on their backs, and under their arms, and flee; and Zion's people will have to send out relief to them, for they will come when the judgments come on the nations.[7]

> The time is not far distant when the curtain will be dropped between us and the United States. . . . It behooves us to be saving and to prepare for the time to come. The day will come when the people of the United States will come lugging their bundles under their arms, coming to us for bread to eat.[8]

Regarding the Salt Lake valley as a place of safety, President Brigham Young remarked,

> By and by there will be a gulf between the righteous and the wicked so that they cannot trade with each other, and national intercourse will cease [probably because the Armageddon "beast" will control buying and selling].[9]

> We are blessed in these mountains; this is the best place on earth

for the Latter-day Saints. Search for the history of all nations and every geographical position on the face of the earth, and you cannot find another situation so well adapted for the Saints as are these mountains. Here is the place in which the Lord designed to hide His people.... It has been designed for many generations, to hide up the Saints in the last days until the indignation of the Almighty be over.[10]

The latter-day apostle, Melvin J. Ballard, also indicated that Utah will be a place of refuge: "Do you not know, my brethren and sisters, that God knew what was coming; that he brought this people into these mountain valleys as a place of refuge when the storm shall come. We only hear the beginning of that storm. Dismal and distressful as has been its approach, while its thunders and its flashings have filled our hearts with terror, it is but the beginning of the storm."[11]

Elder Orson Pratt remarked,

> The time will come when there will be no safety in carrying on the peaceful pursuits of farming or agriculture . . . people will think themselves well off if they can flee from city to city, from town to town and escape with their lives. . . .
>
> But what will become of this people? Shall we be swept off in the general ruin? Shall desolation come upon us? . . . That will depend altogether upon our conduct. . . . By doing that which is right . . . prosperity will be upon the inhabitants of Utah. . . . [The Lord] will send forth the missionaries of this people to the four quarters of the earth to publish peace . . . and proclaim that there is still a place left in the heart of the American continent where there are peace and safety and refuge from the storms, desolations, and tribulations coming upon the wicked.[12]

Besides Utah, another part of Zion has been specifically designated as a place of safety.

> And it shall be called the New Jerusalem, a land of peace, a city of refuge, a place of safety for the saints of the most High God;
> And the glory of the Lord shall be there, and the terror of the Lord also shall be there, insomuch that the wicked will not come unto it, and it shall be called Zion.
> And it shall come to pass among the wicked, that every man that will not take his sword against his neighbor must needs flee unto Zion for safety.
> And there shall be gathered unto it out of every nation under

heaven; and it shall be the only people that shall not be at war one with another.

And it shall be said among the wicked: Let us not go up to battle against Zion, for the inhabitants of Zion are terrible; wherefore we cannot stand.

And it shall come to pass that the righteous shall be gathered out from among all nations, and shall come to Zion, singing with songs of everlasting joy. (D&C 45:66–71)

The Lord told Joseph Smith that "the purpose of purchasing lands [is for] building up of the New Jerusalem. . . . That my covenant people may be gathered in one in that day when I shall come to my temple" (D&C 42:35–36).

In the meantime, the Saints have been instructed to continue establishing stakes of Zion throughout the world until the time comes for the building of the New Jerusalem. The Lord commanded, "Ye shall build up my church in every region—until the time shall come when it shall be revealed unto you from on high, when the city of the New Jerusalem shall be prepared" (D&C 42:8–9).

Elder Alvin R. Dyer taught that the current gathering to stakes is a diversionary plan until the time comes for the gathering to the New Jerusalem. He stated, "The Lord . . . indicated the diversionary plan for the gathering of the Saints until such time as they would return to build up the waste places of Zion, [the New Jerusalem]."[13]

Before the Saints return there, the area will be cleansed of its evil inhabitants. The Lord declared,

> Behold, the destroyer I have sent forth to destroy and lay waste mine enemies; and not many years hence they shall not be left to pollute mine heritage, and to blaspheme my name upon the lands which I have consecrated for the gathering together of my saints. (D&C 105:15)

> And it shall be said in days to come that none is able to go up to the land of Zion . . . but he that is upright in heart. (D&C 61:16)

Quoting the Lord, Brigham Young remarked, " 'I will purge the land,' saith the Lord, 'cut off the evil doer, and prepare a way for the return of my people to their inheritance.' We pray for this."[14]

Even after the cleansing of the area, the return to build Zion will apparently be during a time of danger, for it will be necessary for heavenly armies to protect the Saints in their return. The Prophet Joseph Smith recorded that his scribe "saw, in a vision, the armies of heaven protecting the Saints in their return to Zion."[15]

The Lord promised that he will also be with the Saints when they return.

> Behold, I say unto you, the redemption of Zion must needs come by power.... Ye must needs be led out of bondage by power, and with a stretched-out arm. And as your fathers were led at the first [out of Egypt], even so shall the redemption of Zion be ... I said unto your Fathers: Mine angel shall go up before you, but not my presence. But I say unto you: Mine angels shall go up before you, and also my presence, and in time ye shall possess the goodly land. (D&C 103:15, 17–20)

> Behold, I will go before you and be your rearward; and I will be in your midst. (D&C 49:27)

Elder Orson Pratt taught that the Lord's presence would be manifest in a cloud and a pillar of fire:

> I expect that when the Lord leads forth his people to build up the city of Zion, his presence will be visible. When we speak of the presence of the Lord we speak of an exhibition of power.... We shall go back to Jackson County [and] ... when we go back, there will be a very large organization consisting of thousands, and tens of thousands, and they will march forward, the glory of God overshadowing their camp by day in the form of a cloud, and a pillar of flaming fire by night, the Lord's voice being uttered forth before his army....
>
> Will not this produce terror upon all the nations of the earth? Will not armies of this description, though they may not be as numerous as the armies of the world, cause a terror to fall upon the nations? The Lord says the banners of Zion shall be terrible.... But when the Lord's presence is there, when his voice is heard, and his angels go before the camp, it will be telegraphed to the uttermost parts of the earth and fear will seize upon all people, especially the wicked, and the knees of the ungodly will tremble in that day.[16]

Not only will the Saints return under the protection of the Almighty, even after the New Jerusalem is built, the "mount Zion" city and its inhabitants will continue to be protected by the Lord. Scriptures tell us that "the Lord will create upon every dwelling place of mount Zion, and upon her assemblies, a cloud and smoke by day and the shining of a flaming fire by night; for upon all the glory of Zion shall be a defense. And there shall be a tabernacle for a shadow in the daytime from the heat, and for a place of refuge, and a covert from storm and from rain" (2 Nephi 14:5–6; see also Isaiah 4:5–6).

Not only will there be deliverance in the New Jerusalem (mount Zion), but there will also be deliverance in Jerusalem in the land of Israel. The Lord said through his prophets,

> And it shall come to pass, that whosoever shall call on the name of the Lord shall be delivered: for in mount Zion and in Jerusalem shall be deliverance. (Joel 2:32)

> For it is ordained that in Zion and in her stakes, and in Jerusalem, [will be] those places which I have appointed for refuge. (D&C 124:36)

> In that day it shall be said to Jerusalem, Fear thou not: and to Zion . . . Let not thine hands be slack. The Lord thy God in the midst of thee is mighty; he will save, he will rejoice over thee. (Zephaniah 3:16)

President Wilford Woodruff observed that the gathering for safety will be just as important in our day as it was in the days of Noah: "And as the Lord has said by the ancient prophets, in the last days there should be deliverance in Jerusalem and in Mount Zion; and . . . pointed out the location of Zion and commanded the Saints among the Gentiles to gather thereunto and build it up, while the Jews gather to Jerusalem. The safety of the Saints depends as much upon their fulfilling His commandments as the safety of Noah and Lot depended upon their obedience to the commands of God in their day and generation."[17]

If we expect to have God's protection when he sends desolation upon the wicked, we must be a Zion people and stand in the holy places which he has designated for safety. The Lord said, "This is Zion—the pure in heart; therefore, let Zion rejoice, while all the wicked shall mourn" (D&C 97:21).

Notes
1. *Doctrine and Covenants Student Manual*, 95.
2. Ibid., 98.
3. Smith, *Teachings of the Prophet Joseph Smith*, 71.
4. Ibid., 160–61.
5. *Journal of Discourses*, 20:266.
6. Ibid., 20:135.

7. Ibid., 4:106.
8. Ibid., 5:10.
9. Ibid., 12:284.
10. Lund, *The Coming of the Lord*, 90.
11. Ibid., 91.
12. *Journal of Discourses*, 12:344–45.
13. Alvin R. Dyer, *The Refiner's Fire: The Significance of Events Transpiring in Missouri* (Salt Lake City: Deseret Book, 1968), 69.
14. *Journal of Discourses*, 9:270.
15. Lund, *The Coming of the Lord*, 109.
16. *Journal of Discourses*, 15:364.
17. Ludlow, *Latter-day Prophets Speak*, 242.

Nineteen

RETURN OF THE LOST TRIBES

It has been prophesied that the time will come when "every man that will not take his sword against his neighbor must needs flee to Zion for safety. And there shall be gathered unto it out of every nation under heaven; and it shall be the only people that shall not be at war one with another" (D&C 45:68–69). That might be the time when the "lost tribes" of Israel will flee from the north. The Lord will say to them, "Ho, Ho, come forth, and flee from the land of the north, saith the Lord" (Zechariah 2:6). And "they shall come together out of the land of the north" (Jeremiah 3:18).

Ten of the twelve tribes of Israel (the northern kingdom of Israel) became "lost" after they were forcefully taken into Assyrian captivity in 721 BC. Some time later, some managed to leave the land of their captivity, and they traveled to a land north of Assyria. That northern land was anciently called Arsareth,[1] but its current name is unknown. However, it could be somewhere in Russia. Elder George Reynolds explained, "Skirting along the Black Sea, they would pass the Caucasian range, cross the Kuban River, be prevented by the Sea of Azof from turning westward and would soon reach the present home of the Don Cossaks' [in southern Russia]."[2] Today millions of people are living in Russia and its neighboring countries, any of whom could be descendants of the lost tribes.

The descendants are considered lost today because they are no longer recognized as Israelites; they are now simply known as citizens of the country or countries, in which they reside. Elder James E. Talmage observed that "while many of those belonging to the Ten Tribes were diffused among the nations, a sufficient number to justify the retention of the original name were led away as a body and are now in existence in some place where the Lord has hidden them."[3]

The apocryphal writer, Esdras, indicated that many descendants of the lost tribes are still in the land of Arsareth today and will remain there until the time comes for their return. He recorded,

> Those are the ten tribes, which were carried away prisoners out of their own land. . . . But they took this counsel among themselves, that they would leave the multitude of the heathen, and go forth into a further country, where never mankind had dwelt, that they might there keep their statutes, which they had never kept in their own land. And they entered into Euphrates [River] by the narrow passage of the river. For the most High . . . held still the flood, till they were passed over. For through that country there was a great way to go, namely of a year and a half: and the same region is called Arsareth. Then dwelt they there until the latter times; and now when they shall begin to come, The Highest shall stay the stream again, that they may go through.[4]

Joseph Fielding Smith taught that when they return, they will return together as a body:

> The Ten Tribes were taken by force out of the land the Lord gave them. Many of them mixed with the peoples among whom they were scattered. A large portion, however, departed in one body into the north and disappeared from the rest of the world. Where they went and where they are we do not know. That they are intact we must believe, else how shall the scripture be fulfilled? There are too many prophecies concerning them and their return as a body for us to ignore the fact.[5]

Jeremiah also prophesied that "they shall come together out of the land of the north" (Jeremiah 3:18).

John the Revelator is probably among the main body of the lost tribes to prepare them for their return. Hyrum M. Smith, a latter-day apostle (along with Janne M. Sjodahl), wrote, "At a conference of the church held in June 1831, the Prophet said that John the Revelator was then among the ten tribes of Israel who had been led away . . . to prepare them for their return from their long dispersion."[6]

While exiled to the isle of Patmos, John was told by an angel that he would "prophesy again before many peoples" (which peoples include the lost tribes). John wrote, "And [the angel] said unto me, Thou must prophesy again before many peoples, and nations, and tongues, and kings" (Revelation 10:11).

It was revealed to Joseph Smith that John's mission was to gather the tribes of Israel in the last days (see D&C 77:14). And it was revealed to John that in order to fulfill his latter-day mission, he would not die but would minister as an angel. The Lord said to him, "John, my beloved, what desirest thou? For if you shall ask what you will, it shall be granted unto you. And I said unto him: Lord, give unto me power over death, that I may live and bring souls unto thee. And the Lord said unto me: Verily, verily, I say unto thee, because thou desirest this, thou shalt tarry until I come in my glory, and shalt prophesy before nations, kindreds, tongues and people. . . . Therefore I will make [thee] as flaming fire and a ministering angel" (D&C 7:1–3, 6).

Jesus was referring to John when he said to his disciples, "There be some standing here which shall not taste of death, till they see the Son of man coming in his kingdom" (Matthew 16:28). While discussing John's mission among the ten tribes, Elder Orson Pratt said that "in the last days the spirit and power of Elias will attend [John's] administrations among these ten tribes, and he will assist in preparing them to return to this land."[7]

Not only was John to visit and minister among the lost tribes, but Jesus also promised to visit them after his resurrection. He said, "Now I go unto the Father, and also to show myself unto the lost tribes of Israel" (3 Nephi 17:4); "them also I must bring, . . . and there shall be one fold, and one shepherd" (3 Nephi 15:17).

The southern kingdom of Israel, which consisted primarily of the tribe of Judah (Jews), did not travel north with the other tribes because that kingdom had not been taken captive into Assyria. However, the southern kingdom was destroyed in AD 70, and the Jews were scattered into all parts of the world. Interestingly, over the centuries they managed to maintain their identity as Jews. In 1948, when the land of Israel was officially declared to be their homeland, many Jews returned from their dispersion to the land of their inheritance.

It has been prophesied that the day will come when the lost tribes will also be gathered back to their land of promise. Speaking of that day, the Lord said, "Verily I say unto you, at that day shall the work of the Father commence among all the dispersed of my people, yea, even the tribes which have been lost, which the Father hath led away out of Jerusalem.

Yea, the work shall commence among all the dispersed of my people . . . in preparing the way whereby [they] may be gathered home to the land of their inheritance" (3 Nephi 21:26–28).

Not all the tribes will return to the land of Israel, for there are to be two gathering places, one in Israel and one in America. America is the gathering place and the promised land for the tribe of Joseph. The Prophet Joseph Smith said, "Descendants from that Joseph who was sold into Egypt . . . the land of America is a promised land unto them."[8]

The lost tribes will gather initially with the tribe of Joseph in America before they return to the land of Israel. The Lord said through the prophet Jeremiah, "I will bring them from the north country . . . a great company shall return thither. They shall come with weeping, and with supplications . . . they shall come and sing in the height of Zion" (Jeremiah 31:8–9, 12). Elder LeGrand Richards remarked, "Note that Jeremiah did not say that they will return hither [here] . . . but [he said] thither [there] or to a distant place. He understood that [the tribe of] Joseph was to be given a new land in the 'utmost bound of the everlasting hills.' "[9]

The Prophet Joseph Smith taught, "The ransomed of the Lord shall return and come to [America's] Zion . . . and then they will be delivered from the overflowing scourge that shall pass through the land. . . . But [the tribe of] Judah shall obtain deliverance at Jerusalem."[10]

The Lord also indicated through the prophet Isaiah that the lost tribes will go first to America's Zion.

> In those days, and in that time, saith the Lord, the children of Israel shall come . . . going and weeping: they shall go, and seek the Lord their God. They shall ask the way to Zion with their faces thitherward. (Isaiah 50:4–5)

> And the ransomed of the Lord shall return, and come to Zion with songs and everlasting joy upon their heads: they shall obtain joy and gladness, and sorrow and sighing shall flee away. (Isaiah 35:10)

In America the tribes of Israel will receive their priesthood blessings through the tribe of Ephraim (the son of Joseph). They shall "be crowned with glory, even in Zion, by the hands of the servants of the Lord, even the children of Ephraim" (D&C 133:32).

The keys for leading the ten tribes from the north were first committed to the Prophet Joseph Smith in 1836 (see D&C 110:11), so the gathering of those tribes will take place under the direction of whichever prophet is the president of the Church at the time of the gathering, for he holds the keys.

Because the ten tribes will return under the direction of the President who holds the keys, they must return before the priesthood meeting at Adam-ondi-Ahman when all priesthood keys will be delivered back to the Lord.[11] So it is likely that the lost tribes will flee from the north during the war of Armageddon, for the war will be raging in the Middle East when the meeting at Adam-ondi-Ahman takes place (see chapter 23 of this book).

The time of Armageddon is also the time when the river Euphrates will be dried up enough for the tribes to pass over. For "they entered into Euphrates by the narrow passage of the river" in their journey northward, and "when they shall begin to come [back], The Highest shall stay the stream again, that they may go through."[12] The book of Revelation states that during Armageddon, "the sixth angel poured out his vial upon the great river Euphrates; and the water thereof was dried up" (Revelation 16:12).

The Prophet Joseph Smith taught that when the tribes "flee unto Zion for safety" (D&C 45:68), they will "be delivered from the overflowing scourge that shall pass through the land."[13]

Joseph Fielding Smith indicated that they will return after much destruction of the wicked: "The great day of the coming of the lost tribes would be after the preparatory work had been accomplished in the destruction of the wickedness in very great measure, and the way prepared in part for the coming of the Lord."[14]

Joseph Smith indicated that the wicked in the United States will be swept from off the land to prepare the way for the return of the lost tribes. He prophesied, "And now I am prepared to say by the authority of Jesus Christ, that not many years shall pass away before the United States shall present such a scene of bloodshed as has not a parallel in the history of our nation; pestilence, hail, famine, and earthquake will sweep the wicked of this generation from off the face of the land, to open and prepare the way for the return of the lost tribes of Israel from the north country."[15]

At that time the Lord's words regarding them will be fulfilled. He prophesied,

> Behold, I will bring them from the north country . . . with them the blind and the lame, the woman with child and her that travaileth with child together: a great company shall return thither. . . . For the Lord hath . . . ransomed him from the hand of him that was stronger

than he. Therefore they shall come and sing in the height of Zion. . . . I will turn their mourning into joy, and will comfort them, and make them rejoice from their sorrow . . . and they shall come again from the land of the enemy. (Jeremiah 31:8, 11–13, 16)

Their enemies shall become a prey unto them. (D&C 133:28)

They shall make great noise by reason of the multitude of men. (Micah 2:12)

Thy children shall make haste against thy destroyers . . . all these gather themselves together . . . and they that swallowed thee up shall be far away. (1 Nephi 21:17–19)

At that time there will be prophets among the lost tribes who shall lead the people back in a great show of power. Latter-day scripture reads,

And they who are in the north countries shall come in remembrance before the Lord; and their prophets shall hear his voice, and shall no longer stay themselves; and they shall smite the rocks, and the ice shall flow down at their presence. . . .
Their enemies shall become a prey unto them. . . .
And the boundaries of the everlasting hills [in America] shall tremble at their presence. And there shall they fall down and be crowned with glory, even in Zion, by the hands of the servants of the Lord, even the children of Ephraim. (D&C 133:26, 28, 31–32)

The prophet Isaiah indicated that the tribes will need to cross the ocean in order to reach their destination. This is evidence they will come to America, and not simply to the nearby land of Israel, for there is no ocean between Israel and the northern land of Arsareth, where they are currently residing (according to Esdras who was quoted previously). Isaiah said, "Art thou not it which hath dried the sea, the waters of the great deep; that hath made the depths of the sea a way for the ransomed to pass over? Therefore the redeemed of the Lord shall return" (Isaiah 51:10–11). "And there shall be an highway for the remnant of his people, which shall be left from Assyria" (Isaiah 11:16). Anther scripture also states that "An highway shall be cast up in the midst of the great deep" (D&C 133:27).

The *Doctrine and Covenants* student manual defines "the great deep" as the ocean:

That the "great deep" means the ocean or sea is attested to by the Old Testament prophet Isaiah. . . . How a highway will be cast up in the midst of the deep for the ten tribes to come to Zion has not been made known by the Lord; however, an interesting parallel is the story of Moses parting the Red Sea. With Pharaoh and his army at their backs and the Red Sea in front of them, Israel had come to an impasse. Then a great miracle took place: a highway was cast up in the midst of the deep, and Israel crossed over on dry ground (see Exodus 14; Isaiah 11:15-16). How the Lord will bring the ten tribes to Zion is not fully clear, but that he will do it is a certainty.[16]

The highway could be above the ocean because it is quite possible the tribes will be transported to America via translation (see next two chapters). That idea is not beyond the realm of possibility when viewed in the context of scripture. Isaiah tells us that the highway on which they will travel is called, "the way of holiness," and only the redeemed will walk upon it. He recorded, "And an highway shall be there, and a way, and it shall be called The way of holiness; the unclean shall not pass over it . . . but the redeemed shall walk there: And the ransomed of the Lord" (Isaiah 35:8–9). "And the Lord have removed men far away, and there shall be a great forsaking in the midst of the land" (Isaiah 6:12).

The transporting of the tribes from the north will probably occur at the time when all righteous souls are translated. Thus angels will assist in gathering them. Scriptures tell us, "The Son of Man shall come, and he shall send his angels before him . . . and they shall gather together the remainder of his elect from the four winds" (Joseph Smith—Matthew 1:37).

The return of the lost tribes will be so miraculous that the Lord declared, "Therefore, behold, the days come, saith the Lord, that it shall no more be said, The Lord liveth that brought up the children of Israel out of the land of Egypt; But the Lord liveth, that brought up the children of Israel from the land of the north, and from all the lands whither he had driven them" (Jeremiah 16:14–15). Thus the Lord exclaimed, "O Israel, Fear not: for I have redeemed thee. . . . When thou passest through the waters, I will be with thee; and through the rivers, they shall not overflow thee: when thou walkest through the fire, thou shalt not be burned" (Isaiah 43:1–2).

The Lord not only promised to help the ten tribes when they return, but also all the righteous who will be forced to flee Armageddon's desolation.

> And it shall come to pass in that day that the Lord shall beat off from the channel of the river unto the stream of Egypt, and ye shall be gathered. . . . And it shall come to pass in that day, that the great

trumpet shall be blown, and they will come which were ready to perish in the land of Assyria [in the Middle East], and the outcasts in the land of Egypt. (Isaiah 27:12–13)

And the Lord shall utterly destroy the tongue of the Egyptian sea; and with his mighty wind shall he shake his hand over the river, and shall smite it in the seven streams, and make men go over dryshod. (Isaiah 11:15)

The Lord declared,

I will make all my mountains a way, and my highways shall be exalted. Behold, these shall come from far: and, lo, these from the north and from the west; and these from the land of Sinim. . . .
Behold: all these gather themselves together. (Isaiah 49:11–12, 18)

Go through, go through the gates; prepare ye the way of the people; cast up, cast up the highway; gather out the stones; lift up a standard for the people . . . And they shall call them, The holy people, The redeemed of the Lord. (Isaiah 62:10, 12)

It appears, however, that before the highway is prepared, some people will flee from Armageddon's desolation in airplanes. Isaiah recorded,

And [God] will lift up an ensign to the nations from far [America], and will hiss unto them from the end of the earth: and behold, they shall come with speed swiftly:
None shall be weary nor stumble among them; none shall slumber nor sleep; neither shall the girdle of their loins be loosed, nor the lachet of their shoes be broken:
Whose arrows are sharp, and all their bows bent, their horses hoofs shall be counted like flint, and their wheels like a whirlwind: Their roaring shall be like a lion, they shall roar like young lions: yea, they shall roar, and lay hold of the prey, and shall carry it away safe . . .
And if one look to the land, behold darkness and sorrow, and the light is darkened in the heavens thereof. (Isaiah 5:26–30)

They shall fly upon the shoulders of the Philistines toward the west; they shall spoil them of the east together. (Isaiah 11:14)

Who are these that fly as a cloud, and as doves to their windows. (Isaiah 60:8)

Because scriptures often have dual meaning, it is possible that these passages might be referring to the translation of the righteous as well as transportation by airplanes.

Isaiah prophesied that the tribes will be transported initially to the New Jerusalem in America (mount Zion).

> Therefore the redeemed of the Lord shall return, and come with singing unto Zion; and everlasting joy shall be upon their head: they shall obtain gladness and joy; and sorrow and mourning shall flee away. (Isaiah 51:11)

> In that time shall the present be brought unto the Lord of hosts of a people scattered and peeled, and from a people terrible from their beginning hitherto; a nation meted out and trodden under foot . . . to the place of the name of the Lord of hosts, the mount Zion [New Jerusalem]. (Isaiah 18:7)

> In that day shall the branch of the Lord be beautiful and glorious, and . . . the earth shall be excellent and comely for them that are escaped of Israel. . . .
> And the Lord will create upon every dwelling place of mount Zion, and upon her assemblies, a cloud and smoke by day, and the shining of a flaming fire by night. . . .
> And there shall be a tabernacle for a shadow in the daytime from the heat, and for a place of refuge. (Isaiah. 4:2, 5–6)

Modern scripture discusses the reaction of the wicked to the Zion city where the redeemed will be taken. "And it shall be said among the wicked: Let us not go up to battle against Zion, for the inhabitants of Zion are terrible; wherefore we cannot stand . . . and they shall stand afar off and tremble. And all nations shall be afraid because of the terror of the Lord" (D&C 45:70, 74–75). "The nations of the earth shall tremble because of her, and shall fear because of her terrible ones" (D&C 64:43).

After the war of Armageddon is ended by the Lord, all but the tribe of Joseph will return to Israel, the land of their of inheritance. The Church-published *Old Testament Student Manual 2* states, "The ten tribes . . . are to eventually receive their land inheritance with Judah and not with Ephraim (see Ether 13:11). . . . After they have received their priesthood blessings . . . they will go to Jerusalem."[17] In that day the Lord's words will be fulfilled: "In those days the house of Judah [southern kingdom] shall walk with the house of Israel [northern kingdom], and they shall come . . . to the land that I have given for an inheritance unto your fathers" (Jeremiah 3:18).

The time when the ten tribes will go back to the land of Israel will be after their resurrection.

> Thus saith the Lord God; Behold, O my people, I will open your graves, and cause you to come up out of your graves, and bring you into the land of Israel. . . . And I shall place you in your own land. (Ezekiel 37:12, 14)

> And I will make them one nation in the land upon the mountains of Israel; and one king shall be king to them all: and they shall be no more two nations, neither shall they be divided into two kingdoms any more at all. . . .
> And my servant David shall be their prince for ever. (Ezekiel 37:22, 25)

David is Jesus Christ. He will inherit King David's throne and rule over Israel during the Millennium.[18] The *Doctrine and Covenants Student Manual* states, "The king who shall reign personally upon the earth during the Millennium shall be the Branch who grew out of the house of David. . . . That the Branch of David is Christ is perfectly clear. . . . He is . . . called David . . . a new David, an Eternal David, who shall reign forever on the throne of his ancient ancestor."[19]

Notes

1. McConkie, *Mormon Doctrine*, 456.
2. Ibid., 457.
3. James E. Talmage, *A Study of the Articles of Faith* (Salt Lake City: Deseret Book), 340.
4. McConkie, *Mormon Doctrine*, 456.
5. Joseph Fielding Smith, *The Way to Perfection,* (Salt Lake City: Deseret Book, 1978), 130.
6. Hyrum M. Smith and Janne M. Sjodahl, *Doctrine and Covenants Commentary* (Salt Lake City: Deseret Book, 1978), 843–44.
7. *Journal of Discourse,* 18:26.
8. Smith, *Teachings of the Prophet Joseph Smith,* 17.
9. LeGrand Richards, *Israel! Do You Know?* 177–78.
10. Smith, *Teachings of the Prophet Joseph Smith,* 17.
11. See JST, Luke 3:8.
12. *Doctrine and Covenants Student Manual,* 341.
13. Smith, *Teachings of the Prophet Joseph Smith,* 17.
14. R. Clayton Brough, *The Lost Tribes,* 96.
15. Smith, *Teachings of the Prophet Joseph Smith,* 17.
16. *Doctrine And Covenants Student Manual,* 341.

17. *Old Testament Student Manual,* 2:116.
18. See Isaiah 9:7 and Jeremiah 23:3–6.
19. *Old Testament Student Manual,* 2:148.

Twenty

A Solemn Assembly

Near the end of the three and one-half year siege of Jerusalem, the Saints will know that the coming of the Lord is imminent. "Behold, the day of the Lord cometh . . . All nations [will be] against Jerusalem to battle" (Zechariah 14:1–2). "Then shall [the Saints] know that the hour is nigh. . . . They shall behold blood, and fire, and vapors of smoke" (D&C 45:38, 41).

The Lord said, "Mine elect, when they shall see all these things, they shall know that he is near, even at the doors" (JS–M 1:39). For "when ye shall see Jerusalem compassed with armies, then know that [my] desolation thereof is nigh. Then let them which are in Judea flee to the mountains; and let them which are in the midst of it depart out" (Luke 21:20–21). President Spencer W. Kimball remarked, "When the world is full of tribulation and help is needed, but it seems the time must be past and all hope is vain, then Christ will come."[1]

Just before the Lord comes, the two prophets in Jerusalem will be holding the evil Armageddon army at bay. "These two sons are come unto thee . . . as a wild bull in a net, they are full of the fury of the Lord" (2 Nephi 8:19–20). But as their three and a half-year mission comes to a close, the Lord's servants will finally be killed.

> And when they have finished their testimony, the beast that ascendeth out of the bottomless pit shall make war against them, and shall overcome them, and kill them. And their dead bodies shall lie in the street of that great city [Jerusalem]. . . . And they of the people and kindreds and tongues and nations shall see their dead bodies three days

and an half, and shall not suffer their dead bodies to be put in graves. And they that dwell upon the earth shall rejoice over them, and make merry, and shall send gifts one to another; because these two prophets tormented them that dwelt on the earth. (Revelation 11:7–10)

> There is [now] none to guide [Israel] among all the sons whom she hath brought forth; neither is there any that taketh her by the hand . . . These two things are come unto thee; . . . [but] thy sons have fainted, they lie at the head of all the streets. (Isaiah 51:18–20)

With the two prophets out of the way, Gog and his beast will be able to rush in to conquer the city.

> They shall run to and fro in the city; they shall run upon the wall, they shall climb up upon the houses; they shall enter in at the windows like a thief. (Joel 2:9)

> And the city shall be taken, and the houses rifled, and the women ravished . . . and the residue of the people shall not be cut off from the city. (Zechariah 14:2)

> And [Gog] shall plant the tabernacles of his palace between the seas and the glorious holy mountain. (Daniel 11:45)

> Then will the Lord . . . pity his people. (Joel 2:18)

When it appears the remaining Jews are about to be overcome, the Lord will prepare to destroy Gog and his beastly army (as well as all their supporters). Just before his hand falls upon the wicked armies, the righteous will undoubtedly be fasting and praying for deliverance. Assurance of God's help can be found in the scriptures:

> Therefore also now, saith the Lord, turn ye even to me with all your heart, and with fasting, and with weeping, and with mourning. And rend your heart, and not your garments, and turn unto the Lord your God. . . .
> Let the priests, the ministers of the Lord, weep between the porch and the altar, and let them say, Spare thy people, O Lord. (Joel 2:12–13, 17)

> O Jerusalem . . . lift up thy voice with strength; lift it up, be not afraid; say unto the cities of Judah, Behold your God! Behold, the Lord God will come with strong hand, and his arm shall rule for him. (Isaiah 40:9–10)

And it shall come to pass, that whosoever shall call on the name of the Lord shall be delivered: for in mount Zion, and in Jerusalem shall be deliverance, as the Lord hath said. (Joel 2:32)

The Mighty God shall deliver his covenant people. (2 Nephi 6:17)

For thus saith the Lord, I will cut my work short in righteousness, for the days come that I will send forth judgment unto victory. (D&C 52:11)

And except those days should be shortened, there should no flesh be saved: but for the elect's sake those days shall be shortened. (Matthew 24:22)

At that time, the Lord will send angels ahead of him to alert the righteous to prepare for deliverance and gather in a solemn assembly.

The Son of man . . . shall send his angels before him with the sound of a great trumpet. (JS–M 1:37)

And angels shall fly through the midst of heaven, crying with a loud voice, sounding the trump of God, saying: Prepare ye, prepare ye, O inhabitants of the earth; for the judgment of our God is come. Behold, and lo, the Bridegroom cometh. (D&C 88:92)

The marriage of the Lamb is come, and his wife hath made herself ready. (Revelation 19:7)

The Lord declared,

In that day it shall be said to Jerusalem, Fear thou not: and to Zion, Let not thine hands be slack. The Lord thy God in the midst of thee is mighty; he will save [thee] . . . I will gather them that are sorrowful for the solemn assembly. (Zephaniah 3:16–18)

Blow the trumpet in Zion, sanctify a fast, call a solemn assembly: Gather the people, sanctify the congregation, assemble the elders, gather the children, and those that suck the breast. (Joel 2:15–16)

Blow ye the trumpet in Zion, and sound an alarm in my holy mountain: let all the inhabitants of the land tremble: for the day of the Lord cometh, for it is nigh at hand. (Joel 2:1)

For a nation is come up upon my land, strong, and without number whose teeth are the teeth of a lion . . . He hath laid my vine waste . . .

The meat offering and the drink offering is cut off from the house of the Lord; the priests, the Lord's ministers, mourn. . . .

Sanctify ye a fast, call a solemn assembly, gather the elders and all the inhabitants of the land into the house of the Lord your God, and cry unto the Lord, Alas for the day! For the day of the Lord is at hand, and as a destruction from the Almighty shall it come. (Joel 1:6–7, 9, 14–15)

Wherefore, stand ye in holy places, and be not moved, until the day of the Lord come; for behold, it cometh quickly, saith the Lord. (D&C 87:8)

One of the angels who will be sent to prepare the righteous for deliverance will be Michael, the archangel. Scriptures tell us that "Michael [is] the seventh angel, even the archangel" (D&C 88:112). And "the Holy One of Zion . . . hath appointed Michael your prince, and established his feet, and set him upon high, and given unto him the keys of salvation under the counsel and direction of the Holy One" (D&C 78:15–16).

Joseph Smith taught that Michael is the same person as Adam, the first man placed upon the earth. The prophet declared, "The Lord appeared unto [Adam and his righteous posterity] and they rose up and blessed Adam, and called him Michael, the Prince, the Archangel. And the Lord administered comfort unto Adam, and said unto him, I have set thee to be at the head [of] a multitude of nations . . . thou art a Prince over them forever."[2]

Adam will return to Earth as Michael, the archangel, a resurrected person and messenger from God. The prophet Daniel said this about Adam's role during the winding up scenes of Armageddon: "And at that time shall Michael stand up, the great prince which standeth for the children of thy people: and there was a time of trouble, such as never was since there was a nation even to that same time: and at that time thy people shall be delivered, every one that shall be found written in the book [of life]" (Daniel 12:1).

John the Revelator also stated,

[And] in the days of the seventh angel [Michael], when he shall begin to sound, the mystery of God should be finished. (Revelation 10:7)

And [the] mighty angel came down from heaven, clothed with a cloud: and a rainbow was upon his head, and his face was as it were the sun, and his feet as pillars of fire . . . and he set his right foot upon the sea, and his left foot on the earth, And cried with a loud voice, as when a lion roareth: and when he had cried, seven thunders uttered their voices. . . . And the angel . . . lifted up his hand to heaven, And sware by him that liveth for ever and ever . . . that there should be time no longer. (Revelation 10:1–3, 5–6)

Adam's message will be so important that Isaiah declared, "All ye inhabitants of the world and dwellers on the earth . . . when he bloweth a trumpet, hear ye" (Isaiah 18:3). But only the Saints will hear, for it is they to whom Adam will come. He will undoubtedly appear to the prophet of the Church first, for "surely the Lord God will do nothing, but he [first] revealeth his secret unto his servants the prophets" (Amos 3:7). Then instructions will be given to the Saints.

Notes
1. *Doctrine and Covenants Student Manual,* 97.
2. Smith, *Teachings of the Prophet Joseph Smith,* 38–39.

Twenty-one

GATHERING TO ONE PLACE

Near the end of Armageddon, Michael (Adam) will sound his trump, meaning he will make an important announcement. He will announce to the Saints that they are going to be removed to a safe place out of harm's way—they will be gathered from all the stakes of Zion into one place.

President Joseph Fielding Smith remarked, "It appears from the revelation, that there must be a time when Zion—the pure in heart—will be isolated from the rest of the world. . . . There must come a time, for the Lord has spoken it, when by some miraculous manner, he will gather from the four ends of the earth his people in a gathering which does not have to do with that which has already taken place."[1]

The apostle Orson Pratt also stated that preparatory to the coming of Jesus, there will be a universal gathering of the Saints from the four quarters of the earth. He said, "There is to be a grand gathering of all [the Lord's] people from the four quarters of the earth into one body, one family as it were; one people consolidated in one region of country, before he shall come."[2]

Prophets have revealed where that final gathering place will be. Joseph Smith taught,

> God will gather out His Saints from the Gentiles, and then comes desolation and destruction, and none can escape except the pure in heart who are gathered.[3]
>
> Wherefore, the decree hath gone forth from the Father that they shall be gathered in unto one place upon the face of this land, to prepare

their hearts and be prepared in all things against the day when tribulation and desolation are sent forth upon the wicked. (D&C 29:8)

[Therefore,] Zion is to be prepared, even a new Jerusalem, for the elect that are to be gathered from the four quarters of the earth.[4]

Elder Robert D. Hales, of the quorum of the twelve apostles, also stated that "when the Savior comes to His temple [in the New Jerusalem] . . . those who are true and faithful will be there."[5]

The Lord himself declared,

Before the great day of the Lord shall come . . . Zion shall . . . be assembled together unto the place which I have appointed. (D&C 49:24–25)

Yea, [the Lord] has spoken by the mouth of his prophets . . . for the gathering of his saints to stand upon mount Zion, which shall be the city of New Jersalem. (D&C 84:2)

For in mount Zion, and in Jerusalem shall be deliverance, as the Lord hath said. (Joel 2:32)

[And] they shall not be beaten down by the storm at the last day; yea, neither shall they be harrowed up by the whirlwinds; but when the storm cometh they shall be gathered together in their place, that the storm cannot penetrate to them. . . .

They are in the hands of the Lord of the harvest, and they are his; and he will raise them up at the last day. (Alma 26:6–7)

Because of the life-threatening situation posed by the Armageddon beast, it will be necessary for angels to help transport the Saints to the New Jerusalem (Joseph Smith—Matthew 1:37). And it appears that the means of transportation will be "translation." Not only will the Saints be translated to the New Jerusalem, but according to President John Taylor, "the city [itself] will [also] be translated."[6] (Apparently it will not be taken to heaven, but it will be lifted into the clouds directly above the earth, a safe distance from the destruction below and the desolation which God will pour out upon the wicked; see 1 Thessalonians 4:16–17).

Regarding the angelic assistance at that time, the Lord has said to the Saints, "Ye must be led out of bondage by power, and . . . mine angels shall go up before you, and also my presence" (D&C 103:17, 20).

The gathering of translated mortals to the New Jerusalem will be the final harvesting of the righteous from God's vineyard. Scriptures indicate what the angel reapers will do:

> [They will] first gather out the wheat from among the tares, and after gathering the wheat, behold and lo, the tares are bound in bundles, and the field remaineth to be burned. (D&C 86:7)

> The harvest is the end of the world; and the reapers are the angels. (Matthew 13:39)

> [For] the time cometh speedily that the righteous must be led up as calves of the stall, and the Holy One of Israel must reign in dominion, and might, and power, and great glory. And he gathereth his children from the four quarters of the earth. (1 Nephi 22:24–25)

The Lord said,

> Wherefore, seeing that I, the Lord, have decreed all these things upon the face of the earth, I will that my saints should be assembled upon the land of Zion, [the New Jerusalem]. (D&C 63:36)

> That ye may be gathered in one, that ye may be my people and I will be your God. . . . That my covenant people may be gathered in one in that day when I shall come to my temple. (D&C 42:9, 36)

> [Therefore,] I will bring thy seed from the east, and gather thee from the west. I will say to the north, Give up; and to the south, Keep not back . . . Let all the nations be gathered together, and let the people be assembled. (Isaiah 43:5–6, 9)

Not only will the seventh angel's trump be heard, announcing to the Saints that they are going to be transported to safety, the Lord's voice will also be heard.

> The Lord shall roar from on high, and utter his voice from his holy habitation; he shall mightily roar upon his habitation; he shall give a shout, as they that tread the grapes, against all the inhabitants of the earth. (Jeremiah 25:30)

> Our God . . . shall not keep silence . . . He shall call to the heavens from above, and to the earth. . . . Gather my saints together unto me; those that have made a covenant with me by sacrifice. And the heavens shall declare his righteousness. (Psalm 50:3–6)

Following the Lord's voice and the trump of the archangel, the translation will begin. It will be accompanied by the resurrection of the righteous from their graves. The resurrected and the translated will be caught up together to the New Jerusalem as the Lord descends toward it.

> For the Lord himself shall descend from heaven with a shout, with the voice of the archangel, and with the trump of God: and the dead in Christ shall rise first. (1 Thessalonians 4:16)
>
> Awake and arise and go forth to meet the Bridegroom; behold and lo, the Bridegroom cometh. (D&C 133:10)
>
> For a trump shall sound both long and loud . . . and all the earth shall quake, and they shall come forth . . . to receive a crown of righteousness. . . .
> Michael, [the] archangel, shall sound his trump, and then shall all the [righteous] dead awake. (D&C 29:13, 26)
>
> [And] the graves of the saints shall be opened; and they shall come forth and stand on the right hand of the Lamb, when he shall stand upon mount Zion, and upon the holy city, the new Jerusalem. (D&C 133:56)
>
> And . . . men shall be awakened by the power of God when the trump shall sound. (Mormon 9:13)
>
> [And] the Son of Man shall come down in heaven, clothed in the brightness of his glory, to meet the kingdom of God which is set up on the earth. (D&C 65:5)
>
> The Son of Man shall come, and he shall send his angels before him with the sound of a trumpet, and they shall gather together the remainder of his elect from the four winds, from one end of heaven to the other. (JS–M 1:37)
>
> [For] in those days . . . the sun shall be darkened, and the moon shall not give her light, and the stars of heaven shall fall, and the powers that are in heaven shall be shaken. . . .
> And then shall he send his angels, and shall gather together his elect from the four winds, from the uttermost part of the earth to the uttermost part of heaven. (Mark 13:24–25, 27)
>
> [And] the dead shall hear the voice of the Son of God: and they that hear shall live. . . . And shall come forth. (John 5:25, 28)

Regarding that event, scriptures tell us,

> The dead in Christ shall rise first: Then we which are alive and

> remain shall be caught up together with them in the clouds, to meet the Lord in the air. (1 Thessalonians 4:16–17)
>
> And the saints that are upon the earth, who are alive, shall be quickened and be caught up to meet him. And they who have slept in their graves shall come forth, for their graves shall be opened; and they also shall be caught up to meet him in the pillar of heaven—They are Christ's, the first fruits . . . who are first caught up to meet him; and all this by the voice of the sounding of the trump of the angel of God. (D&C 88:96–98)
>
> In Christ shall all be made alive. But every man in his own order: Christ the firstfruits; afterward they that are Christ's at his coming. (1 Corinthians 15:22–23)

This is probably the time when the lost tribes will also come on the highway to the New Jerusalem.

This is also likely the time when the two prophets, who will have been lying dead in the streets of Jerusalem for three and one-half days, will be resurrected and stand upon their feet before the eyes of the people.

> And after three days and an half the Spirit of life from God entered into them, and they stood upon their feet; and great fear fell upon them which saw them.
>
> And [the prophets] heard a great voice saying unto them, Come up hither. And they ascended up to heaven [the atmosphere above the earth] in a cloud; and their enemies beheld them.
>
> And the same hour there was a great earthquake, and the tenth part of the city fell, and in the earthquake were slain of men seven thousand: and the remnant were affrighted, and gave glory to the God of heaven. (Revelation 11:11–13)
>
> And there were voices, and thunders, and lightnings; and there was a great earthquake, such as was not since men were upon the earth, so mighty an earthquake, and so great.
>
> And that great city was divided into three parts, and the cities of the nations fell. (Revelation 16:18–19)
>
> For the day cometh that the Lord shall utter his voice out of heaven; the heavens shall shake and the earth shall tremble, and the trump of God shall sound both long and loud, and shall say to the sleeping nations: Ye saints arise and live; ye sinners stay and sleep until I shall call again. (D&C 43:18)

The lifting up of the righteous to the New Jerusalem, in the clouds above the earth, will fulfill Jesus' prophetic words:

> The saints that have slept shall come forth to meet me in the cloud . . . [they] shall come forth from the four quarters of the earth. . . .
> The righteous shall be gathered out from among all nations, and shall come to Zion, singing with songs of everlasting joy. (D&C 45:45–46, 71)

> [They shall be lifted up] in the clouds, to meet the Lord in the air. (1 Thessalonians 4:17)

> [And the] cloud shall rest upon [the New Jerusalem temple], which cloud shall be even the glory of the Lord, which shall fill the house. (D&C 84:5)

> Then shall be fulfilled that which is written, that in the last days, two shall be in the field, the one shall be taken, and the other left; two shall be grinding at the mill, the one taken and the other left. (JS—Matthew 1:44–45)

At that time, it will dawn upon complacent and foolish procrastinators that they are being left behind. Frantically, "the foolish [will say] unto the wise, Give us of your oil; for our lamps are gone out. But the wise [will answer], saying, Not so; lest there be not enough for us. . . . And while [the foolish] went to buy, the bridegroom came; and they that were ready went in with him to the marriage: and the door was shut" (Matthew 25:8–10). In vain the foolish will cry, "Lord, Lord, open to us." But he will answer, "Verily I say unto you, I know you not" (Matthew 25:11–12). Thus their fate will be sealed for all eternity, for the Lord said,

> He that watches not for me shall be cut off. (D&C 45:43)

> [And the wicked] shall be cut off from among the people. (D&C 1:14)

> [And] all they who fight against Zion shall be cut off. (1 Nephi 22:19)

> [But] mine elect hear my voice and harden not their hearts; wherefore . . . they shall be gathered in unto one place upon the face of this land . . . when tribulation and desolation are sent forth upon the wicked. (D&C 29:7–8)

> And even so will I gather mine elect from the four quarters of the

earth, even as many as will believe in me, and hearken unto my voice. (D&C 33:6)

For they will hear my voice, and shall see me, and shall not be asleep, and shall abide the day of my coming; for they shall be purified, even as I am pure. (D&C 35:21)

Notes
1. Smith, *The Signs of the Times,* 199.
2. *Journal of Discourses,* 15:56.
3. *Doctrine and Covenants Student Manual,* 371.
4. Smith, *Teachings of the Prophet Joseph Smith,* 84.
5. Robert D. Hales, "Holy Scriptures: The Power of God unto Our Salvation," *Ensign,* Nov. 2006, 27.
6. *Journal of Discourses,* 21:253.

Twenty-two

WHERE THE EAGLES ARE GATHERED

When Jesus told his disciples about the day when "the one shall be taken, and the other shall be left" (Luke 17:34), his disciples asked him, "Where, Lord, shall they be taken? And he said unto them, wheresoever the body is gathered, or, in other words, whithersoever the saints are gathered, thither will the eagles be gathered together; or thither will the remainder be gathered together" (JST, Luke 17:36–37).

The scriptures tell us that the resurrected righteous and the translated "remainder" will not be taken directly to heaven, but they will be transported to the New Jerusalem (which most likely includes the clouds and atmosphere above it). The "graves of the saints shall be opened; and they shall come forth and stand on the right hand of the Lamb, when he shall stand upon mount Zion, and upon the holy city, the New Jerusalem" (D&C 133:56).

Speaking of the gathering to the New Jerusalem, Brigham Young said, "We shall be there when Jesus comes; and if we are not there, we will come with him: in either case we shall be there when he comes. . . . We look forward with all the anticipation and confidence . . . that we shall be there when Jesus comes."[1]

It is probably there where the marriage of the Lamb will take place. Jesus, the Bridegroom, will be united with his bride, the Church, which will "come forth out of the wilderness of darkness, and shine forth fair as the moon, clear as the sun, and terrible as an army with banners. And be adorned as a bride for that day when [the Lord] shalt unveil the heavens" (D&C 109:73). And "the bridegroom [will] go forth of his chamber, and the bride out of her closet" (Joel 2:16).

Thus it is in the New Jerusalem where the gathered elect will have their first glimpse of Jesus Christ. Waiting for the Lord's appearance there will undoubtedly be a solemn and anxious moment for the gathered Saints. The Lord prophesied of that day when he said, "I [will] sweep the earth as with a flood, to gather out mine elect from the four quarters of the earth, unto a place which I shall prepare, an Holy City, that my people may gird up their loins and be looking forth for the time of my coming; for there shall be my tabernacle, and it shall be called Zion, a New Jerusalem" (Moses 7:62).

Just before Jesus appears to the gathered Saints, a "sign" will be seen, for "there shall appear a great sign in heaven, and all people shall see it together" (D&C 88:93). This sign will likely be the glory emminating from Jesus as he descends toward the earth "in a pillar of fire" (D&C 29:12), with "all the holy angels" (Matthew 25:31).

Jesus' glory will be like the glow of a sunrise on the horizon just before the sun appears. The scriptures say,

> Immediately after the tribulation of those days . . . shall the powers of heaven be shaken: And then shall appear the sign of the Son of man in heaven. (JS—Matthew 1:36–37)

> For as the light of the morning cometh out of the east, and shineth even unto the west, and covereth the whole earth, so shall also the coming of the Son of Man be. (JS—Matthew 1:26)

> The light shall not be clear nor dark: but it shall be one day . . . that at evening time it shall be light. (Zechariah 14:6–7)

Joseph Smith remarked that some people, seeing the glowing manifestation, will believe it to be a comet or something similar. He said, "Then will appear one grand sign of the Son of Man in heaven. But what will the world do? They will say it is a planet, a comet, etc. But the Son of Man will come as the sign of the coming of the Son of Man, which will be as the light of the morning out of the east."[2]

When the sign begins to appear, heaven will be silent. This could result from Jesus and his heavenly host no longer being in heaven. Or the silence could be a manifestation of reverence and respect for the Son of God as he makes his descent to the earth. There will undoubtedly be a solemn and reverent silence among the Saints as they await Jesus' appearance. The scriptures say,

> Be silent, O all flesh, before the Lord: for he is raised up out of his holy habitation. (Zechariah 2:13)

> The Lord is in his holy temple: let all the earth keep silence before him. (Habakkuk 2:20)

> [And] there shall be silence in heaven for the space of half an hour; and immediately after shall the curtain of heaven be unfolded, as a scroll is unfolded after it is rolled up, and the face of the Lord shall be unveiled [to the righteous]. (D&C 88:95)

> And the Lord whom ye seek, shall suddenly come to his temple [in the New Jerusalem]. (Malachi 3:1)

> And a cloud shall rest upon it, which cloud shall be even the glory of the Lord which shall fill the house. (D&C 84:5)

> [For the] Son of Man shall come down in heaven, clothed in the brightness of his glory, to meet the kingdom of God which is set up on the earth. (D&C 65:5)

Although the whole world will see the sign, only the elect will see Jesus at that time. The Lord himself declared, "My covenant people [will] be gathered in one in that day when I shall come to my temple" (D&C 42:36), and "the veil shall be rent and [they] shall see me and know that I am" (D&C 67:10).

The Lord indicated that when the faithful are transported to the New Jerusalem, he will hasten the building of the city. He said,

> Behold, I, the Lord, will hasten the city in its time, and will crown the faithful with joy and with rejoicing. (D&C 52:43)

> [For] the city New Jerusalem shall be built by the gathering of the saints. (D&C 84:4)

> And the nations of the earth shall honor her, and shall say: Surely Zion is the city of our God, and surely Zion cannot fall, neither be moved out of her place, for God is there, and the hand of the Lord is there; And he hath sworn by the power of his might to be her salvation and her high tower. (D&C 97:19–20)

There in New Jerusalem, the saints will be safely hidden away while the Lord takes vengeance upon the wicked. Scriptures indicate he will say to the righteous,

> Come, my people, enter thou into thy chambers, and shut thy doors about thee: hide thyself as it were for a little moment, until the indignation be overpast. For, behold, the Lord cometh out of his place to punish the inhabitants of the earth for their iniquity: the earth also shall disclose her blood, and shall no more cover her slain. (Isaiah 26:20–21)

> Gather yourselves together, yea, gather together... before the decree bring forth, before the day pass as the chaff, before the fierce anger of the Lord come upon you....
> Seek righteousness, seek meekness: it may be ye shall be hid in the day of the Lord's anger. (Zephaniah 2:1–3)

> And my people shall dwell in a peaceable habitation, and in sure dwellings, and in quiet resting places; when it shall hail, coming down on the forest. (Isaiah 32:18–19)

When Jesus descends to the New Jerusalem, the Zion city of Enoch, which had been translated anciently, will descend with him. The translated and resurrected Saints from all ages will meet together in the clouds. President John Taylor stated, "When the time comes that these calamities we read of shall overtake the earth, those that are prepared will have the power of translation, as they had in former times, and the city will be translated. And Zion that is on the earth will rise, and the Zion above will descend, as we are told, and we will meet and fall on each other's necks and embrace and kiss each other. And thus the purposes of God to a certain extent will then be fulfilled."[3]

Scriptures inform us,

> By faith Enoch was translated that he should not see death; and was not found, because God had translated him. (Hebrews 11:5)

> And it came to pass that Enoch saw the day of the coming of the Son of Man, in the last days, to dwell on earth. (Moses 7:65)

> And the Lord said unto Enoch... [I will] gather out mine elect from the four quarters of the earth, unto a place which I shall prepare, an Holy City... and it shall be called Zion, a New Jerusalem.
> And the Lord said unto Enoch: Then shalt thou and all thy city meet them there, and we will receive them into our bosom, and they shall see us; and we will fall upon their necks, and they shall fall upon our necks, and we will kiss each other;
> And there shall be mine abode, and it shall be Zion, which shall

come forth out of all the creations which I have made. (Moses 7:60, 62–64)

Other scriptures also refer to the meeting of the two Zion cities: "The Lord hath brought again Zion; the Lord hath redeemed his people, Israel.... The Lord hath gathered all things in one. The Lord hath brought down Zion from above. The Lord hath brought up Zion from beneath. The earth hath travailed and brought forth her strength; and truth is established in her bowels; and the heavens have smiled upon her; and she is clothed with the glory of her God; for he stands in the midst of his people" (D&C 84:99–101).

Only people who come forth in the first resurrection will have citizenship in the combined Zion cities, for the first resurrection will include only the just. The just are the righteous living and dead whom the Lord will elect to meet him in the New Jerusalem.

> These are they who shall have part in the first resurrection. These are they who shall come forth in the resurrection of the just. These are they who are come to Mount Zion, and unto the city of the living God, the heavenly place, the holiest of all. These are they who have come to an innumerable company of angels, to the general assembly and church of Enoch, and of the Firstborn....
>
> These are they who are just men made perfect through Jesus the mediator of the new covenant, who wrought out this perfect atonement through the shedding of his own blood. (D&C 76:64–67, 69)

The Lord said of them,

> Ye are come unto mount Sion and unto the city of the living God, the heavenly Jerusalem, and to an innumerable company of angels, to the general assembly and church of the firstborn, which are written in heaven, and to God the Judge of all, and to the spirits of just men made perfect, and to Jesus the mediator of the new covenant. (Hebrews 12:22–23)
>
> For ye are the church of the Firstborn, and he will take you up in a cloud. (D&C 78:21)

Scriptures tell us that once righteous mortals have been transported to the New Jerusalem,

> Houses [shall be] without man, and the land be utterly desolate. And the Lord have removed men far away, and there be a great forsaking in the midst of the land. (Isaiah 6:11–12)

At that hour cometh an entire separation of the righteous and the wicked. (D&C 63:54)

For the time cometh that the Lord God shall cause a great division among the people, and the wicked will he destroy; [but] he will spare his people. (2 Nephi 30:10)

For the marriage of the Lamb is come, and his wife hath made herself ready. And to her was granted that she should be arrayed in fine linen, clean and white: for the fine linen is the righteousness of saints. And . . . blessed are they which are called unto the marriage supper of the Lamb. (Revelation 19:7–9)

The Lord said,

And at that day . . . shall the parable be fulfilled which I spake concerning the ten virgins. For they that are wise and have received the truth, and have taken the Holy Spirit for their guide, and have not been deceived—verily I say unto you, they shall not be hewn down and cast into the fire, but shall abide the day. (D&C 45:56–57)

[Therefore] be faithful until I come, and ye shall be caught up, that where I am ye may be also. (D&C 27:18)

[For] if thou art faithful in keeping my commandments, thou shalt be lifted up at the last day. (D&C 5:35)

Notes
1. Widtsoe, *Discourses of Brigham Young*, 120.
2. Smith, *Teachings of the Prophet Joseph Smith*, 287.
3. *Journal of Discourses*, 21:253.

Twenty-three

ADAM-ONDI-AHMAN

During Jesus' heavenly convocation with the Saints in New Jerusalem, the people left behind will see only the glowing sign of his presence there. The glory of the translated city will probably be part of the sign, "For . . . the glory of the Lord shall be upon [the Zion city]" (D&C 64:41). "And she is clothed with the glory of her God; for he stands in the midst of his people" (D&C 84:101). Not realizing the significance of this sign, those left behind will be completely unaware that Jesus Christ will be meeting with the Saints in the holy city. That meeting will be kept secret from the rest of the world because it will precede Jesus' Second Coming to the rest of the world "as a thief in the night" (2 Peter 3:10).

When the rest of earth's inhabitants see the sign, "they shall stand afar off and tremble. And all nations shall be afraid" (D&C 45:74–75). "The nations . . . shall fear because of [Zion's] terrible ones" (D&C 64:43). "And it shall be said among the wicked: Let us not go up to battle against Zion, for the inhabitants of Zion are terrible; wherefore we cannot stand" (D&C 45:70).

While the wicked tremble, the faithful will be gazing upon the face of the Lord in the greatest Church conference ever held. The scriptures tell us that among the faithful will be the 144,000 priesthood leaders. For "the Lamb shall stand upon Mount Zion [the New Jerusalem], and with him a hundred and forty-four thousand, having his Father's name written on their foreheads. . . . And he shall utter his voice out of Zion. . . . And the Lord, even the Savior, shall stand in the midst of his people" (D&C 133:18, 21, 25).

John the Revelator recorded,

> And I looked, and, lo, a Lamb stood on the mount Sion, and with him an hundred forty and four thousand, having his Father's name written in their foreheads. . . .
>
> And they sung as it were a new song before the throne . . . and no man could learn that song but the hundred and forty and four thousand, which were redeemed from the earth.
>
> These are they which were not defiled with women; for they are virgins [pure]. These are they which follow the Lamb whithersoever he goeth. These were redeemed from among men, being the firstfruits [the first to be resurrected] unto God and to the Lamb. (Revelation 14:1, 3–4)

At that great conference, the priesthood leaders will give an offering and sacrifice.

> [They will] offer an acceptable offering and sacrifice in the house of the Lord. . . .
>
> And the sons of Moses and of Aaron shall be filled with the glory of the Lord, upon Mount Zion in the Lord's house . . .
>
> For whoso is faithful in obtaining [the] two priesthoods . . . are sanctified by the Spirit unto the renewing of their bodies.
>
> They become the sons of Moses and of Aaron and the seed of Abraham and the church and kingdom, and the elect of God. (D&C 84:31–34)
>
> Behold . . . he [the Lord] shall purify the sons of Levi, and purge them as gold and silver, that they may offer unto the Lord an offering in righteousness. (D&C 128:24)

Because of the large number of people who will be caught up to be with the Lord in the New Jerusalem, the translated city could extend not only over the area of Jackson County, Missouri, but also over the area of Adam-ondi-Ahman, which is near Jackson County. Adam-ondi-Ahman is significant because that is where Adam and Eve lived after they were driven from the Garden of Eden. It is about ninety miles north of where the ancient garden was located.

Brigham Young taught that the Garden of Eden was in the land of America. He said, "Men have supposed that because [Noah's] Ark rested on Ararat that . . . it was from thence the Ark started to sail. But God in His revelations has informed us that it was on the choice land of

Joseph where Adam was placed and the Garden of Eden was laid out."[1] Elder Orson F. Whitney also stated, "The 'Choice Seer' declared that the Garden of Eden was in Missouri, on the very spot where the New Jerusalem is yet to rise."[2]

Scriptures tell us,

> Three years previous to the death of Adam, he called . . . the residue of his posterity who were righteous, into the valley of Adam-ondi-Ahman, and there bestowed upon them his last blessing.
>
> And the Lord appeared unto them, and they rose up and blessed Adam, and called him Michael, the prince, the archangel.
>
> And the Lord administered comfort unto Adam, and said unto him, I have set thee to be at the head; a multitude of nations shall come of thee, and thou art a prince over them forever.
>
> And Adam stood up in the midst of the congregation; and notwithstanding he was bowed down with age, being full of the Holy Ghost, predicted whatsoever should befall his posterity unto the latest generation.
>
> These things were all written in the book of Enoch, and are to be testified of in due time. (D&C 107:53–57)

Just as Adam's righteous posterity gathered to Adam-ondi-Ahman anciently, they will all gather there again as part of the New Jerusalem conference. According to a statement printed in the March 2005, *Ensign*, "the Prophet [Joseph Smith] designated Adam-ondi-Ahman as a gathering place."[3] In the scriptures we read that "Spring Hill is named by the Lord Adam-ondi-Ahman, because, said he, it is the place where Adam shall come to visit his people, or the Ancient of Days shall sit, as spoken of by Daniel the prophet" (D&C 116:1).

Daniel, while speaking of Armageddon, related,

> I beheld till the thrones were cast down, and the Ancient of days [Adam] did sit, whose garment was white as snow, and the hair of his head like the pure wool: his throne was like the fiery flame, and his wheels as burning fire.
>
> A fiery stream issued and came forth from before him: thousand thousands ministered unto him, and ten thousand times ten thousand stood before him: the judgment was set, and the books were opened.
>
> I beheld even till the beast [of Armageddon] was slain, and his body destroyed, and given to the burning flame. (Daniel 7:9–11)
>
> I beheld, and the same horn [Gog] made war with the saints and

prevailed against them; until the Ancient of days [Adam] came, and judgment was given to the saints of the most High. (Daniel 7:21–22)

> And [Gog] shall . . . come to his end, and none shall help him.
> And at that time shall Michael [Adam] stand up, the great prince which standeth for the children of thy people: and there shall be a time of trouble, such as never was since there was a nation even to that same time. (Daniel 11:45, 12:1)

Joseph Smith commented on that event, saying, "Daniel in his seventh chapter speaks of the Ancient of Days; he means the oldest man, our Father Adam, Michael; he will call his children together and hold a council with them to prepare them for the [second] coming of the Son of Man."[4]

Elder Orson Pratt explained that the Lord "makes this preparation beforehand, so that there may be a people ready to receive him. People of mortality [who will have been translated], as well as immortal beings, all knowing their positions, will form the grand Council, and they will be organized ready to receive Jesus when he comes."[5]

Elder Bruce R. McConkie said of that event, "One of the greatest spiritual gatherings of all the ages took place in the Valley of Adam-ondi-Ahman some 5,000 years ago, and another gathering—of even greater importance relative to this earth's destiny—is soon to take place in that same location,"[6] and "all the faithful saints of all ages will assemble with the Lord Jesu. . . . It will be the greatest congregation of faithful saints ever assembled on planet earth."[7]

Speaking of that event, Joseph Fielding Smith said,

> Not many years hence there shall be another gathering of high priests and righteous souls in this same valley of Adam-ondi-Ahman. At this gathering Adam, the Ancient of Days, will again be present. At this time the vision which Daniel saw will be enacted. The Ancient of Days will sit [as] . . . the first patriarch of the race, who holds the keys of salvation. This shall be a day of judgment and preparation . . . .[This meeting] shall precede the coming of Jesus Christ as a thief in the night, unbeknown to all the world.[8]

The scriptures tell us how many people will be in attendance at that meeting. Adam, "the Ancient of days did sit. . . . Thousand thousands ministered unto him, and ten thousand times ten thousand stood before him" (Daniel 7:9–10). John the Revelator also said, "The number of them was ten thousand, and thousands of thousands" (Revelation 5:11). Modern apostles have also commented on the number:

> This gathering of the children of Adam, where the thousands, and the tens of thousands are assembled . . . will be one of the greatest events this troubled earth has ever seen.[9] [Joseph Fielding Smith]

> A certain person [Adam] is to come, accompanied by a great host; the name of this person is the Ancient of Days . . . and he will have the oversight of this host. . . . This 'ten thousand times ten thousand' spoken of will be the faithful of his own posterity.[10] [Orson Pratt]

> And who are the "ten thousand times ten thousand" who stand before him? Are not these the one hundred million and more who have been faithful and true in the days of their mortal probation? . . . All the faithful members of the Church then living [who will have been translated] and all the faithful saints of all the ages past will be present. It will be the greatest congregation of faithful saints ever assembled on planet earth . . . at a place called Adam-ondi-Ahman.[11] [Bruce R. McConkie]

Sometime during that heavenly general conference, all church leaders who have held priesthood "keys" will return them to Adam, who in turn will deliver them back to the Lord. The Prophet Joseph Smith taught, "Our Father Adam, Michael . . . is the father of the human family, and presides over the spirits of all men, and all that have had the keys must stand before him in this grand council. . . . The Son of Man stands before him. . . . Adam delivers up his stewardship to Christ, that which was delivered to him as holding the keys of the universe, but retains his standing as the head of the human family."[12] Joseph Fielding Smith also said, "There will stand before him those who have held the keys of all dispensations, who shall render up their stewardship to the first patriarch of the race, who holds the keys of salvation."[13]

After that task is completed, the priesthood leaders will receive new assignments. They will be called to reign with Jesus as "kings and priests" John the Revelator recorded, "Thou . . . hast made us unto our God kings and priests: and we shall reign on the earth" (Revelation 5:10).

The Saints will also be given new assignments or callings, for "the saints of the most High shall take the kingdom . . . and judgment was given to the saints of the most High" (Daniel 7:18, 22), "and the saints arose, and were crowned at the right hand of the Son of Man, with crowns of glory" (Moses 7:56).

The apostle Orson Pratt observed, "[Adam] comes to set in order the councils of the Priesthood pertaining to all dispensations, to arrange the Priesthood and the councils of the Saints of all former dispensations in one grand family and household.... Then every family that is in the order of the Priesthood, and every man and every woman, and every son or daughter whatever their kindred, descent or Priesthood, will know their place."[14]

One of the most important things on Adam's agenda will be to call for the sustaining of Jesus Christ as the rightful ruler of the earth. Adam will announce the official beginning of Jesus' long-awaited reign as "King of kings, and Lord of lords" (1 Timothy 6:15). The apostle John wrote about that momentous event:

> And the seventh angel [Adam] sounded, and there were great voices in heaven, saying, The kingdoms of this world are become the kingdoms of our Lord, and of his Christ; and he shall reign for ever and ever. (Revelation 11:15)
>
> The four and twenty elders fall down before him that sat on the throne, and worship him that liveth for ever and ever, and cast their crowns before the throne, saying, Thou art worthy, O Lord, to receive glory and honour and power. (Revelation 4:10–11)

John continued,

> And after these things I heard a great voice of much people in heaven, saying Alleluia; Salvation, and glory, and honour, and power, unto the Lord our God....
>
> And I heard as it were a great multitude, and as the voice of many waters, and as the voice of mighty thunderings, saying, Alleluia: for the Lord God omnipotent reigneth. (Revelation 19:1, 6)
>
> And I saw ... them that had gotten the victory over the beast, and over his image, and over his mark, and over the number of his name....
>
> And they sing ... the song of the Lamb, saying, Great and marvelous are thy works, Lord God Almighty; just and true are thy ways, thou King of saints. Who shall not fear thee, O Lord, and glorify thy name? For thou only art holy: for all nations shall come and worship before thee. (Revelation 15:2–4)

The prophet Daniel also wrote of that event. He recorded,

And at that time shall Michael [Adam] stand up, the great prince which standeth for the children of the people. (Daniel 12:1)

And, behold, one like the Son of Man came with the clouds of heaven, and came to the Ancient of days, and they brought him near before him. And there was given [Jesus] dominion, and glory, and a kingdom, that all people, nations, and languages, should serve him: his dominion is an everlasting dominion, which shall not pass away, and his kingdom that which shall not be destroyed. (Daniel 7:13–14)

Other scriptures state,

The Savior shall stand in the midst of his people, and shall reign. (D&C 133:25)

For the Lord shall be in their midst, and his glory shall be upon them, and he will be their king and their lawgiver. (D&C 45:59)

Now unto the King eternal, immortal, invisible, the only wise God, be honor and glory for ever and ever. (1 Timothy 1:17)

The Lord reigneth, he is clothed with majesty . . . the world also is established, that it cannot be moved. Thy throne is established. . . .

Thy testimonies are very sure: holiness becometh thine house, O Lord, for ever. (Psalm 93:1–2, 5)

Elder Alvin R. Dyer summarized that event with these words: "Our Lord will then assume the reigns of the government; directions will be given to the priesthood, and he, whose right it is to rule, will be installed officially by the voice of the priesthood there assembled. This grand council of priesthood will not only be composed of those who are faithful who now dwell on the earth, but also the prophets and apostles of old, who have any directing authority."[14]

That momentous day will be "the great day of the Lord," for it will be a turning point in the history of the world. Although one of the most horrific events (Armageddon) will still be raging in the Middle East, the sustaining of Jesus Christ at the meeting of Adam-ondi-Ahman will be one of the greatest events ever to occur, because when Jesus takes charge of the earth, the violence of Armageddon will be stopped, Satan will be deposed, and his reign of tyranny will come to an end. It is no wonder that Elder Neal A. Maxwell exclaimed, "Yes, Armageddon lies ahead. But so does Adam-ondi-Ahman!"[15]

Joseph Fielding Smith expressed these words:

> Until this grand council is held, Satan shall hold rule in the nations of the earth; but at that time thrones are to be cast down and man's rule shall come to an end.[16]

> Christ will . . . be installed as the rightful Ruler of this earth.[17]

> At that time there will be a transfer of authority from the usurper and imposter, Lucifer, to the rightful King, Jesus Christ. . . . Our Lord will then assume the reins of government.[18]

> Following this event every government in the world, including the United States, will have to become part of the government of God. Then righteous rule will be established. The earth will be cleansed; the wicked will be destroyed; and the reign of peace will be ushered in.[19]

The prophet Daniel also saw that all worldly thrones and governments will lose their dominion at that time. He said, "I beheld till the thrones were cast down, and the Ancient of days did sit" (Daniel 7:9).

That grand conference with the Lord will also include a sacrament meeting. Jesus told his disciples, "The hour cometh that I will drink of the fruit of the vine with you on the earth. . . . And also with all those whom my Father hath given me out of the world" (D&C 27:5,14).

Elder McConkie tells us,

> Jesus is going to partake of the sacrament again with his . . . disciples on earth. But it will not be with [them] only. He names others who will be present [see D&C 27]. . . . The grand summation . . . comes in these words: "And also with all those whom my Father hath given me out of the world." (D&C 27:4–14). The sacrament is to be administered in a future day on the earth, when the Lord Jesus is present, and when all the righteous of all ages are present. This, of course, will be a part of the grand council at Adam-ondi-Ahman.[20]

Only people who, prior to that meeting, have worthily partaken of the sacrament upon the earth, and also have repented of their sins and kept the Lord's commandments, will be privileged to participate in the sacrament meeting at Adam-ondi-Ahman. We can only imagine what it will be like to partake of the sacrament in the presence of the Savior himself, by whom and for whom the sacrament was instituted.

That glorious meeting will only be eclipsed by the Second Coming of the Lord Jesus Christ to the rest of the world. Jesus said that before that day comes, "He that feareth me shall be looking forth for the great day of the Lord to come, even for the signs of the coming of the Son of Man" (D&C 45:39). And "they that are with him are called, and chosen, and faithful" (Revelation 17:14).

Notes
1. *Journal of Discourses*, 11:337.
2. N. B. Lundwall, comp. *Temples of the Most High*, (Salt Lake City: Bookcraft, 1949), 275–76.
3. Fred E. Woods, " 'We Wanted to Come to Zion,' " *Ensign*, March 2005, 33.
4. Smith, *Teachings of the Prophet Joseph Smith*, 157.
5. *Journal of Discourses*, 18:344.
6. McConkie, *Mormon Doctrine*, 21.
7. McConkie. *Millennial Messiah*, 579.
8. Smith, *The Way to Perfection*, 289, 291.
9. Smith, *The Progress of Man*, 481.
10. *Journal of Discourses*, 18:341–42.
11. McConkie, *Millennial Messiah*, 579, 585.
12. Smith, *Teachings of the Prophet Joseph Smith*, 157.
13. *Doctrine and Covenants Student Manual*, 404.
14. Dyer, *The Refiner's Fire*, 182.
15. Neal A. Maxwell, "O, Divine Redeemer," *Ensign*, November 1981, 10.
16. Smith, *The Way to Perfection*, 290.
17. Smith, *The Progress of Man*, 482.
18. *Doctrine and Covenants Student Manual*, 288.
19. Smith, *Doctrines of Salvation*, 3:13–14.
20. McConkie, *The Millennial Messiah*, 587.

Twenty-four

THE SECOND COMING OF JESUS

Once Jesus is sustained as King of kings and Lord of lords, he will appear to the rest of the world. At that time any wicked people who still remain on the earth will be destroyed so Jesus can begin his millennial reign of peace. The unsuspecting sinners will not know, until it is too late, that Jesus' appearance will mark the end of their mortal lives.

> The Lord . . . shall come in a day when [the unrepentant] looketh not for him and in an hour that he is not aware. (JS—Matthew 1:53)
>
> [For] as it was in the days of Noe, so shall it be also in the days of the Son of man. . . .
> Likewise also as it was in the days of Lot; they did eat, they drank, they bought, they sold. . . . But the same day that Lot went out of Sodom it rained fire and brimstone from heaven, and destroyed them all. Even thus shall it be in the day when the Son of man is revealed. (Luke 17:26, 28–30)

That day will be the "dreadful day of the Lord" (Malachi 4:5) for the unrepentant who will have rejected every opportunity to overcome their iniquitous ways.

> [For] the indignation of the Lord is upon all nations, and his fury upon all their armies. (Isaiah 34:2)
>
> [Because] the rest of the men which were not killed by [Armageddon's] plagues . . . repented not. (Revelation 9:20)
>
> [Thus] the Lord . . . shall come down upon the world with a curse

to judgment; yea, upon all the nations that forget God, and upon all the ungodly. (D&C 133:2–3)

Behold, the day of the Lord cometh, cruel both with wrath and fierce anger, to lay the land desolate; and he shall destroy the sinners thereof out of it. (2 Nephi 23:9)

[And he will] destroy all the nations that come against Jerusalem. (Zechariah 12:9)

At that time, Satan's plot to annihilate God's people will unravel, for Jesus, the mighty conqueror "on a white horse," will appear with his heavenly army to rescue the suffering Jews (Revelation 19:11–16), and "he will avenge his saints speedily" (JST, Luke 18:18).

Jesus' army will consist of the resurrected and translated Saints from all ages. The scriptures state,"Behold the Lord cometh with ten thousands of his saints, to execute judgment upon all" (Jude 1:14); "these are they whom he shall bring with him when he shall come in the clouds" (D&C 76:63). "They are Christ's, the first fruits, they who shall descend with him" (D&C 88:98). The prophet, Zechariah, exclaimed, "The Lord my God shall come, and all the saints with thee" (Zechariah 14:5).

The apostle John indicated that by that time,

The second woe [of Armageddon] is past; and, behold, the third woe cometh quickly. And the seventh angel [Adam] sounded; and there were great voices in heaven, saying, The kingdoms of this world are become the kingdoms of our Lord, and of his Christ; and he shall reign for ever and ever.

And the four and twenty elders . . . worshipped God, saying . . . thou hast taken to thee thy great power, and hast reigned.

And the nations were angry, and thy wrath is come, and . . . thou shouldest . . . destroy them which destroy the earth.

And the temple of God was opened in heaven . . . and there were lightnings, and voices, and thunderings. (Revelation 11:14–19)

Before the Lord destroys the sinners, his voice will be heard.

[He] shall cause his glorious voice to be heard, and shall shew the lightning down of his arm, with the indignation of his anger. (Isaiah 30:30)

And the Lord shall utter his voice before his army: for his camp is very great. (Joel 2:11)

And he shall utter his voice out of Zion, and he shall speak from Jerusalem, and his voice shall be heard among all people. (D&C 133:21)

A voice of noise from the city, a voice from the temple, a voice of the Lord that rendereth recompense to his enemies. (Isaiah 66:6)

And all the ends of the earth shall hear it: and the nations of the earth shall mourn, and they that have laughed shall see their folly. (D&C 45:49)

For it is the day of the Lord's vengeance. (Isaiah 34:8)

The Lord's words at that time will be a searing reminder to the wicked of why they are going to be destroyed.

The Lord shall utter his voice out of heaven, saying: . . . O, ye nations of the earth, how often would I have gathered you together as a hen gathereth her chickens under her wings, but ye would not!
How oft have I called upon you by the mouth of my servants, and by the ministering of angels, and by mine own voice, and by the voice of thunderings, and by the voice of lightnings, and by the voice of tempests, and by the voice of earthquakes, and great hailstorms, and by the voice of famines and pestilences of every kind, and by the great sound of a trump, and by the voice of judgment, and by the voice of mercy all the day long, and by the voice of glory and honor and the riches of eternal life, and would have saved you with an everlasting salvation, but ye would not!
Behold, the day has come, when the cup of the wrath of mine indignation is full. (D&C 43:23–26)

[Now] because of the wickedness of the world . . . I will take vengeance upon the wicked, for they will not repent. (D&C 29:17)

Behold, and lo, there are none to deliver you: for ye obeyed not my voice when I called you out of the heavens; ye believed not my servants, and when they were sent to you ye received them not. (D&C 133:71)

[Now] the day of vengeance is in my heart, and the year of my redeemed is come. (Isaiah 63:4)

After the Lord announces to the world what he intends to do, "the glory of the Lord shall be revealed, and all flesh shall see it together" (Isaiah 40:5).

And then shall they see the Son of man coming in a cloud with power and great glory. (Luke 21:27)

Behold, he cometh with clouds and every eye shall see him. (Revelation 1:7)

And . . . heaven opened, and behold a white horse; and he that sat upon him was called Faithful and True, and in righteousness he doth judge and make war. His eyes were as a flame of fire, and on his head were many crowns; and he had a name written, that no man knew, but himself. And he was clothed with a vesture dipped in blood: and his name is called The Word of God.

And the armies which were in heaven followed him upon white horses, clothed in fine linen, white and clean.

And out of his mouth goeth a sharp sword, that with it he should smite the nations . . . and he treadeth the winepress of the fierceness and wrath of Almighty God.

And he hath on his vesture and on his thigh a name written, KING OF KINGS, AND LORD OF LORDS. (Revelation 19:11–16)

[For] the Son of God cometh in his glory, and his might, majesty, power, and dominion. . . . Behold the glory of the King of all the earth. (Alma 5:50)

[And] then shall all the tribes of the earth mourn. (Matthew 24:30)

And they also which pierced him: and all kindreds of the earth shall wail because of him. (Revelation 1:7)

The Lord hath opened his armoury, and hath brought forth the weapons of his indignation. . . .

Woe unto them! For their day is come, the time of their visitation [and] . . . the vengeance of the Lord our God. (Jeremiah 50:25, 27–28)

And so great will be the glory of his presence that the sun shall hide his face in shame, and the moon shall withhold its light, and the stars shall be hurled from their places. (D&C 133:49)

And the Lord shall be red in his apparel, and his garments like him that treadeth in the wine-vat. (D&C 133:48)

Who is this that cometh from Edom, with dyed garments from Bozrah? This that is glorious in his apparel, traveling in the greatness of his strength? I that speak in righteousness, mighty to save. Wherefore art thou red in thine apparel, and thy garments like him that treadeth in the winefat? (Isaiah 63:1–2)

> And his voice shall be heard: I have trodden the wine-press alone, and have brought judgment upon all people; and none were with me; and I have trampled them in my fury, and I did tread upon them in mine anger, and their blood have I sprinkled upon my garment, and stained all my raiment; for this was the day of vengeance which was in my heart. (D&C 133:50–51)

Just before Jesus destroys the wicked, the devil and his beastly army, in a last-ditch effort to defeat the Lord and destroy his people, will begin to fight Earth's new king. The apostle John recorded, "And I saw the beast, and the kings of the earth, and their armies, gathered together to make war against him that sat on the horse and against his army" (Revelation 19:19). "These [ten horns] shall make war with the Lamb, [but] the Lamb shall overcome them" (Revelation 17:14).

The prophet Zechariah also wrote of that event. He recorded,

> Then shall the Lord go forth, and fight against those nations, as when he fought in the day of battle. (Zechariah 14:3)

> And the Lord shall be seen over them, and his arrow shall go forth as the lightning: and the Lord God shall blow the trumpet, and shall go with whirlwinds of the south. (Zechariah 9:14)

> In that day shall the Lord defend the inhabitants of Jerusalem; and he that is feeble among them at that day shall be as David [who slew Goliath]; and the house of David shall be as God, as the angel of the Lord before them. (Zechariah 12:8)

Elder Charles W. Penrose explains what will happen next. "[T]he distressed and nearly vanquished sons of Judah, at the crisis of their fate, when the hostile troops of several nations are ravaging the city and all the horrors of war are overwhelming the people of Jerusalem, [Jesus] will set his feet upon the Mount of Olives, which will cleave and part asunder at his touch. Attended by a host from heaven, he will overthrow and destroy the combined armies of the Gentiles."[1]

That event is also recorded in the scriptures.

> And the seventh angel poured out his vial into the air; and there came a great voice out of the temple of heaven, from the throne, saying, It is done. (Revelation 16:17)

Then shall the arm of the Lord fall upon the nations. And then shall the Lord set his foot on this mount. (D&C 45:47–48)

And his feet shall stand in that day upon the mount of Olives, which is before Jerusalem on the east. (Zechariah 14:4)

And there were voices, and thunders, and lightnings; and there was a great earthquake, such as was not since men were upon the earth, so mighty an earthquake, and so great. And the great city was divided into three parts, and the cities of the nations fell . . . and every island fled away, and the mountains were not found. (Revelation 16:18–20)

And the mount of Olives "shall cleave in twain, and the earth shall tremble, and reel to and fro, and the heavens also shall shake" (D&C 45:48).

The mount of Olives shall cleave in the midst thereof toward the east and toward the west, and there shall be a very great valley: and half of the mountain shall remove toward the north, and half of it toward the south. And [the Jews] shall flee to the valley of the mountains; for the valley of the mountains shall reach unto Azel. (Zechariah 14:4–5)

[And] all the men that are upon the face of all the earth, shall shake at [the Lord's] presence, and the mountains shall be thrown down, and the steep places shall fall, and every wall shall fall to the ground. (Ezekiel 38:20)

And [the wicked] shall go into the holes of the rocks, and into the caves of the earth, for the fear of the Lord shall come upon them, and the glory of his majesty shall smite them, when he ariseth to shake terribly the earth. (2 Nephi 12:19)

Then the Lord will destroy Gog and his beastly army with fire.

Yea, the Lord will answer and say unto his people . . . I will no more make you a reproach among the heathen: But I will remove far off from you the northern army, and will drive him into a land barren and desolate, with his face toward the east sea, and his hinder part toward the utmost sea, and his stink shall come up, and his ill savor shall come up, because he hath done great things. (Joel 2:19–20)

[And] with an overrunning flood [I] will make an utter end of the place thereof, and darkness shall pursue [my] enemies . . . .they shall be devoured as stubble fully dry. (Nahum 1:8, 10)

And I will send a fire on Magog, and among them that dwell carelessly in the isles: and they shall know that I am the Lord. (Ezekiel 39:6)

> For, behold, the day cometh that shall burn as an oven, and all the proud, yea, and all that do wickedly, shall be stubble. (D&C 133:64)

The Lord's fiery glory will apparently combine with the fires of Armageddon to burn the evil armies and the rest of earth's sinful people. As Jesus descends toward them "in a pillar of fire" (D&C 29:12), "a fire goeth before him, and burneth up his enemies round about" (Psalm 97:3).

> [For he] shall be revealed from heaven with his mighty angels, In flaming fire taking vengeance on them . . . that obey not the gospel of our Lord Jesus Christ. (2 Thessalonians 1:7–8)

> For the presence of the Lord shall be as the melting fire that burneth, and as the fire which causeth the waters to boil. (D&C 133:41)

> And the earth is burned at his presence, yea, the world, and all that dwell therein. (Nahum 1:5)

> Therefore . . . the inhabitants of the earth are burned, and few men left. (Isaiah 24:6)

Even Gog, the "wicked counselor . . . shall be cut down, when he shall pass through" (Nahum 1:11), and "he shall be broken without hand" (Daniel 8:25); "he shall come to his end, and none shall help him" (Daniel 11:45). And "the captives of the mighty shall be taken away, and the prey of the terrible shall be delivered" (1 Nephi 21:25).

Then will the Lord's prophetic warning to Gog be fulfilled:

> I am against thee, O Gog, chief prince of Meshech and Tubal; And I . . . will bring thee upon the mountains of Israel:
> And I will smite thy bow out of thy left hand, and will cause thy arrows to fall out of thy right hand.
> Thou shalt fall upon the mountains of Israel, thou, and all thy bands, and the people that is with thee: I will give thee unto the ravenous birds of every sort, and to the beasts of the field to be devoured.
> Thou shalt fall upon the open field: for I have spoken it, saith the Lord God. (Ezekiel 39:1–5)

> And it shall come to pass in that day, that I will give unto Gog a place there of graves in Israel, the valley of the passengers [travelers] on the east of the sea: and it shall stop the noses of the passengers: and

there shall they bury Gog and all his multitude: and they shall call it The valley of Hamon-gog.

And seven months shall the house of Israel be burying them, that they may cleanse the land.

Yea, all the people of the land shall bury them. . . .

And they shall sever out men of continual employment, passing through the land to bury with the passengers those that remain upon the face of the earth, to cleanse it: after the end of seven months shall they search. And the passengers that pass through the land, when any seeth a man's bone, then shall he set up a sign by it, till the buriers have buried it in the valley of Hamon-gog. . . .

Thus shall they cleanse the land. (Ezekiel 39:11–16)

And they that dwell in the cities of Israel shall go forth, and shall set on fire and burn the weapons . . . and they shall burn them with fire seven years: so that they shall take no wood out of the field, neither cut down any out of the forests; for they shall burn the weapons with fire: and they shall spoil those that spoiled them, and rob those that robbed them, saith the Lord God. (Ezekiel 39:9–10)

Thus Armageddon's "beast" will be destroyed. Scriptures tell us that "the beast was taken, and with him the false prophet that wrought miracles before him, with which he deceived them that had the mark of the beast, and them that worshipped his image. These both were cast alive into a lake of fire burning with brimstone" (Revelation 19:20–21).

[And] the beast was slain, and his body destroyed and given to the burning flame. As concerning the rest of the beasts [earthly governments], they had their dominion taken away: yet their lives were prolonged for a season and a time. (Daniel 7:11)

If any man worship the beast and his image, and receive his mark in his forehead, or in his hand, the same shall drink of the wine of the wrath of God, which is poured out without mixture . . . and he shall be tormented with fire and brimstone in the presence of the holy angels, and in the presence of the Lamb:

And the smoke of their torment ascendeth up for ever and ever: and they have no rest day nor night, who worship the beast and his image, and whosoever receiveth the mark of his name. (Revelation 14:9–11)

And the multitude of all the nations that fight against Zion . . . and that distress her, shall be as a dream of a night vision. . . . he waketh and his soul is empty. (2 Nephi 27:3)

[For] it is the day of the Lord's vengeance, and the year of recompences for the controversy of Zion. And the streams thereof shall be turned into pitch, and the dust thereof into brimstone. (Isaiah 34:8–9)

The Lord declared,

Every nation which shall war against thee, O house of Israel . . . shall fall into the pit which they digged to ensnare the people of the Lord. And all that fight against Zion shall be destroyed. (1 Nephi 22:14)

And ye [Israel] shall tread down the wicked; for they shall be ashes under the soles of your feet. (3 Nephi 25:3)

And the slain of the Lord shall be at that day from one end of the earth unto the other end of the earth. (Jeremiah 25:33)

For in those days shall be affliction, such as was not from the beginning of the creation which God created unto this time, neither shall be. (Mark 13:19)

For, behold, the Lord will come with fire, and with his chariots like a whirlwind, to render his anger with fury, and his rebuke with flames of fire . . . and the slain of the Lord shall be many. (Isaiah 66:15–16)

And thus . . . shall the inhabitants of the earth be made to feel the wrath, and indignation, and chastening hand of an almighty God, until the consumption decreed hath made a full end of all nations. (D&C 87:6)

Notes

1. *Doctrine and Covenants Student Manual,* 340.

Twenty-five

THE MILLENNIUM AND BEYOND

From the ashes of Armageddon will arise the great Millennium, a thousand-year period of peace on earth.

> [And] the nations . . . shall beat their swords into plowshares, and their spears into pruninghooks: nation shall not lift up sword against nation, neither shall they learn war anymore. (Isaiah 2:4)

> They shall hunger no more, neither thirst any more . . . For the Lamb which is in the midst of the throne shall feed them . . . and God shall wipe away all tears from their eyes. (Revelation 7:16–17)

Enmity will cease even within the animal kingdom. "The wolf and the lamb shall feed together, and the lion shall eat straw like the bullock: and dust shall be the serpent's meat. They shall not hurt nor destroy in all my holy mountain, saith the Lord" (Isaiah 65:25).

Thus peace will prevail. "And that same sociality which exists among us here will exist among us there, only it will be coupled with eternal glory, which glory we do not now enjoy" (D&C 130:2). Everyone who cannot endure glory will have been burned by the glory of the Lord, and thus Babylon, the world of evil, will no longer exist.

> Babylon the great is fallen, is fallen. . . .
> For her sins have reached unto heaven, and God hath remembered her iniquities. . . .
> Therefore shall her plagues come in one day . . . and she shall be utterly burned with fire. . . .
> Alas, alas, that great city Babylon, that mighty city! For in one

hour is thy judgment come. . . .

> For by thy sorceries were all nations deceived. And in her was found the blood of prophets, and of saints, and of all that were slain upon the earth. (Revelation 18:2, 5, 8, 10, 23–24)

At that time the identity of the king of Babylon will be revealed. He will be none other than the person who was known as Lucifer in our pre-earth life, and whom we now call Satan; he is the anti-Christ who has opposed God and his Beloved Son from the beginning of time.

> For . . . he it is who now worketh, and Christ suffereth him to work, until the time is fulfilled that he shall be taken out of the way. And then shall that wicked one be revealed, whom the Lord shall consume with the spirit of his mouth, and shall destroy with the brightness of his coming. (JST, 2 Thessalonians 2:7–8)

> Lucifer . . . thou shalt be brought down to hell, to the sides of the pit. They that see thee shall narrowly look upon thee, and consider thee, saying, Is this the man that made the earth to tremble, that did shake kingdoms? (Isaiah 14:12, 15–16)

> Art thou also become weak as we? Art thou become like unto us? Thy pomp is brought down to the grave. . . .
> But thou art cast out of thy grave . . . Thou shalt not be joined with them in burial [because Satan is a spirit]. (Isaiah 14:10–11, 19–20)

> Yet thou shalt be brought down to hell, to the sides of the pit. (Isaiah 14:15)

At that time Satan shall be bound, and he "shall have no more power over the hearts of the children of men; for . . . they who do wickedly shall be as stubble" (1 Nephi 22:15).

> And because of the righteousness of the people [who remain], Satan has no power; wherefore, he cannot be loosed for the space of many years. (1 Nephi 22:26)

> [An angel] laid hold on the dragon, that old serpent, which is the Devil, and Satan, and bound him a thousand years, and cast him into the bottomless pit. (Revelation 20:2–3)

President George Q. Cannon explained how both the power of God and the righteousness of the people will be necessary to bind Satan. He said, "We talk about Satan being bound. Satan will be bound by the power of God; but he will be bound also by the determination of the people of God not to listen to him."[1]

Once Satan is bound and Babylon is removed, the curse upon the earth will also be removed. The curse was placed when Adam and Eve, while in the Garden of Eden, succumbed to the devil's temptation. As a result of their transgression, they fell spiritually and physically, and the earth fell with them. The Lord said to them, "Cursed is the ground for thy sake; in sorrow shalt thou eat of it all the days of thy life; thorns also and thistles shall it bring forth to thee" (Genesis 3:17–18). Thus the curse changed the earth from a terrestrial paradise to its present condition, a telestial planet.

However, during the Millennium the earth will be restored to its paradisiacal state (see Articles of Faith 1:10). And "the Lord shall . . . make her wilderness like Eden, and her desert like the garden of the Lord" (Isaiah 51:3). Jesus declared,

> And also that of element shall melt with fervent heat; and all things shall become new, that my knowledge and glory may dwell upon the earth. (D&C 101:25)
>
> For, behold, I create new heavens and a new earth: and the former shall not be remembered, nor come into mind. (Isaiah 65:17)

To transform the earth, the Lord "shall break down the mountains, and the valleys shall not be found. He shall command the great deep [ocean], and it shall be driven back into the north countries, and the islands shall become one land; And the land of Jerusalem and the land of Zion shall be turned back into their own place, and the earth shall be like as it was in the days before it was divided" (D&C 133:22–24).

> A fountain shall come forth of the house of the Lord, and shall water the valley of Shittim. (Joel 3:18)
>
> These waters issue out toward the east country, and go into the desert, and go into the [Dead] sea: which being brought forth into the sea, the waters shall be healed. And . . . every thing that liveth, which moveth, whithersoever the rivers shall come, shall live. . . .
>
> And by the river upon the bank thereof, on this side and on that side, shall grow all trees for meat [food] . . . it shall bring forth new fruits, because their waters they issued out of the sanctuary: and the fruit thereof shall be for meat, and the leaf thereof for medicine. (Ezekiel 47:8–10, 12)

After the earth is made into a paradise, the New Jerusalem will return from its translated location "in the clouds" above the earth (1 Thessalonians 4:17), and Jesus, the God of Israel, will then dwell with his people. John the Revelator said,

> And I John saw the holy city, New Jerusalem, coming down . . . prepared as a bride adorned for her husband. And I heard a great voice out of heaven saying, Behold, the tabernacle of God is with men, and he will dwell with them, and they shall be his people. (Revelation 21:2–3)

> These are they which came out of great tribulation, and have washed their robes, and made them white in the blood of the Lamb. (Revelation 7:14)

> And God shall wipe away all tears from their eyes; and there shall be no more death, neither sorrow, nor crying, neither shall there be any more pain: for the former things are passed away. (Revelation 21:4)

With Satan and his followers gone, Jesus Christ will reign with undisputed authority. "In that day shall there be one Lord, and his name one" (Zechariah 14:9). "For . . . the government shall be upon his shoulder: and his name shall be called Wonderful, Counsellor, The mighty God, The everlasting Father, The Prince of Peace" (Isaiah 9:6). Jesus himself declared, "Ye shall have no laws but my laws when I come, for I am your lawgiver" (D&C 38:22).

The law will go forth from the two world capital cities, "for out of Zion shall go forth the [political] law, and the word of the Lord [ecclesiastical law] from Jerusalem" (Isaiah 2:3), for "the Lord of hosts shall reign in mount Zion, and in Jerusalem" (Isaiah 24:23).

At that time, Satan's church (the great and abominable church) will be replaced by the true church of God. For "that great and abominable church, which is the whore of all the earth, shall be cast down by devouring fire . . . for abominations shall not reign" (D&C 29:21). "And . . . that great whore, who hath perverted the right ways of the Lord, yea, that great and abominable church, shall tumble to the dust and great shall be the fall of it" (1 Nephi 22:14).

Under the sovereign rule of Jesus Christ, priesthood holders will assist in directing the affairs of the Lord's kingdom. Scriptures tell us,

> They are they who are priests and kings, who have received of his fullness and of his glory. (D&C 76:56)

> They shall be priests of God and of Christ, and shall reign with him a thousand years. (Revelation 20:6)

> [And they are they who have received] the fullness of the priesthood. . . . Those so attaining shall have exaltation and be kings, priests, rulers, and lords in . . . the eternal kingdoms of the great King.[2]

Also reigning with the Lord during the millennial era will be the saints. The apostle John wrote,

> And I saw thrones, and they sat upon them, and judgment was given unto them: and I saw the souls of them that were beheaded for the witness of Jesus, and for the word of God, and which had not worshipped the beast, neither his image, neither had received his mark upon their foreheads, or in their hands; and they lived and reigned with Christ a thousand years. (Revelation 20:4)

> He that overcometh, and keepeth [the Lord's] works unto the end, to him will [He] give power over the nations. (Revelation 2:26)

Those over whom Jesus and his Saints will rule will be people of a terrestrial order. Having lived honorable and upright lives, the terrestrials will be spared from the burning, but they will not be worthy to rule, for they will have failed to live all the requirements of God's higher celestial law, the law contained in the gospel of Jesus Christ.

Joseph Fielding Smith said, "Some members of the church have an erroneous idea that when the millennium comes, all of the people are going to be swept off the earth except righteous members of the Church. That is not so. There will be millions of people . . . of all beliefs . . . who have lived clean lives."[3]

Even though they will have lived honorably, the terrestrials are referred to as "wicked" in the scriptures. Joseph Fielding Smith explained that "the Lord speaks of those who have not received the gospel as being 'wicked' as they are still under the bondage of sin, having not been baptized. 'The inhabitants of the terrestrial order will remain on the earth during the Millennium, and this class is without the gospel ordinances.' "[4]

Joseph Smith was referring to terrestrials when he said, "There will be wicked men on the earth during the thousand years. The heathen nations who will not come up to worship will be visited with the judgments of God, and must eventually be destroyed from the earth" unless they accept Jesus Christ and his gospel.[5]

For eventually "all shall bow the knee, and every tongue shall confess to him who sits upon the throne" (D&C 76:110). "And they shall come which were ready to perish in the land of Assyria [in the Middle East], and the outcasts in the land of Egypt, and shall worship the Lord in the holy mount at Jerusalem" (Isaiah 27:13).

People who convert during the Millennium will not be able to change their status to that of a celestial being if they had the opportunity to hear the gospel while in mortality and rejected it. They will be resurrected with a terrestrial body that will not be able to endure the glory of the celestial kingdom (which the earth will be changed to at the end of the Millennium). Thus they will never be able to advance to a higher degree of glory.

We learn from the scriptures that once a person receives his resurrected body, it will never die or change. "The spirit and the body shall be reunited again in its perfect form; both limb and joint shall be restored to its perfect frame . . . and . . . they can die no more; their spirits uniting with their bodies, never to be divided; thus the whole becoming . . . immortal and unchanging for all eternity" (Alma 11:43, 45).

Everyone will go through the resurrection process, even the wicked, but the latter will not be given their bodies until the end of the Millennium. Jesus "suffereth . . . that the resurrection might pass upon all men" (2 Nephi 9:22). Celestials "are they who shall have part in the first resurrection" (D&C 76:64), and terrestrials will come forth next (D&C 88:99). But "the rest of the dead . . . live not again until the thousand years are ended" (D&C 88:101).

Hence when the Lord calls the Saints in the first resurrection, to meet him in the New Jerusalem, the opportunity for other people to become part of that select group will be irredeemably lost forever, for they will have failed to qualilfy in time. In fact, that opportunity will be gone the moment a person dies (unless he did not have a chance to hear and accept the gospel before his death). Death for many people comes sooner than anticipated, so every day should be lived as if it were the last. For all shall die and then "all that are in the graves . . . shall come forth; they that have done good, unto the resurrection of life; and they that have done evil, unto the resurrection of damnation" (John 5:28–29).

Included among the people who will remain on the earth during the millennium will be Jews and other Israelites. The unconverted among them will be converted at that time, for the Lord declared,

> Behold, I will save my people . . . and they shall dwell in the midst

of Jerusalem: and they shall be my people, and I will be their God, in truth and in righteousness. (Zechariah 8:7–8)

[For] then shall the Jews look upon me and say: what are these wounds in thine hands and in thy feet? Then shall they know that I am the Lord; for I will say unto them: These wounds are the wounds with which I was wounded in the house of my friends. I am he who was lifted up. I am Jesus that was crucified. I am the Son of God. And then shall they weep because of their iniquities; then shall they lament because they persecuted their king. (D&C 45:51–53)

And . . . they shall look upon me whom they have pierced, and they shall mourn for him, as one mourneth for his only son, and shall be in bitterness for him as one that is in bitterness for his firstborn. In that day shall there be a great mourning in Jerusalem. (Zechariah 12:10–11)

[But] the Lord shall comfort Zion: he will comfort all her waste places . . . and [soon] joy and gladness shall be found therein, thanksgiving, and the voice of melody. (Isaiah 51:3)

[And] Jerusalem shall be called a city of truth; and the mountain of the Lord of hosts the holy mountain. (Zechariah 8:3)

In that day shall the Lord of hosts be for a crown of glory, and for a diadem of beauty, unto the residue of his people. (Isaiah 28:5)

The Lord said,

I will sanctify my great name, which was profaned among the heathen, which you [Israel] have profaned in the midst of them . . . I shall be sanctified in you before their eyes. . . .

And I will put my spirit within you, and cause you to walk in my statutes, and ye shall keep my judgments, and do them . . .

And ye shall be my people, and I will be your God. (Ezekiel 36:23, 27–28)

And all flesh shall know that I the Lord am thy Savior and thy Redeemer, the mighty One of Jacob. (Isaiah 49:26)

[And] the house of Israel shall know that I am the Lord their God from that day and forward. (Ezekiel 39:22)

Repentant Israel will finally understand Jesus' atonement for their sins.

He is despised and rejected of men; a man of sorrows, and

acquainted with grief: and we hid as it were our faces from him; he was despised, and we esteemed him not.

Surely he hath borne our griefs, and carried our sorrows: yet we did esteem him stricken, smitten of God, and afflicted.

But he was wounded for our transgressions, he was bruised for our iniquities: the chastisement of our peace was upon him; and with his stripes we are healed.

All we like sheep have gone astray; we have turned every one to his own way; and the Lord hath laid on him the iniquity of us all. (Isaiah 53:3–6)

The terrestrial and celestial residents of the earth during the Millennium will be either mortal or immortal. Immortals will be the resurrected; mortals will be translated beings, as well as terrestrial survivors of God's wrath. Elder Orson Pratt said of the translated, "a partial change will be wrought upon them, [but] not a change to immortality."[6]

The Lord revealed the following about the Millennium:

Children shall grow up until they become old; old men shall die; but they shall not sleep in the dust, but they shall be changed in the twinkling of an eye. (D&C 63:5)

In that day an infant shall not die until he is old; and his life shall be as the age of a tree. (D&C 101:30)

There shall be no more thence an infant of days, nor an old man that hath not filled his days: for the child shall die an hundred years old. (Isaiah 65:20)

[For] it is appointed to him to die at the age of man . . . but they shall not sleep in the dust, but they shall be changed in the twinkling of an eye [from mortality to immortality]. (D&C 63:50–51)

Those who die as children before the Millennium begins will be resurrected as children, for, as Joseph Smith said, "the body will come forth as it is laid to rest, for there is no growth or development in the grave."[7] And because Satan will no longer be able to tempt children, they "shall grow up without sin unto salvation" (D&C 45:58).

Joseph Smith taught that righteous people who have lost children through death, or who have been deprived of other blessings while in mortality, will have all those losses made up to them during the Millennium, if they are faithful. He said, "All your losses will be made up to you in the resurrection, provided you continue faithful."[8]

And thus, during the great millennial era, happiness and peace will prevail over the entire earth. The Lord declared,

> I will rejoice in Jerusalem, and joy in my people: and the voice of weeping shall be no more heard in her, nor the voice of crying. . . .
> And they shall plant vineyards, and eat the fruit of them.
> They shall not build, and another inhabit: they shall not plant, and another eat: for all the days of a tree are the days of my people, and mine elect shall long enjoy the work of their hands . . . and their offspring with them. (Isaiah 65:19, 21–23)
>
> [And the righteous] shall rest from all their troubles and from all care and sorrow. (Alma 40:12)
>
> [For] whoso repenteth and hardeneth not his heart . . . these shall enter into [God's] rest. (Alma 12:34)

The earth will also finally rest, as the Lord promised Enoch: "As I live, even so will I come in the last days . . . to fulfill the oath which I have made unto you . . . And the day shall come that the earth shall rest" (Moses 7:60–61). Hence the Millennium will be a one-thousand-year-long Sabbath day of rest for both the earth and its righteous inhabitants.

At the end of the Millennium, this earth will become a celestial planet, and only celestial people will be allowed to remain upon it. All others will be removed to lower kingdoms. In the scriptures we read that "when the thousand years are ended, . . . the earth shall be consumed and pass away, and there shall [again] be a new heaven and a new earth" (D&C 29:22–23).

> [And the earth] must needs be sanctified from all unrighteousness, that it may be prepared for a celestial glory; for after it hath filled the measure of its creation, it shall be crowned with glory, even with the presence of God the Father; that bodies who are of the celestial kingdom may possess it forever and ever; for, for this intent was it made and created, and for this intent are they sanctified. . . .
> Wherefore, it shall be sanctified . . . and the righteous shall inherit it. (D&C 88:18–20, 26)

Not only will the righteous inherit the earth, but they, along with Jesus Christ, will inherit "all things." The apostle Paul taught that the "Son . . . hath [been] appointed heir of all things" (Hebrews 1:2), and "the Spirit beareth witness with our spirit, that we are the children of God:

And if children, then heirs; heirs of God, and joint-heirs with Christ . . . that we may be also glorified" (Romans 8:16–17).

Other scriptures tell us,

> The saints shall be filled with [Jesus'] glory, and receive their inheritance and be made equal with him. (D&C 88:107)

> For [they] are the church of the Firstborn, and he will take [them] up in a cloud, and appoint every man his portion. And he that is a faithful and wise steward shall inherit all things. (D&C 78:21–22)

When the earth is celestialized, it will become "a globe like a sea of glass and fire . . . made like unto crystal" (D&C 130:7, 9). The sea of glass "is the earth, in its sanctified, immortal, and eternal state" (D&C 77:1). The new earth will have no need of the sun because it will be like a sun in glory. Scriptures tell us,

> And the [earth] had no need of the sun, neither of the moon, to shine in it; for the glory of God did lighten it. (Revelation 21:23)

> There is one glory of the sun. (1 Corinthians 15:41)

> [And those who will inhabit the sun-like earth] are they whose bodies are celestial, whose glory is that of the sun, even the glory of God. (D&C 76:70)

> Then shall the righteous shine forth as the sun in the kingdom of their Father. (Matthew 13:43)

> Therefore are they before the throne of God. . . . They shall hunger no more, neither thirst any more; neither shall the sun light on them. (Revelation 7:15–16)

> The sun shall be no more thy light by day; neither for brightness shall the moon give light unto thee: but the Lord shall be unto thee an everlasting light, and thy God thy glory. (Isaiah 60:19)

The apostle John described the celestialized earth.

> And I heard a great noise out of heaven saying, Behold, the tabernacle of God is with men, and he will dwell with them, and they shall be his people, and God himself shall be with them. (Revelation 21:3)

> And I saw a great white throne, and him that sat on it, from whose face the [former] earth and the heaven fled away. (Revelation 20:11)

And there was a rainbow round about the throne, in sight like unto an emerald. And round about the throne were four and twenty seats: and upon the seats I saw four and twenty elders sitting clothed in white raiment; and they had on their heads crowns of gold. . . .

And before the throne there was a sea of glass like unto crystal. (Revelation 4:3–4, 6)

And I saw a new heaven and a new earth: for the first heaven and the first earth were passed away; and there was no more sea. (Revelation 21:1)

John also described the new earth as a world-wide New Jerusalem.

And I John saw the holy city, new Jerusalem . . .

Having the glory of God: and her light was like unto a stone most precious, even like a jasper stone, clear as crystal; and had a wall great and high, and had twelve gates, and at the gates twelve angels, and names written thereon, which are the names of the twelve tribes of the children of Israel. (Revelation 21:2, 11–12)

And the wall of the city had twelve foundations, and in them the names of the twelve apostles of the Lamb. . . .

And the city lieth foursquare, and the length is as large as the breadth. . . . The length and the breadth and the height of it are equal [like the earth]. . . .

And the building of the wall of it was of jasper, and the city was pure gold, like unto clear glass. And the foundations of the wall of the city were garnished with all manner of precious stones. (Revelation 21:14, 16, 18–19)

And the twelve gates were twelve pearls . . . and the street of the city was pure gold. . . . And I saw no temple therein: for the Lord God Almighty and the Lamb are the temple of it. And the city had no need of the sun, neither of the moon, to shine in it for the glory of God did lighten it, and the Lamb is the light thereof. . . .

And the gates of it shall not be shut at all by day: for there shall be no night there. (Revelation 21:21–23, 25)

Blessed are they that do [keep the] commandments, [for] they . . . may enter in through the gates of the city. (Revelation 22:14)

And [there was] a pure river of water of life, clear as crystal, proceeding out of the throne of God and of the Lamb. In the midst of the street of it, and on either side of the river, was there the tree of life, which bare twelve manner of fruits, and yielded her fruit every month: and the leaves of the tree were for the healing of the nations. And there shall be no more curse: but the throne of God and of the Lamb shall be in it. (Revelation 22:2–3)

> And there shall be no night there; and they need no candle, neither light of the sun, for the Lord God giveth them light: and they shall reign for ever and ever. (Revelation 22:5)

The Prophet Joseph Smith also saw the celestialized earth in vision. He related, "I saw the transcendent beauty of the gate through which the heirs of that kingdom will enter, which was like unto circling flames of fire; also the blazing throne of God, whereon was seated the Father and the Son. [And] I saw the beautiful streets of that kingdom, which had the appearance of being paved with gold."[9]

The Lord told the prophet Joseph that "[angels] reside in the presence of God, on a globe like a sea of glass and fire . . . The place where God resides is a great Urim and Thummim. This earth, in its sanctified and immortal state, will be made like unto crystal and will be a Urim and Thummim to the inhabitants who dwell thereon" (D&C 130:7–9).

Brigham Young indicated that when the earth becomes a celestialized Urim and Thummin, "it will be like the sun. . . . it will not then be an opaque body as it now is, but . . . will be full of light and glory."[10]

And "a person, by looking into it, can know things past, present, and to come; though none but celestialized beings can enjoy this privilege. They will look into the earth, and the things they desire to know will be exhibited to them, the same as the face is seen by looking into a mirror."[11]

Celestial people will also be given a personal Urim and Thummim in the form of a white stone. "And a white stone is given to each of those who come into the celestial kingdom" (D&C 130:11), "and in the stone a new name written, which no man knoweth saving he that receiveth it" (Revelation 2:17).

Scriptures tell us, "The new name is the key word" (D&C 130:11). "Then the white stone . . . will become a Urim and Thummim to each individual who receives one, whereby things pertaining to a higher order of kingdoms will be made known" (D&C 130:10).

Thus those who inherit the celestialized earth will enjoy and experience many things which we cannot now even envision. Referring to those who will inherit the Celestial Kingdom, the Lord said,

He that endureth in faith and doeth my will, the same shall overcome, and shall receive an inheritance upon the earth when the day of transfiguration shall come. (D&C 63:20)

Him that overcometh will I make a pillar in the temple of my God, and he shall go no more out: and I will write upon him the name of my God, and the name of the city of my God, which is new Jerusalem. (Revelation 3:12)

[For it is] the righteous, the saints of the Holy One of Israel, they who have believed in the Holy One of Israel, they who have endured the crosses of the world, and despised the shame of it, [who] shall inherit the kingdom of God, which was prepared for them from the foundation of the world, and their joy shall be full forever. (2 Nephi 9:18)

[And] great and marvelous are the . . . mysteries of his kingdom which . . . surpasses all understanding in glory, and in might, and in dominion. (D&C 76:114)

Wherefore, as it is written, they are gods, even the sons of God—Wherefore, all things are theirs. . . .
These shall dwell in the presence of God and his Christ forever and ever. . . .
These are they who are just men made perfect through Jesus . . . who wrought out this perfect atonement. . . .
These are they whose bodies are celestial, whose glory is that of the sun, even the glory of God, the highest of all. (D&C 76:58, 62, 69–70)

And thus the righteous shall have joy in the Celestial Kingdom of God forever. That was the very reason the earth was created and man was placed upon it, for "men are that they might have joy" (2 Nephi 2:25). The mortal earth was to be a school wherein God's children could learn from personal experience with evil that only righteousness brings happiness, and "wickedness never was happiness" (Alma 41:10). The Prophet Joseph Smith taught, "Happiness is the object and design of our existence; and will be the end thereof, if we pursue the path that leads to it."[12]

The great King Benjamin also declared, "I would desire that ye should consider on the blessed and happy state of those that keep the commandments of God. For behold, they are blessed in all things, both temporal and spiritual; and if they hold out faithful to the end they are received into heaven, that thereby they may dwell with God in a state of never-ending happiness" (Mosiah 2:41). The Lord also said,

> Ye cannot behold with your natural eyes, for the present time, the design of your God concerning those things which shall come hereafter, and the glory which shall follow after much tribulation. For after much tribulation come the blessings. Wherefore the day cometh that ye shall be crowned with much glory. (D&C 58:3–4)
>
> And, if you keep my commandments and endure to the end, you shall have eternal life, which gift is the greatest of all the gifts of God. (D&C 14:7)
>
> All thrones and dominions, principalities and powers, shall be revealed and set forth upon all who have endured valiantly for the gospel of Jesus Christ. (D&C 121:29)
>
> Eye hath not seen, nor ear heard, neither have entered into the heart of man, the things which God hath prepared for them that love him. (1 Corinthians 2:9)
>
> Great shall be their reward and eternal shall be their glory. (D&C 76:6)

Everyone who follows the gospel path, which leads to eternal life in the kingdom of God, will one day reach that glorious destination, and there the Lord's words of welcome will be heard: "Well done, thou good and faithful servant: thou hast been faithful over a few things, I will make thee ruler over many things: enter thou into the joy of thy Lord" (Matthew 25:21).

Thus our journey through life, culminating in a victorious triumph over sin, can be summarized in the simple words of the poet Robert Frost: "Two roads diverged . . . I took the one less traveled by, and that has made all the difference."[13]

Notes

1. *Doctrine and Covenants Student Manual*, 89.
2. McConkie, *Mormon Doctrine*, 425.
3. Smith, *Doctrines of Salvation*, 1:86.
4. Smith, *Answers to Gospel Questions*, 1:110.
5. Smith, *Teachings of the Prophet Joseph Smith*, 268–269.
6. *Journal of Discourses*, 16:319.
7. Smith, *Teachings of the Prophet Joseph Smith*, 200.
8. Ibid., 296.

9. Ibid., 107.
10. *Journal of Discourses,* 7:163.
11. Ibid., 9:87.
12. Smith, *Teachings of the Prophet Joseph Smith,* 255.
13. Edward Connery Lathem, *The Poetry of Robert Frost* (New York: Henry Holt and Company, 1975), 105.

ABOUT THE AUTHOR

Connie Joslin, a native of Utah, spent her early years in Roosevelt. After high school, she attended Utah State University in Logan, where she graduated with honors in 1966. She then moved to Southern California where she taught high school English for several years. In 1970 she married Gary James Joslin in the Los Angeles Temple. They eventually moved back to Utah where they raised their family. After her husband passed away in 1998, she became the Director of Washington Institute for Graduate Studies.

Since her retirement, she has stayed busy with family and church responsibilities. She has served in such capacities as ward organist, Young Women president, Relief Society president, and Gospel Doctrine teacher.